Windows to the World

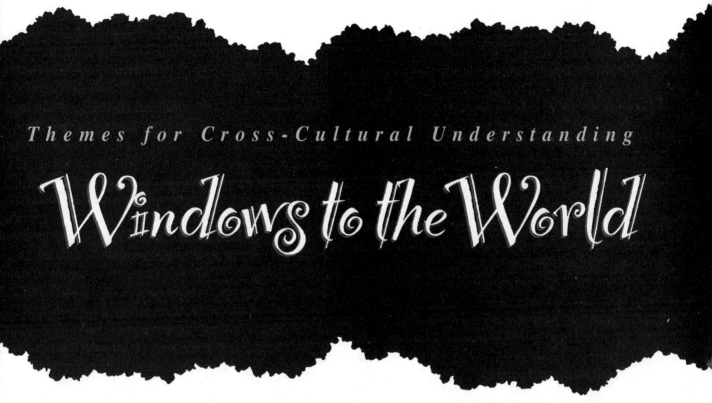

Themes for Cross-Cultural Understanding

Windows to the World

PHYLLIS KEPLER • BROOKE SARNO ROYSE • JOHN KEPLER

GoodYearBooks

An Imprint of ScottForesman
A Division of Harper Collins*Publishers*

Richard Ammentorp of Schaumburg Elementary School District 54, Schaumburg, Illinois,
realized the potential in this cross-cultural approach to understanding those who are
different, and was the first to permit us to introduce the program in the classroom.
For his sensitivity, encouragement, and foresight, we are deeply grateful.

GoodYearBooks

are available for most basic curriculum subjects plus many enrichment areas.
For more GoodYearBooks, contact your local bookseller or educational dealer.
For a complete catalog with information about other GoodYearBooks, please write:

GoodYearBooks
ScottForesman
1900 East Lake Avenue
Glenview, IL 60025

Book design by Foster Design.

ISBN 0-673-36153-5
1 2 3 4 5 6 7 8 9–MH–02 01 00 99 98 97 96

ACKNOWLEDGMENTS

Any book dealing with cross-cultural understanding requires input and guidance from sources throughout the world, and the authors have been blessed with help from many culturally smart friends and business associates in writing this one. We also have been fortunate to have access to several of the faculty members and the use of the magnificent library and other research facilities of our alma mater, Northwestern University.

We acknowledge our gratitude, particularly, to the following individuals and institutions who encouraged this effort and unhesitatingly were on call to answer any questions and keep us from straying from our task: Inamul Haq, principal of the Islamic Foundation School in Villa Park, Illinois, whose knowledge of Islam and the Muslim world is encyclopedic; Lynn Min, an invaluable source on Korea; Hope Barrone, who critiqued the material on Japan; Abdul Wahab Kassim, director of the Mid-West Regional Office of the Malaysian Students Department in Evanston, Illinois; Vera Yin, expert on both Chinas; Joyce Wandawa and Grace Bayona, who provided excellent material on Central Africa; and Susan Diehl of the Glen Ellyn, Illinois, Public Library for her personal and in-depth expertise on Nigeria.

This book could not have been completed without the aid of many staff members of these consular and other national offices in Chicago: France, People's Republic of China, Indonesia, India, Thailand, Philippines, Greece, Afghanistan Tourists Information Office, and the Mexican Tourist Office.

The Chicago Hindu Society and the Buddhist Temple in Hinsdale, Illinois, guided us through the intricacies of these religions with patience and skill.

Finally, we are grateful for the inspiration and confidence throughout the writing of this book of our editors at GoodYear Books, especially Bobbie Dempsey.

Table of Contents

Chapter 1:
LANGUAGE

Chapter 2:
SPACE

Chapter 4: RELATIONSHIPS

Chapter 5: THE INDIVIDUAL AND THE GROUP

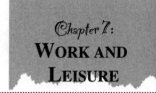

Chapter 7:
WORK AND LEISURE

Chapter 6:
MORAL VALUES

A FINAL WORD

Opening Your Windows to the World

There's more to the world than you can see through your window; get outside and you'll see more.

—RUSSIAN PROVERB

This proverb says a lot about cross-cultural understanding. It tells us that we need to get out into the world to understand what is beyond our limited range of vision. But, more than that, it also implies that the window through which we perceive the world around us may not always give us the best, truest, and fullest picture.

The purpose of this book is to help you equip your students with some of the concepts, attitudes, and skills for successful cross-cultural understanding. Its aim is to help students get outside their own windows, not only to see more of the world and its many diverse cultures, but also to be able to look back through their windows and see what their own world may look like to others, to people from other cultural perspectives. They will learn to view people from other cultures with less prejudice and ethnocentrism as they start to understand how people from other cultures might view them. This is a dual vision essential to cross-cultural understanding.

Preparing for Global Citizenship

More than ever, today's students need to be prepared for global citizenship. As the world grows closer, socially, economically, and technologically, they will need to be more and more cross-culturally adept, equipped with the interpersonal skills and the open-minded attitudes necessary for healthy and successful interaction with people from other cultures and cultural backgrounds. Knowing facts about foreign countries simply will not be enough. Nor will matching the test scores of Japanese and German students so that students can "compete" in the global mar-

ketplace. Students need the cross-cultural attitudes and skills that can take them beyond the classroom, out into the world where they can cooperate with people from other cultures and participate in decision-making for the global community.

Becoming Cross-Culturally Adept

How does one become more cross-culturally adept? Plenty of people go off to live abroad and travel the world and yet are just as biased and ethnocentric as they were to begin with. Plenty of other people never leave their communities yet are tolerant, accepting, and able to interact well with people who are different from them. What this shows is that your students do not need to travel to foreign cultures to learn cross-cultural understanding. They can learn it in their own schools and neighborhoods while still being able to see outside their cultural windows.

Whenever they buy their gum at the Korean American-owned grocery store on the corner, play video games manufactured in Japan, listen to rap music with its African American roots, or eat a Mexican burrito for lunch, our students experience the world in their own neighborhoods. Yet making kids aware of the global economy that brings products to their lives and homes is still not enough. Cross-cultural education is not a matter of simply understanding the characteristics of a particular culture or even of achieving an "awareness" of other cultures. Rather, it involves the development of attitudes and behavioral skills that facilitate open, non-biased, respectful and creative interaction with people from any culture. Students can learn these attitudes and skills as they are given the opportunity to interact creatively with others across social and cultural lines—lines already found within their multicultural classrooms.

From *Windows to the World: Themes for Cross-Cultural Understanding.* Copyright © 1996 by Phyllis Kepler, Brooke Sarno Royse, and John Kepler

Cultures constantly influence each other, sharing and exchanging discoveries, beliefs, values, languages, and new perspectives. In this way, they are dependent on one another, for without the interaction with other cultures, they may stagnate and die out. Like cultures, people are always changing and influencing each other. Humans are social animals who are dependent on one another for survival and quality of life, indeed for our very identities. If we can bring this point home to our students and help them experience it, they will begin to accept and appreciate others. They may learn to see that our cultural differences make the world more colorful, more enriching, and much more fun.

Cross-Cultural Outcomes

The purpose of this book is to help teachers and students attain the following goals:

1. To learn to interact in healthy, productive, and creative ways across cultural lines.

2. To celebrate, not deprecate, cultural differences.

3. To see oneself from another's perspective.

4. To think more critically about how one's own culture shapes one's identity.

5. To learn to look for the social, historical, economic, ethical, religious, and political reasons for another's cultural behavior and beliefs, rather than to dismiss them, unthinkingly, as strange.

6. To comprehend the rich interdependence of cultures, within the United States and around the world.

7. To develop the desire to pursue an understanding of other specific cultures.

8. To appreciate and understand one's own cultural heritage.

9. To promote healthy civic culture within the classroom.

10. To prepare oneself for global citizenship.

Why "Cross-Cultural" and not "Multicultural"?

A note about definitions: This is a cross-cultural book, not a multicultural book. It concerns itself with world cultures, not just the cultures represented in the United States. Moreover, while the word "multicultural" has a variety of meanings for many uses, its primary meaning is "being of many cultures." It celebrates the fact that there are many different cultures and cultural orientations in the U.S. and in other countries. The word "cross-cultural," on the other hand, implies that some kind of beneficial action is occurring: we are crossing over the cultural barriers and boundaries that exist in our multicultural world, barriers that too often promote prejudice, racism, ethnocentrism, and violence. By crossing these boundaries, we can learn to accept and understand one another. We hope that this book meets some of the multicultural needs of classrooms while using a global perspective.

Using Themes as the Focus of Cross-Cultural Study

This book is not divided into chapters devoted to specific cultures around the world, but rather into chapters devoted to particular themes. This is what makes the book's approach different from most approaches to multicultural and cross-cultural education. Treating cultures as separate prepackaged "units" provides a misleading picture of what cultures are and how they work. A culture is a system of beliefs, values, and behavior by means of which a group of people perceive and experience the world. Cultures are always changing and growing; they are dynamic organisms. Cultures almost always are rubbing against each other, influencing each other's beliefs and values in complex and fascinating ways.

You can compare this process not to a melting pot or even to a salad bowl—two popular but inaccurate images used to describe a multicultural society—but rather to looking through a kaleidoscope. In a melting pot, all the ingredients lose their individual color and flavor to become one mass. In a salad bowl, the ingredients retain their individual color and flavor but the salad remains a salad. With a kaleidoscope, the many glass pieces represent various cultures or the people from various cultures. As you turn the kaleidoscope, the pieces move and fall into different combinations of designs and colors, creating an endlessly fascinating, beautifully textured picture.

That picture is the world of people from many cultures whose interaction keeps the world always new and always interesting. Indeed, it is the world of our multicultural classrooms. Therefore, to teach cultures as distinct, fixed units of study, as if they stand alone from other cultures, is to do a disservice to the people of those cultures—and to our students, who are quickly bored with such an approach. Facts and fixed knowledge alone do not lead to healthy cross-cultural attitudes and skills.

Teaching cultures by themes gives a more complete picture of what cultures are, reflects a sound interdisciplinary curricular model, helps students make productive comparisons and contrasts between other cultures and their own, and, we have found, interests students far more than other approaches. The general themes you will find in this book are important aspects of living that each culture holds, perceives, interprets, and expresses in its own way. Since the themes are common to all cultures, they indicate that we all share some basic aspects of living but that each culture will perceive and express its experience of these themes in a different way. By learning about cultures in terms of themes, students gain a richer, more contextual understanding of how cultures fit together from within and without. And the themes provide a useful means for students to think about other cultures and their own, to categorize the ways cultures are different and alike.

Because our focus is on cultural themes rather than on individual cultures, our goal is not to be exhaustive, covering as many cultures as we can, but rather to focus on cultures only insofar as they illustrate the central theme. And because we happen to know more about some cultures than others, you will find more information on a handful of particular cultures (Japan, Mexico, and the Arab World, to name a few) than on others. Furthermore, we want to stress a major point: we do not in any way mean to imply that everyone in a certain culture thinks, acts, or expresses the theme in the same way. We simply have tried to locate some dominant characteristics found in the culture for the sake of learning and discussion. These dominant characteristics are those by which individuals in a culture, more often than not, are judged, rewarded, and punished within their culture. Making general observations about a culture can be dangerous and can lead to stereotyping, yet there has to be a way to study and talk about the beliefs and behaviors of people in other cultures. The point is to walk the fine line between accuracy and generalization. Some cultures are more homogeneous than others: making general observations about relatively homogeneous Japan, for example, is probably more reliable than making general observations about the more heterogeneous and multicultural United States. If you disagree with some of our statements about cultural traits in the U.S., we encourage you to use those statements for discussion and debate with your students. Nevertheless, in our discussion of each culture, we have tried as much as possible not to imply that all people in one culture are the same.

How Culture Shapes Us

Our culture plays an enormous role in defining our beliefs, values, and behavior, in constructing who we are. The themes and activities in this book are meant to help students become more aware of how culture shapes so much about them—their personalities, their perspectives, and their perceptions. By becoming more aware, they can start on the road to becoming active participants and contributors to their cultures rather than simply being receptacles of all they inherit. In other words, as they become more aware of the power of culture to shape them, they will learn not to take their worlds for granted and instead can begin to question what they inherit as unchallenged cultural tradition. They will develop their critical thinking skills so that they can distinguish between those aspects of their culture that need to be changed (i.e., racism) and those that are worth preserving (i.e., the value placed on individual life). As they develop these skills, they will begin to see themselves as able to bring beneficial changes to their communities and the world.

Cross-Cultural Attitudes and Skills

You might call such awareness a cross-cultural attitude or skill, for if students can understand how culture shapes them, then they may see how a different culture can shape someone else to be different from them, and therefore be better able to accept the other person for who he or she is. One of the main objectives of this book is to equip students with the cross-cultural attitudes and skills needed for healthy interaction with those who are culturally different. Such attitudes and skills are essential building blocks for achieving the general outcomes of this book. They include:

- recognizing and defining biases
- suspending judgment when encountering someone who is different

- seeing oneself as different, too; recognizing and respecting a mutual difference
- developing the curiosity to learn why others are different
- seeing and treating others as people of equal worth
- being able to see oneself from the other's perspective
- understanding one's need for others, that individuals and cultures have a mutual interdependency
- developing a social and cross-cultural sense of identity
- developing the ability both to prevent and resolve cross-cultural misunderstanding

These attitudes and skills are best brought out by instructional techniques that include student self-examination, role-playing, peer instruction, cooperative learning, problem-based activities, cultural content instruction, and the use of literature and arts from other cultures.

Activities

The activities in this book are designed to illustrate the cultural information and concepts offered in each lesson. But, more importantly, they are opportunities for your students to learn and practice essential cross-cultural interactive attitudes and skills. Each activity is designated by one or two cross-cultural "competencies" that are tapped by the activity: *collaborative, interpretive, constructive,* or *cross-cultural.* These competencies are really cross-cultural skills that the activity is designed to promote.

Activities that are designated *collaborative* focus on group work and cooperative learning. By working together in groups, students learn to practice significant cross-cultural skills: to negotiate differing perspectives, to listen sensitively, to be diplomatic, to figure out their own perspectives, to respect others' opinions, to build consensus, and to work as a team.

Activities that are labeled *interpretive* tend to include the following: discussing and questioning their own cultural assumptions and the influence of their culture on their beliefs, analyzing cultural messages through advertising and the media, reading and understanding stories, interpreting the beliefs and behaviors of people from other cultures, trying to understand how people from other cultures might view them, analyzing the behavior of their peers and people in their communities, and doing experiments in perception.

These activities encourage students to engage in higher-order thinking skills, to work hard to understand what others say and mean, to be open and receptive to other perspectives, and to learn to see themselves from the other's point of view.

Activities termed *constructive* involve the students in creating or generating some sort of product, new knowledge, or new opinion. They encourage hands-on participation in constructing things through various media and using various ways of knowing (or "multiple intelligences," in the words of Howard Gardner). Some of the projects are drawn and painted, some written, some debated, some acted out, some computed, etc. These project-oriented activities help students to practice the cross-cultural skills of cooperation, creativity, and respect for other forms of creativity and knowledge.

Finally, activities that encourage students to compare and contrast cultures, to imagine standing in the shoes of someone from another culture, to role-play behavior from another culture, or to imitate an art form from another culture are designated *cross-cultural.* These activities allow students to practice the cultural perspectives and behaviors of others, and by pretending to be other people, they may gain a deeper empathy and understanding of those who are different from them.

Turning Windows Into Doors

By learning to practice cross-cultural attitudes and skills in the classroom, students should be able to internalize them and then transfer them to real-world situations, to the cross-cultural encounters that will surely be more common as the world grows closer. We hope this book will help your students make *doors* out of their windows to the world.

How to Use This Book

ach chapter consists of a General Introduction to introduce you to the chapter's theme and some introductory exercises called "What Went Wrong?" followed by three to six lessons. Each lesson includes some information about particular cultures for you to share and discuss with the students, and these are interspersed with student activities.

Windows to the World is meant to be a resource book for you, so feel free to skip around and use only those chapters that fit your curricular needs. Some teachers may find that the book makes a useful year-long course of study. In any case, each chapter represents a course section, usually taking three weeks. Before you begin each chapter, or course section, read it thoroughly to familiarize yourself with the content. When you begin the course section, present the "What Went Wrong?" exercises to the students. These exercises introduce the course theme with word problems designed to get the students thinking about the subject. Don't forget to use a globe or world map to familiarize students with the locations of the cultures you will be discussing.

Then go lesson by lesson, sharing the cultural information and using the class activities to illustrate and explore the concepts with the students. You might want to skip some lessons if they do not meet your needs. And some activities may not be appropriate for your students' grade level. The first chapters contain more activities than the later chapters, primarily to get your students familiar with the kinds of issues and concepts about which they will be learning. Use the activities as they are or as prompts or suggestions, extend them, or create your own. Some of the activities may take an hour or less, and others may take a day or even a week to complete. You will want to plan your course with this in mind.

We encourage you to have the students keep cross-cultural portfolios, consisting of their student worksheets, written work, artwork, videos or photos of staged events, and log or journal entries—whatever you (and they) feel gives the best overall picture of their work during the course. To lend a sense of perspective to the portfolio, it is interesting to have the students write their expectations and assumptions about the course and other cultures beforehand and then have them write what they have learned after the course is finished. Include these statements in the portfolio. Portfolios can be shared with par-

ents and other classes, and can be used for assessment and evaluation as well.

When students meet in groups for various activities, we recommend that you help them apply a cooperative learning model. There are many such models in the vast literature on cooperative learning. In some models, the students take on particular roles within the group, such as Recorder, Encourager, Repeater, Troubleshooter, Reporter, etc. This way, each person contributes constructively to the process and product of the team.

On some pages, you will find "Sidebars" filled with quotations, proverbs, new words, and lists, as well as "Did You Know?" boxes. The "Did You Know?" boxes contain interesting or humorous facts about beliefs and behavior in other cultures. Often they will contain some advice on what to do and what not to do when visiting a particular culture. During the course, you might want to copy (or have the students copy) some of the quotations, proverbs, new words, lists, or boxes onto signs to hang around the room. Or you could use them to create bulletin board designs or to decorate the door of your classroom so that the rest of the school can see what your class is studying.

Language

Goals

This chapter explores the verbal and non-verbal aspects of language in cross-cultural understanding. The stories, explanations, examples from various cultures, and student activities are designed to help students achieve the following goals:

1. To understand that a culture's use of language helps shape how its members perceive and describe the world; that a culture's language can influence the way one interprets his or her experience.

2. To grasp some principal characteristics of language use in various cultures.

3. To develop a basic understanding of how language and culture influence each other.

4. To understand how differences in language use among cultures can lead to crucial misunderstandings.

5. To see that even language similarity can create misunderstanding.

6. To understand how different languages develop, change, and interdepend.

7. To grasp the importance of body language in communication; to learn some rudiments of communicating across cultural lines even without speaking the same verbal language.

Cross-Cultural Attitudes and Skills

As students work towards these goals, they will develop the following cross-cultural attitudes and skills:

1. They will begin to shed their prejudices toward other people's use of language as they develop an open-minded sensitivity to the many different styles people use in communication around the world.

2. They will develop an ability to think not simply about what others say, but about what others mean.

3. They will develop a sense of their own difference from others as they encounter the frustrations in making themselves understood.

4. They will hone their communicative skills as they practice trying to make themselves understood by others, and their interpretive skills as they practice understanding others.

GENERAL INTRODUCTION

Sign posted near an elevator in a Paris hotel lobby: THE LIFT IS BEING FIXED FOR THE NEXT DAY. DURING THAT TIME WE REGRET THAT YOU WILL BE UNBEARABLE.

Line from a report in an East African newspaper for English speakers:
"A new swimming pool is rapidly taking shape since the contractors have thrown in the bulk of their workers."

A language is more than a way for people to talk with one another. Since humans began to speak with simple grunts, language has developed into a very complicated system that does far more than permit people to express their ideas verbally. The philosopher Wittgenstein once wrote that the limits of our language are the limits of our world. Language determines how we see the world; while enabling us to describe what we see, it also sets limits on how much and exactly what we can observe and describe.

Simply learning to translate a foreign language from books and in classes does not ensure that the learner can communicate effectively with people from other cultures.

Languages are finely nuanced systems of communication that express attitudes, values, and ways of looking at the world that are different for each particular culture. When important international business or political negotiations are to take place, for example, those in charge of selecting a translator search for someone who is not only bilingual but also *bi-cultural*—that is, someone who has had direct experience of the two cultures and can understand the nuances of each. Students who are examining foreign cultures for the first time or interacting with other young people from a variety of ethnic groups in their own classrooms, however, do not need to become bi-cultural in order to understand people from different cultural backgrounds. If they take the time to study *how* and *why* other people use their languages, students can acquire invaluable skills and sensitivities necessary for cross-cultural understanding.

Language can be a marvelous tool for bringing people together. While actually learning another language is an excellent way to begin bridging cultural gaps, all students can take giant steps toward cross-cultural understanding by exploring the more subtle dimensions of the ways in which people speak.

One problem in cross-cultural communication is that the order in which people put their words together often varies from culture to culture, making those who attempt to translate the language wonder what the other person really is trying to say. And the words themselves cannot always be directly interpreted. Their subtle, hidden, and implied meanings often escape a foreigner, even one who has learned the language well. Thousands of stories persist concerning misinterpretations of foreign tongues. Thai employees of a European firm based in that Southeast Asian country translated a sign which really meant "Out of sight, out of mind" into "Invisible things are insane." In his book *Mother Tongue: English and How It Got That Way* (1990), Bill Bryson relates how a Japanese attempt to assist foreign motorists went awry with the following advisory:

> When a passenger of the foot heave in sight, tootle the horn. Trumpet at him melodiously at first, but if he still obstacles your passage, then tootle him with vigor.

If nothing else, the instructions demonstrate the Japanese propensity for politeness and formality in using their language.

Rumors have existed since the end of World War II that the conflict in the Pacific might have ended quite differently if the interpreters had been aware of the *implied* meaning of a specific word. The Allies had demanded an unconditional surrender from the Japanese, and they replied that they were maintaining their policy of *mokusatsu* (moh-koo-sah-tsoo). The literal translation of this word is "to kill with silence," but its more common meaning to a Japanese usually is *either* "to ignore" *or* "to withhold from comment." Tragically, the translators chose "ignore." A week later, the atomic bomb exploded over Hiroshima.

In addition, we must not forget that language involves more than verbal communication. Students will discover that a raised eyebrow, a crossed leg, or a simple hand movement can be an offensive gesture in some cultures. A smile is certainly *not* the same in every language, for it sometimes disguises anger or vents frustration. Students will learn that actions are another form of communication known as *body language*, and these actions often are as important as verbal communication. While people in some societies rely heavily on body language to make their points, others use gestures very sparingly, but their lack of movement can be loaded with meaning as well.

Of course, like all other aspects of culture, not every member of a particular culture will use the language in the same way. In the lessons that follow, we have simply introduced some general traits of language use in several cultures, traits that you might find a large number of people in a particular culture displaying when communicating.

It is important for students to become aware of the great diversities in cultures and how these variations influence the use of language. We should never assume that everyone uses his or her language the same way nor that what we hear people from other areas of the world say is exactly what they mean. In order to ascertain what others mean, students must remember to consider many factors:

- Who is saying it
- How it is being said
- When it is being said
- Where it is being said
- Why it is being said

Context is all-important when it comes to cross-cultural understanding and interaction. Effective communication requires a perceptive eye, a patient ear, and an open mind.

What Went Wrong?

These introductory activities are designed to introduce the students to the ways language can act as a stumbling block in cross-cultural understanding. Most students will not know the correct answer to the question posed in each activity, but that is not the point. The point is to initiate curiosity and discussion and to stir their interest in pursuing this topic.

    Teacher's Instructions: Divide your class into groups of four or five students. Hand each group a copy of each of the following worksheets. Have each group work together to decide which answer best explains the behavior described in "What Went Wrong?" Then, as a class, each group will explain its reason for choosing the answer. After each group has spoken, reveal the correct answer and discuss it. An explanation to each one has been given below. Do the same with each "What Went Wrong?"

Some discussion questions include:

1. Why did your group choose this answer over the other answers? Were there clues given, did you simply eliminate the other answers, did you choose by instinct, or did you apply some assumptions you already had about the cultures mentioned? If you applied some assumptions, what did you already assume about the people from that culture?

2. How would you have felt in this situation?

3. What would you have done next?

4. What does this exercise show you about the different ways people from different cultures respond to the same situation?

Answers and Explanations

WHAT WENT WRONG? #1 = Answer #3
Mr. Sawyer did not understand that young Insu, because of his own culture's different use of language, interpreted the phrase, "I can't wait," to mean that his teacher literally could not wait for his report and wanted to see it immediately. East Asians are not given to exaggeration and overstatement in their languages. That, coupled with their deep reverence for educators, led Insu to fear that he had risked Mr. Sawyer's disapproval. And since East Asians rarely show their emotions overtly, Insu assumed a blank face to hide his anxiety.

WHAT WENT WRONG? #2 = Answer #4
Suzie Jones waited and waited in vain for her Mexican friend to arrive. She thought her friend possibly did not like her. This was not the case at all. Suzie did not understand the Mexican culture's different standard of politeness and different way of making appointments. Suzie's friend was simply being courteous by offering to take her shopping; but if she had been serious about the appointment she would have been much more specific about the logistics of the date. What she said was the equivalent of "let's do lunch" in the United States.

WHAT WENT WRONG? #3 = Answer #2
After the Japanese mother's response to her compliment, Mrs. Johnson worried that her Japanese third grader was not getting the support and encouragement he needed from his parents. Indeed, she thought he would not be able to achieve academic success because his parents had no faith in his intellectual abilities. But Mrs. Johnson did not understand that Japanese parents traditionally do not praise their children in public and do not feel comfortable setting themselves or their children off from others. The Japanese mother was probably quite proud of her son but embarrassed by Mrs. Johnson's calling attention to his achievement. Therefore she responded with the respectful humility the Japanese employ when using their language.

WHAT WENT WRONG? #4 = Answer #3
Tina was uncomfortable accepting such a valuable gift from her Arab friend. After all, she was simply being polite in admiring the gold cup. Tina didn't understand that Arab standards of hospitality go much further than customary politeness in the U.S. Admiring something verbally in an Arab's home will frequently result in an extravagant gift.

Each of these scenarios highlights the embarrassing or troubling events that can occur when members of one culture are not sensitive to the different use of language by members of another culture.

From *Windows to the World: Themes for Cross-Cultural Understanding.* Copyright © 1996 by Phyllis Kepler, Brooke Sarno Royse, and John Kepler

Student

Worksheet

NAME _____

DATE _____

WHAT WENT WRONG? #1

Mr. Sawyer, a fifth-grade teacher in a Chicago school, watches Insu Kim, a newly arrived ten-year-old from Korea, working eagerly on his social studies report. "I can't wait to see your report," comments Mr. Sawyer. The other students and Mr. Sawyer notice that, instead of looking pleased, Insu responds to the remark with a blank, unreadable face.

Why did Insu respond the way he did? (Circle the answer that best explains Insu's behavior.)

1. He was excited that Mr. Sawyer was interested in his report but since Koreans tend to hide their feelings, he tried to cover his excitement with a blank face.

2. He knew that his report was going to be brilliant and did not care what his teacher thought of it.

3. He thought Mr. Sawyer literally could not wait to see his report and wanted it immediately. He hid his fear behind a blank face.

4. He was embarrassed that Mr. Sawyer singled him out from the other students and did not want his classmates to see that he was really excited about the attention his teacher was showing him.

NAME _____

DATE _____

WHAT WENT WRONG? #2

Suzie Jones, a sixteen-year-old from Birmingham, Alabama, is living temporarily in Mexico City with her family. A Mexican friend says, "I shall be over tomorrow morning to take you shopping." The next morning Suzie waits and waits, but the friend never arrives.

Why did Suzie's Mexican friend never show up for their appointment? (Circle the answer that best explains Suzie's friend's behavior.)

1. Suzie's Mexican friend was not really a friend. In fact she did not really like Suzie and wanted to play a trick on her.

2. Suzie's Mexican friend got sick the next morning and did not bother to call up Suzie to tell her she could not make it.

3. Suzie's Mexican friend did not like people from the United States.

4. Suzie's Mexican friend liked Suzie very much and was simply being polite by making a date with her, but if she had really been serious about the date, she would have been much more specific about the details of their shopping trip.

Student
Worksheet

NAME _____

DATE _____

WHAT WENT WRONG? #3

Mrs. Johnson, an elementary school teacher in Des Moines, Iowa, compliments a Japanese mother on how quickly her third-grade son is learning English. To Mrs. Johnson's astonishment and concern, the mother replies, "Oh, my son is not very smart."

Why did the Japanese mother say that her son was not very smart? (Circle the answer that best explains the mother's behavior.)

1. Because she did not think her son was very smart. She thought Mrs. Johnson was being insincere by complimenting him, and she wanted to set the teacher straight.

2. Because she was embarrassed by Mrs. Johnson's calling attention to her son verbally and publicly. Even though she was pleased to hear that Mrs. Johnson was impressed with her son, the Japanese mother responded with respectful Japanese humility.

3. Because the Japanese never praise their children and the Japanese mother was embarrassed that the teacher was praising her son.

4. Because the mother did not think that learning English was important and certainly not a sign of being smart. If he were really smart, his teacher would have said he was doing well in math and science.

NAME _____

DATE _____

WHAT WENT WRONG? #4

Sixteen-year-old Tina Westmore is invited to the home of a newly arrived Arab student in New York City. "Oh, I love that beautiful gold cup," Tina comments as she looks around the living room. As Tina is leaving, the Arab friend gives her the valuable item.

Why did Tina's Arab friend give her the cup? (Circle the answer that best explains the Arab friend's behavior.)

1. The newly arrived Arab girl did not have any friends in New York, and she wanted to buy Tina's friendship.

2. The cup really wasn't worth much, and if Tina liked it so much, the Arab girl was happy to give it to her.

3. The Arabs are very hospitable and gracious people. No matter what Tina had admired out loud in her friend's home, the Arab girl probably would have offered it to her as a token of friendship and hospitality.

4. The Arab girl misinterpreted Tina's way of admiring the home. She thought that perhaps it was customary in the U.S. to offer as a gift whatever a guest admires verbally in your home. She only wanted to conform to U.S. customs.

Lesson 1

How Language Limits Our Perception

Three baseball umpires were discussing their profession. The first umpire says, "Some are balls and some are strikes, and I call them as they are." The second replies, "Some's balls and some's strikes, and I call 'em as I see 'em." The third thinks about it, then says, "Some's balls and some's strikes, but they ain't nothing 'till I calls 'em!" (Rothwell, 1982)

When it comes to the role language plays in determining our perceptions, the third umpire says it best.

Language both shapes and mirrors the beliefs and values of a culture. Indeed, the language a culture uses determines how that culture sees or perceives the world. Just as attitudes, values, and behavior are determined by one's cultural context, so is perception limited by the kinds of words a person has at his disposal for describing what he experiences. Some of the activities below are designed to help students understand how the language they use, like the language any culture uses, describes not reality but their *perception* of reality. They will discover that they may perceive a color, a taste, a smell, a sound, or a feeling quite differently from a person from another culture simply because they have different kinds of words to do so, and therefore that, when it comes to cultural differences, no one way of describing or perceiving something is necessarily any better or worse than another. They are simply different, and the difference can be an amusing and enriching discovery.

Consider the following example:

Tony, a college-bound high school senior, received a note from the registrar of the university he planned to attend, stating that he would be eligible for C-level courses in the fall. "I was furious," Tony admitted. "I called the registrar and said I definitely was not a C student. I had a straight A average and had never made a C the entire time I was in high school. I was told, of course, that C-level referred to advanced courses, not grades."

We can chuckle over the arrogance of a high school senior, but the incident also illustrates how the language of a high school culture did not transfer readily to that of the university. Our language allows us to define and describe our culture, but, at the same time, it prevents us from experiencing all the world has to offer. Unwittingly, Tony was restricted by his high school cultural language and its perception of a "C," and he failed to interpret it within the context of the collegiate world he was about to enter.

Activity

Share with your students the story about Tony. Ask them if they have ever made a similar mistake and have them share their experiences or write an essay about them. Discuss why these mistakes occur and gear the discussion towards the limits language imposes on their perception of new situations. *(interpretive)*

Perception and the Five Senses

The universal senses—seeing, hearing, smelling, tasting, and feeling—are limited by our language. We do not always see what someone from another culture may see simply because we do not have the same vocabulary to define it. We do not hear all of the world's sounds, are not even aware of them, partly because we have no verbal way to identify them. Smells can seem merely peculiar or odd when we do not have words to define their odor or origin, and one person's spiciness is another person's blandness when it comes to tastes. Feelings, whether physical or emotional, vary from culture to culture simply because of the words available or not available in the language.

What We See

Our eyes permit us actually to see 7,500,000 colors, but our language prevents us from identifying each one. Without a name, it is very difficult to keep a color in mind. Our language allows us to have two responses to color. One is physical, the other psychological.

Physical

Not every culture identifies the same colors verbally, and as a result, pinpointing a color across cultural lines can be difficult. Several tribes in New Guinea classify colors simply as black and white, the only two words in their language for color identification. Therefore, even though they may be able to see many different hues, the lack of words to identify them limits their range of visual perception and their ability to express exactly what they may see. Similarly, an Indian tribal language in northern Mexico does not verbally distinguish between green and blue, so the colors of the cactus and of sky meld into one.

The Japanese do not have a word for pink. When questioned about this, a Japanese woman argued with the authors, "We have pink, but we call it peach." No distinction was made between the two hues. But the Japanese do phonetically adapt English language colors to their vocabulary and therefore can add new colors to their palette. Pink has been introduced as *pinku* (peen-koo), and the term is used sometimes in advertising and promotions. Department stores will hand out a "pink-receipt" to their customers, which is actually a coupon that can be used in a drawing for a prize.

Yet the Korean and Japanese languages can also be far more specific in their definitions of color than can English. A very strong red color in Japanese becomes a precise *akai* (ah-kah), which translates as intense red, while *makkuro* (ma-koo-roh) represents intense black. In the U.S., adjectives are often added to a color (fire-engine red, teal blue, off white, pale yellow), names are borrowed from nature (ochre, seafoam, ivory, aquamarine), or foreign words (terra cotta, mauve, taupe) are imported to describe exactly what is meant, but the Japanese have many exact words. Here are some for the various shades of brown:

chairo (chah-ee-roh)	brown
kuriiro (kuhr-ee-ee-roh)	medium brown
kogechairo (koh-gay-chah-ee-roh)	dark brown

Psychological

People in the United States are *red* with *rage, green* with *envy,* and *yellow* when they are a *coward.* Who is not *blue* when the weekend is over? Brides dress in *white,* and mourners often select *black.* But in many Asian countries *white* is the color of mourning, so gifts should never be wrapped in white paper. Germans delight in a *blue* Monday because it means an extended weekend, while the French know that *green* symbolizes the lack of a grudge towards someone. Speaking of *green,* the Japanese prefer a *green wedding*—in spirit, if not in actuality—because it conjures up images of a new life, a new beginning, and most certainly the development of harmony between the newlyweds. The Japanese also like the *green sauna,* which, rather than bringing to mind pictures of algae, reminds them of the lovely countryside. Brides in India choose *red* over *white,* and in England *black cats* are perceived as *lucky.* The language, perception, and implications of color change from culture to culture, and with the changes come the possibilities of cross-cultural misunderstandings.

Activities

1. Show the students a color chart of the primary and secondary colors, and have them name each color. Then show them three slightly different shades of brown and see if they perceive a difference among them. Can they find names for the three shades or are they all simply variations of "brown"? Explore and discuss how colors are named in English (with adjectives, borrowing from nature or other languages), and then share with them the Japanese exact terms for the shades of brown. Ask them to learn these Japanese words by heart. *(interpretive)*

2. Look at a box of crayons and discuss the way each crayon color has been given a name. Categorize them by the way the colors are named: with an exact English word, with a name modified by an adjective, with a word borrowed from nature, with a word borrowed from another culture's language. Discuss the limits of English in giving exact words for certain colors. *(interpretive)*

3. Have the class look around the room and identify each color they see. Have them try to name each color using only words from nature (ivory, ochre, seafoam, salmon, lime, etc.). *(constructive)*

4. Obtain some color sample strips from a local paint store. Usually the colors on these strips are numbered, not named. If they are named, cross out the names with a magic marker. Divide the class into groups and hand each a sample strip. Have the groups attempt to create names for each color on the strip. Discuss how each group found the names for each color. *(collaborative, constructive)*

5. Make copies of the student worksheet on page 18 and hand one to each of your students. Have the students attempt to match up each of the phrases with the country where it is used. *(cross-cultural)*

6. Ask the students to think of all the ways we in the U.S. associate color with emotions and events. See if they can explain why we associate a certain color with a certain emotion or event. Then see if they can invent reasons why people in other cultures might do so differently. *(interpretive)*

7. Get a book of proverbs from around the world (available in most library reference sections). Find several proverbs from other cultures that have to do with see-

ing, and discuss them with the students. See if they can explain them. Then have them think of all the proverbs they can that have to do with seeing (i.e., "Out of sight, out of mind," "Seeing is believing"), discuss their meaning, and try to draw some conclusions about the value of sight in U.S. culture. If you have a multiethnic class, have the students obtain proverbs about seeing from their own cultures and share them with the class. It is especially interesting to find proverbs that directly contradict those from another culture. In one culture sight may be all-important, but in another culture what one sees may not be as important as what one believes. *(interpretive, cross-cultural)*

8. Cut out random, complex shapes from construction paper. Have the students identify the shapes. Discuss the variety of their responses and explain how everyone may see the same thing but see it differently, depending on the individual and his or her context or cultural background. *(interpretive)*

9. Have the students put nine dots on a piece of paper in the following order:

.   .   .

.   .   .

.   .   .

Ask them to try to connect all the dots with only four lines and without ever picking the pencil off the paper. The only way to do so requires going outside the imagined lines, as such:

Most students will not be able to do the task because they do not think of going outside the perceived square. After showing them how to accomplish the task, discuss why they felt limited by the boundaries of a perceived square. Use this exercise to explain how our perceptions and preconceptions often limit us, and we often have to discard them in order to transcend our limiting prejudices against others. *(constructive)*

10. Play a version of Pictionary®. Divide the class into two teams. Whisper the name of a person, place, thing, or event to a representative from each team. Give them one minute to draw it on the board. As they are drawing, each team will yell out guesses to their representative as to the subject of the sketch. The first team to guess correctly wins. After playing a few rounds, with a different word and different representatives for each round, discuss the different ways each student conceived and drew the item. Point out the different ways each individual pictures and sees certain things. *(collaborative, interpretive)*

11. Play "What Did You See?" Have someone the class has never seen (a friend, a spouse, a parent) dress up in a colorful, detailed, offbeat outfit (include, for example, a hat with a yellow feather, a red bandanna, mismatched socks or shoes, big earrings) and have him or her hold something incongruous for a school setting, such as a dog leash or a bouquet of wilted flowers. Then, without warning the class, have the stranger burst into the room, rush over to the window, and open it; pick up a stack of papers on your desk and move it to the other side; walk all the way around the room; and then abruptly leave. During the entire episode, he or she will be saying and repeating something startling to the students, such as: "The principal has just announced that there will be no spring vacation this year!" or "A snake is loose in the biology lab!" or "They're painting the hallway bright orange!"

Immediately after the person leaves the room, announce that this is all really a game called "What Did You See?" The students will have been so startled by what they have heard that they will not have noticed many of the details of the stranger's outfit and behavior in the classroom. Ask students to remember every detail of what they saw and list the details on the board. When their memories have been exhausted, ask the stranger to re-enact the event. Ascertain all the details the students did not notice earlier. Ask students what it was that limited their powers of observation and why.

Use the game to generate discussion about experiences they have had when they were so engaged with one thing that they completely missed seeing what was before them. Have them share their experiences with the class or write short essays about them. Explain that our perceptions are always necessarily limited by various things—attention span, distractions, prejudices, expectations, etc. *(collaborative, interpretive)*

NAME _____

DATE _____

What Color Is That Feeling?

Instructions: In the left column are phrases that various cultures use to describe emotions or emotional events. In the right column are the countries where these phrases are used. See if you can match up each phrase in the left column with the correct country in the right column.

red with rage	U.S.
blue Monday	India
green sauna	U.S.
mourners wear black	U.S.
green wedding	Germany
brides dress in white	Japan
green with envy	U.S.
red means being in debt	many Asian countries
black cats are lucky	U.S.
white is the color of mourning	U.S.
green means not holding a grudge	Japan
feeling blue when you're sad	France
a coward is yellow	U.S.
brides dress in red	England

What We Hear

Scientists believe that it is possible for the ear to determine approximately 340,000 sounds. But, once again, it is hard to find words to identify many of the sounds we hear. As we cross cultural borders, sounds become *peculiar, grating, cacophonous,* even *unbearable.* To many cultures, U.S.-English speakers sound nasal and flat.

Even animal sounds are heard and imitated quite differently in other cultures. English speakers know that a dog goes *bow-wow* or perhaps *arf-arf,* that a cat *meows,* roosters *cockadoodledoo* and cows *moo.* But animals say different things to a Korean. Dogs go *mong mong* (mawng mawng), cats *ya ong* (yow-**ong**), roosters *gak gok* (**ga**-awk **goh**-awk), and baby chickens *ok* (awk). To a Norwegian, cows say *mø* (the *ø* is pronounced like the *u* in *fur*).

The Language of Music

The language of music also changes across cultures. To the Western ear, the tones of Arab music can sound mysterious and haunting, and the beats of African music can be quite different from Western rhythms. Both Arabs and Africans, however, have made their marks on music in the West.

Arab Music

Western music contains scales of seven notes each. On a piano keyboard, there are white keys and black keys. It is one whole step from white note to white note. Rising just a little above most of the white notes are black keys. If we go from a white note to the nearest black key, we say we have traveled a half-step. When Westerners sing, it is not difficult for them to travel precisely between any of these notes.

Arab music is quite different. It does not have scales; instead its musical notes, or "tones" as the Arabs would say, are placed into "modes." There are many more steps, or closer steps, between each of these tones. Tones can be a quarter, an eighth, or even a sixteenth step apart. Try to imagine eight different notes between the two white notes on the piano keyboard. It would be very difficult, if a Westerner were singing, to land precisely on the correct tone because there would be so little difference between each step. Therefore, Arab music sounds to Westerners as if one is slithering and sliding along a musical course rather than jumping precisely from one note to another.

There also is no harmony in Arab music, at least not as it is defined in the U.S. These components give Arab music a strange sound to Western ears. But remember, Western music can sound very odd to Arabs. An Arab who heard Western music for the first time commented that everyone sounded as if they were off-key.

The Arabs have contributed a number of musical instruments to the Western world. Among them are the guitar, the flute, and the bagpipe. But the Arabs, just like the Africans discussed below, put great emphasis on the human voice. "Most Arabic music is vocal," says Audrey Shabbas in *The Arab World Notebook* (1989). "Arabic songs, for the most part, tend to be love songs," she adds.

African Music

There are more than two thousand different tribes and other cultural entities in sub-Saharan Africa. Although each African tribe has its own indigenous musical style, there are certain characteristics that are present in all African music, characteristics usually not found in many forms of Western music. Most importantly, African music is not meant simply for listening pleasure. Music is woven into all facets of African life, including some of the most minute functions of daily living. One tribe in Dahomey teaches its children to sing a song when they lose their first tooth, and another in Ghana has a special musical rendition that goes along with a ritual that is supposed to cure bed-wetting. There is music for everything, even criminal punishments. A Cameroonian writer named Frances Bebey once said, "The musical art is so much a part of man himself that he has seen no purpose in giving it a separate name" (Roberts, 1972). As a result, Swahili, spoken by more people on the African continent than any other language, has no word for music. Music is everywhere, in everything, It is not part of life. It is life.

Did You Know?

The Sahara Desert is the largest desert in the world, covering approximately three-and-a-half million square miles in northern Africa. It is about the same size as the entire United States. The desert covers about one-third of the African continent. The word "Sahara" is taken from the Arabic word *sahra,* meaning "wilderness." This sea of sand and rock forms an effective barrier between the northern African countries bordering the Mediterranean Sea, such as Morocco and Egypt, and those countries south of the desert, known as sub-Saharan. Rainfall in the desert averages less than ten inches a year, an amount that can fall in just one month in many areas of the U.S.

The human voice and hands are probably the most important instruments in African cultures. People do not simply listen to a musician perform; they nearly always join in to sing along. Composing is done with the human voice, not on pianos or wind or string instruments, as is usually the case in Western cultures. In most African music, a leader sings a line and everyone joins in to answer in a style known as "call and response" (Roberts, 1972). Hand-clapping is even more important to African music than the beat of the drum. Nearly every musical piece is accompanied by human hands beating out a rhythm. Drums, however, do play important roles in most, but not all, African tribes. The players of these percussion instruments are so canny and musically wise that they sometimes are able to make the drums' sounds imitate human voices.

An African musical composition usually carries two different rhythms at the same time. One beat will be for the melody, the other for the accompaniment. This rhythmic interplay is known as cross-rhythms (Roberts, 1972). Imagine listening to a U.S. musical composition that has one drummer following a 4/4 beat (a march) and another drummer beating to the time of a 3/4 rhythm (a waltz) simultaneously.

Today, Western music has infiltrated the large metropolitan areas of Africa and plays an important role along with the more traditional sounds. As in so many cultures around the world, there is a contrast of old and new.

Africa has made monumental contributions to music in the U.S. Several of our most popular musical forms are firmly rooted in Africa. These include jazz (sometimes considered the most important music of the twentieth century), the blues, and spirituals. While being definitive and popular musical styles in their own right, they also have influenced the course of musical innovation in the late twentieth century.

Activities

1. Ask the students what sounds various animals make in the U.S. Then tell them what Koreans and Norwegians hear. Do animals actually make different sounds in other cultures or do people simply hear and pronounce the sounds differently? Discuss why this would be so. Many students have never thought about the fact that how we pronounce various animal sounds in English is not exactly what the animals say. The same goes for the sounds Koreans and Norwegians make to approximate the sounds of animals. The point of this discussion is to make students aware of the ways language determines what we hear and of the role culture plays in this everyday experience. *(interpretive)*

2. Refer to a book of proverbs from around the world (available in most library reference sections). Find several proverbs from other cultures that have to do with hearing, and discuss them with the students. See if they can explain them. Then have them think of all the proverbs or phrases they can that have to do with hearing (i.e., "Don't believe everything you hear"), discuss their meaning, and try to draw some conclusions about the value of hearing in U.S. culture. If you have a multiethnic class, have the students obtain proverbs about hearing from their own cultures and share them with the class. *(cross-cultural, interpretive)*

3. If you have students with Arab backgrounds, ask them to bring tapes of music from their cultures to class. Play the music for the class, and ask the students to describe their responses to the music. Ask the Arab students what they originally thought of U.S. music styles when they first heard them. If you do not have Arab students, obtain tapes from your local library, play them for the class, and discuss the students' responses. *(cross-cultural, interpretive)*

4. How important is music to your students' lives? Discuss with them the significant role music plays in the lives of Africans. *(interpretive)*

5. Obtain a tape of African music from your local library. Play the tape for your students, and discuss the music's unique characteristics. *(interpretive)*

6. Play samples of contemporary African American gospel music, spirituals, jazz, and the blues for your students. Discuss some attributes of each, and list them on the board. What do these musical styles have in common? From what you have shared about African music, can the students see some of the African roots of these musical styles? (Gospel music uses the African "call and response" style, for example.) You may want to discuss the influence of slavery on these forms of music, how the spiritual evolved in the nineteenth-century U.S. South. This is a subject rich with potential for various activities. *(interpretive)*

7. Do a little background research on the roots of rap music (or assign the research to an enthusiastic, music-oriented student). What are those roots? Ask the students if rap music appears to owe any of its characteristics to other African American musical styles and/or to aspects of African music like "call and response" and cross-rhythm. *(interpretive)*

What We Smell

"Phew" is often our word for unpleasant odors, particularly those we cannot identify. "Aroma" becomes our word of choice for the more pleasant smells that waft by our nostrils. But what is "phew" in one culture is an "aroma" in another, and there are often more definitive names to go with it. Most people in the U.S. do not realize that they smell strange to many East Asians. Those who have studied our body odor chalk it up to the large amounts of meat consumed in the U.S. in comparison to the relatively low consumption of the same product by East Asians. To the Koreans, the smell of many people in the U.S. is known as *naimsae* (nayim-**shee**), and any person of their own country who carries such an odor would seriously consider surgery for removal of the underarm sweat glands. Such operations are definitely carried out if the smell is considered too offensive. To a Westerner in Korea, on the other hand, the smell of *kimchee* (kim-**shee**), the spicy pickled cabbage that graces the table daily in nearly every Korean household, might be unpleasant.

Activities

1. Have students visit a local ethnic grocery (Korean, Chinese, Indian, Arab, etc.) or the imported foods section of their local supermarket and bring in various foods with distinctive odors. Line up the items on a table and have the students respond as they take a whiff of each. How do they describe each smell? Note how responses and descriptions vary from student to student. *(cross-cultural, interpretive)*

2. Ask the students to list those things that smell good and those that smell bad. Have them think of all the words in English that describe smells and list them under the good or bad categories (i.e., aroma, scent, stink, fragrance). Explain to them that what they describe as a stink may be an aroma in another culture, as the food exercise has illustrated. *(constructive)*

3. Find several proverbs from other cultures that have to do with smell, and discuss them with the students. See if they can explain them. Then have them think of all the proverbs or phrases they can that have to do with the sense of smell (i.e., "I smell a rat"), discuss their meaning, and try to draw some conclusions about the value of smell in U.S. culture. If you have a multiethnic class, have the students obtain proverbs about the sense of smell from their own cultures and share them with the class. *(cross-cultural, interpretive)*

What We Taste

"Spicy," "hot," "tangy," and "sharp" turn into "mild," "cool," "bland," and "nondescript" as we cross cultures in the food categories. It is all in how we perceive the foods. What is more, even names of edibles can play tricks on our taste buds. If offered a *Toad-in-the-Hole, Bubble and Squeak,* or *Banger and Mash* in England, the hungriest tourist might curb his or her appetite. But these foods are really more edible than they sound. The first is a small sausage tucked under a blanket of popover-like batter; the second, a casserole of mashed potatoes and cabbage that takes its name from the sound it makes while cooking; and the third, a combination of sausage and mashed potatoes. On the other hand, a tourist from the Middle East might get nauseous if offered a *pig-in-a-blanket* or *a hot dog.*

Many from the U.S. perceive ice cream flavors as properly assigned to the fruit and candy genres, but the Japanese view this treat as a prime candidate for more esoteric flavors. In some specialty shops, patrons can be treated to *red bean, tomato and lemon, oolong tea, horseradish, sweet potato,* and *blue cheese* ice creams.

Activities

1. Have students visit a local ethnic grocery (Korean, Chinese, Indian, Arab, etc.) or the imported foods section of their local supermarket and bring in various foods with distinctive tastes. They may also have their parents help them prepare a dish at home. Line up the items on a table, and have the students respond as they take a taste of each food from a different culture. How do they describe the taste? Call their attention to variations in their responses and descriptions. *(cross-cultural, interpretive)*

2. Bring in three different kinds of Mexican salsa (mild, medium, hot), and have the students taste each and describe its level of spiciness. Because of what the students are accustomed to eating at home, their responses will vary. "Mild" may be very hot to one student and "hot" may be very mild to another. Discuss how spiciness may vary from culture to culture, just as it has from individual to individual in the class. *(interpretive)*

3. Tell the students about the different flavors of ice cream in Japan. Would the students ever order these flavors at Baskin Robbins? Why or why not? Discuss how tastes differ from culture to culture. *(cross-cultural)*

4. Ask the students if they would like to eat a "Toad-in-the-Hole," a "Bubble and Squeak," or "Banger and Mash" for lunch. When they are finished saying "Yuk!" explain to them what these foods really are (see above). See if they can think of any foods in the U.S. that would, because of what they are called, sound strange and unappetizing to a foreign visitor. Discuss the significance words have for determining what we think tastes good or bad. *(cross-cultural, constructive)*

5. Find several proverbs from other cultures that have to do with taste, and discuss them with the students. See if they can explain them. Then have them think of all the proverbs or phrases they can that have to do with the sense of taste. Discuss their meaning, and try to draw some conclusions about the value of taste in U.S. culture. If you have a multiethnic class, have the students obtain proverbs about the sense of taste from their own cultures and share them with the class. *(cross-cultural, interpretive)*

What We Feel

A "sweltering" day to someone from the United States may be "refreshing" to an Indian. To say "I feel good" in English would translate literally to something like, "Touch me, my body feels good" in many languages. Many Norwegians use the term *koselig* (**koo**-seh-lee), or "cozy," to refer not only to an inviting mountain cottage with a roaring fire but also to a comfortable gathering of friends or a feeling of warm emotion. People in the United States are quick to say they "love" something—their car, their new shoes, their dinner—while the Japanese refrain from using such a strong emotional term to describe their feelings for an object.

The sense of feeling, whether tactile or emotional, varies from culture to culture and, like the other four senses, often depends on the kinds of words each culture uses to describe what its members can feel.

Activities

1. Explore some of the ways we describe things by how we feel about them. Ask the students to pretend to stand in the shoes of someone from another culture. Discuss what they might think when they hear people in the U.S. constantly say they love something, anything. Do they think we are a warm, loving country? Do they think we are superficial and insincere? Explain that many cultures are confused and put off by the U.S.'s tendency to "love" everything. *(cross-cultural)*

2. Have the students look through magazines at home and find advertisements that attempt to sell an item by evoking certain feelings about it. The students should show their ads to the class and ask their classmates to respond emotionally to the ads. This exercise not only makes young people aware of how the advertising media manipulates their feelings when trying to sell them a product but also highlights the importance of feeling in determining how they perceive something. *(interpretive)*

3. Ask the students to tell or write a story about something that made them happy, sad, or angry recently, but they have to tell the story entirely in slang. Have a few of the students tell or read their stories to the class. As each student reads, mark on the board every slang word that refers to a feeling. Count them and point out how very many slang words we have to describe our feelings. Why do we invent them? Are official English words not enough? Why not? Did everyone in the classroom understand all the slang terms? If not, have the story-teller explain them. Then ask the students to imagine what it would be like trying to understand the story if they were visiting from another culture. *(constructive, cross-cultural)*

Lesson 2

How Language Reflects a Culture's Values and Attitudes

Formality in Language

Activity

Read the following story to the class.

Eleven-year-old David Stone and his parents had recently settled into their new home in Mexico City after moving there from St. Louis. David's dad was assigned to his company's office in that city for a five-year tour. The family was amazed at how friendly everyone seemed to be, and Mr. and Mrs. Stone were surprised to have been invited to a party by some of Mr. Stone's Mexican co-workers. A greater surprise came when the invitation was also extended to include David.

*The night of the party, the Stones practiced their Spanish with the other guests, and the Mexicans seemed very pleased to hear the Stones speaking their language. The Stones, including David, felt so comfortable and at home with their new Mexican friends that they switched from the formal use of the pronoun "you," usted (oo-**sted**), and began to use the informal tu (too).*

The party was still in full swing at two in the morning, but the Stones felt they had to go home, particularly with David along. The three quietly said their good-byes to the hostess without disturbing the other guests and thanked her profusely for the wonderful time they had had. But something seemed very wrong. They sensed that the hostess was not pleased.

Have the class guess what went wrong at the Mexican party. Then explain to them the following information about proper manners around the world.

People in the United States may mistake friendliness among people of other cultures for informality. The two do *not* go hand in hand. Because of its image as a vacation destination with sunny beaches and joyful *mariachi* (**mah**-ree-**ah**-chee) bands, Mexico is often viewed by people in the U.S. as a nation of fun-loving, hence informal, people. Mexicans are warm and friendly, but proper behavior is defined differently than it is in the U.S.

Women rarely appear in shorts or pants on city streets, and many Mexicans frown upon visitors who do not conform to this unwritten rule. While children often are included at adults' parties, certain rules of protocol still must be followed. Usually guests should not quietly slip away from the festivities; instead, they should bid a very polite farewell to each and every guest. Moreover, some Mexicans feel that it is presumptuous for someone to switch from *usted* to *tu* without being invited to do so. By not using the language properly in saying their good-byes and in switching to an informal style of speaking, the Stones had breached some rules of good manners in Mexico.

"Hey, you guys," or its translated equivalent, would not be acceptable in parts of Mexico or many other areas of the world. Europeans are usually more formal by U.S. standards, and the languages of France, Italy, Spain, Germany, Portugal, and Scandinavia incorporate the formal and informal "you." Language formality comes in many forms. The French do not walk into a bakery or any shop, particularly one they visit on a regular basis, and say, "I'll take some. . . ." Rather, they begin their request with a very polite *"Bonjour, Madame, ça va?"* ("Good morning, madam, how are you?").

Asians are generally more formal by Western standards, and, again, the formality is mirrored in their languages. In any conversation between Japanese individuals, the status of the speaker and the person being addressed influence the choice of nouns, verbs, and pronouns. Pronouns, for example, are avoided in polite conversation, so that an employee might ask a superior, "Would Mr.

Did You Know?

In Thailand, the personal pronouns change according to the rank of the person with whom you are speaking. One form of "I" literally means "my hair," and it is used when speaking with someone of a higher or equal rank as a sign of politeness. Its origins go back to the times when the king's subjects had to lower their heads, the most sacred part of their bodies, to a position below the ruler's feet. Out of respect, the subject could not look the king straight in the eye. Instead, he would start his conversation with something to the effect of "My head beneath the dust under your feet addresses you."

Section Chief like a cup of coffee?" In the United States, everyone in the office probably would be on a first-name basis, even with the boss, and the query would be more like, "Hey, Janet, do you want a cup of coffee?"

The title *sensei* (sehn-seh), meaning "teacher" or "master," is attached to a teacher's name in Japan. If this practice were followed in the U.S. classroom, Mr. Jackson would become Jackson-*sensei*. Japanese children also must address students in a higher grade with respect. An eighth grader who called a ninth grader only by name would be in serious trouble. *San* (sahn), an honorific title that is close to "Mr." or "Miss," must follow the older student's name. In the U.S., this would mean that Jimmy, a ninth grader, would become Jimmy-*san* to his eighth-grade friend. Koreans also have a form of honorific speech, and students in that country also must show respect for older classmates. Koreans do not use personal names; instead, the younger child addresses the older one as "older brother" or "older sister." Not to do so can result in serious consequences. Korean students commonly address their teacher by title rather than by name. Thus, they may simply use the English equivalent, "teacher," in the U.S. rather than their instructor's surname.

Activities

1. Ask the students to give examples of formality in the U.S. Tell them that U.S. standards of propriety do not correspond to those in other cultures, and explain what proper behavior might mean to a European, an Arab, or a Japanese person. *(constructive)*

2. Have the students practice proper behavior as a Japanese and a Korean would. Teach them how a Japanese person addresses others, and ask them to spend an entire day practicing. All day, they cannot use the pronoun "you." They must address you, their teacher, with *sensei* attached to your last name. They must address the cafeteria servers as "Ms. or Mr. Cafeteria-Server." They must address the principal as "Mr. Principal." And they must address students in a higher grade with *san* attached to their first names. The following day, they can be Korean and address any older classmates as "older brother" or "older sister." *(cross-cultural)*

JAPANESE TITLES

- chan (attached to a young child's given name, used at home)

- kun (attached to a school-aged boy's given name)

- san (attached to an adult's surname)

- sensei (meaning "teacher," attached to the surname)

What's in a Name?: Language and the Family

One's name often is among the first words spoken to someone you are meeting or introducing to a third party. But calling others by their correct names can be a confusing and embarrassing task when communicating across cultures. An error can display ignorance and insensitivity. Which name is the family name? Does the name need a title? Is the wife called by her husband's name? These are only a few of the problems involved in calling others by name.

Names and their uses are unique to each culture. People in the U.S. should realize that our practice of using first names is considered in very poor taste in most other cultures. In many societies, even the closest of friends refer to each other by last names or by other identifying titles. When someone from the U.S. meets and talks with someone from another culture, he or she should use the other's first name only if specifically invited to do so.

In many East Asian cultures, the family or surname is placed first and is the proper name to use when addressing others. Given names follow. An acceptable way to address East Asians is by using "Mr." together with the surname, for example, "Mr. Kato." A more polite way, however, to introduce a Japanese person (either male or female) is to add the honorific *San* after the surname; Mr. Kato becomes "Kato-San." Younger Japanese children are called by their given name followed by *chan* (chahn)— which implies that they are little—until they enter school. Then things change for boys but not for girls. A boy named Hiroki Kato is called Hiroki-*kun* (koon) (signifying that he is older now) by his elementary school teacher and classmates but still called Hiroki-*chan* at home. A girl named Kuni Kato would still be called Kuni-*chan* both at school and at home. When the children are a bit older they are both called -*kun* and then -*san*.

KOREAN NAMES

Kim	**Sung**	**Ja**
family name, or surname	generational name	given name

Note: When Koreans reside in the U.S., they often will adapt their names to U.S. usage. Kim Sung Ja would become Sung Ja Kim in the U.S.

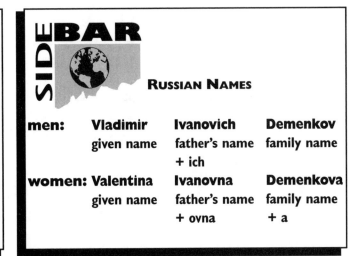

RUSSIAN NAMES

men:	**Vladimir**	**Ivanovich**	**Demenkov**
	given name	father's name + ich	family name
women:	**Valentina**	**Ivanovna**	**Demenkova**
	given name	father's name + ovna	family name + a

The different use of names in Asia is also evident in Korea. Although there are over two hundred surnames in Korea, 21 percent of the population have one surname, "Kim," and 15 percent "Lee/Rhee." Most Koreans have two additional names besides their surname; one is a name identifying the person's generation, and the second is the given name. For example, the name "Kim Sung Ja" consists of Kim, the surname; Sung, identifying the generation; and Ja, the given name. There are no middle names in Korea. This person would use "Sung Ja" as the given name and "Kim" as the family name.

The full Hispanic name includes not only the paternal but also the maternal family names. The father's name is neither first nor last. For example, in the name "Jose Sanchez Santos," the paternal name is "Sanchez" and "Santos" is the mother's family name. The man would be correctly addressed as "Señor Sanchez" or "Señor Sanchez Santos." When a girl marries, she drops her mother's maiden family name and adds her husband's

HISPANIC NAMES

Jose	**Sanchez**	**Santos**
given name	father's family name	mother's family name
Marta	**Acosta**	**Juarez**
given name	father's family name	mother's maiden family name

If Marta marries Jose, her name becomes Marta Acosta de Sanchez.

family name preceded by "de." So if Marta Acosta Juarez marries Jose Sanchez Santos, the bride becomes Marta Acosta de Sanchez.

In some Eastern European countries such as Bulgaria, the female version of the family name is spelled differently from that of the male. If, for example, the male family name is Voukadinov, the wife's name is Voukadinova. This is also true of last names in Russia. Furthermore, Russian names are structured quite differently from names in the U.S. First comes the given name, then the father's given name plus *-ich* for males or *-ovna* for females, and finally the family name. So, a brother and sister, named Vladimir (Vlah-**dee**-meer) and Valentina (Vuh-lun-**tee**-na), respectively, whose father's first name is Ivan and family name is Demenkov, would be: Vladimir Ivanovich (Ee-**vah**-neech) Demenkov and Valentina Ivanovna (Ee-**vah**-nuv-nuh) Demenkova.

Communication Within the Family

Many societies use first names when addressing their family members, a practice they would consider rude and embarrassing with outsiders. Other cultures have different notions of what is a proper way to address another person. In Saudi Arabia, for example, the term "wife" is felt to be too indelicate to use because it carries very intimate connotations, and it is replaced by various euphemisms such as "my lady," or "my cousin" even if they are not related. The wife, in turn, calls her husband "master" or also "cousin." This latter title stems from the attitude that marriage between first cousins is permissible.

Forms of address within African families are sometimes different from those used in the U.S. While children in Nigeria address their parents as *mom* and *dad,* out of deference to age (always an important factor in this West African country), they call an older brother *N'da* [*brother's name*] and an older sister *N'se* [*sister's name*]. *N'da*

Did You Know?

In Russia, when you address someone who is considered to be higher in rank than you, such as a teacher, a professional, an official, or any adult if you are under 30, you would use his or her first name and the patronymic (or, version of the father's given name). You would leave off his or her last name. So, if you met Vladimir Ivanovich Demenkov, your teacher, on the street, you would say, "Good morning, Vladimir Ivanovich!"

and *N'se* mean "my senior" (Harris and Moran, 1988). Because of their extremely close kinship ties, some African tribal languages have no specific words for aunts, uncles, or cousins. Female relatives are called "mother," male relatives are addressed as "father," and cousins are thought of as brothers and sisters.

Koreans often rely on kinship terms to refer to older people. An elder brother would be called *older brother*. Spouses avoid using each other's names and may refer to one another as their child's father or mother. A Korean husband will not use his wife's given name in the presence of others. The term by which he refers to her varies with the status of the person with whom he is speaking. In speaking of another's wife, one refers to her as a "lady" in the highest, most respectful sense.

Activities

1. Share with the students the ways in which families from various cultures name themselves. Ask them to find out from their parents how and why their first and middle names were chosen and what their last names mean, what language they come from, and how they may have been changed through history. Earlier in this century, many immigrants to the U.S. had their names shortened by impatient immigration officials because they were too long or too difficult to pronounce. For example, "Sarno," the maiden name of one of the authors, is an Italian-sounding shortened version of what was really a long Russian name. Have the students research the origins of their family names. Then have them share the information with the class. You could also have them write essays or stories about the origins of their names and compile them in a Class Name Book. *(constructive)*

2. Write the Korean name "Kim Sung Ja" on the board and ask the students to identify the surname, the generational name, and the given name. Write the Mexican name "Jose Sanchez Santos" on the board and ask the students to identify the paternal and maternal names. Then have the students try to liken their father's and their mother's names to Hispanic names. This task is easier to accomplish if they make diagrams of their family names. An example is given below.

Example:

Student's Name:	Joe Louis Brown
Joe's Father's Name:	Bob Andrew Brown
Bob's Mother's Name:	Mary Johnson (her maiden name) Brown
Joe's Mother's Married Name:	Christina Lucas (her maiden name) Brown

Hispanic Equivalent:

Men:	given name	father's family name	mother's family name
Joe:	Joe	Brown	Lucas
Bob:	Bob	Brown	Johnson

Married Women:	given name	father's or maiden family name	husband's family name
Christina's married name:	Christina	Lucas	de Brown

(NOTE: Things get more complicated, of course, for your students with hyphenated last names, single-parent homes, unmarried parents, or unknown parents. These students will need some extra help with this activity and may need to be told that their situations make the activity more challenging and interesting.)

Explain the structure of Russian names, and illustrate them on the board. Discuss the similarities and differences among Korean, Hispanic, Russian, and U.S. names. *(cross-cultural, constructive)*

3. Ask your students how they address members of their families. Do they have close family friends to whom they refer as "aunt" or "uncle"? Tell them about the ways family members address each other in Saudi Arabia, Nigeria, and Korea. What do these forms of address say about the ways people regard each other in those cultures? How are they different from forms of address and the ways family members regard each other in the U.S.? *(interpretive)*

Did You Know?

In Thailand, "please" and "thank you" are rarely said. You do not use "please" when asking someone to pass you something at the table or to hand you something at school. "Thank you" is used only when you have something for which you are very grateful. Thais consider it foolish to say "thank you" to waiters and others who are supposed to be serving you.

Did You Know?

Many in the U.S. say they "speak from the heart." The Japanese, on the other hand, have "belly talk." *Haragei* (hah-rah-geh), the art of belly talk, is the ability to anticipate others' needs without really saying anything about them. The Japanese feel it in their belly; they can simply sense what others want.

Greetings

Most Westerners say "Good morning" or "Hello" to greet each other. Other cultures around the world, however, say very different things in greeting. Africans who speak Swahili say, *"Hujambo"* (hoo-**dyam**-bo) when greeting someone. The other responds, *"Sijambo"* (see-**dyam**-bo). *Jambo* is a contraction which is the equivalent of "Is something bothering you?" in the same way that "Good-bye" is an English contraction of "God be with you." After the other responds, the greeter says *"Asubuhi"* (Ah-soo-boo-hee), which means "How's it going?" The other responds, *"Nzuri"* (Ne-zoo-ree), meaning "Fine."

The Arabs are almost evenly divided in their way of saying "Good morning" to each other. Some do simply give the casual two-word greeting, but others, particularly those who take their religion very seriously, prefer to be more formal by saying, "Peace be on you." It is customary to answer with a more elaborate phrase of "Peace be on you, too. God's mercy and blessing."

The Korean language does not provide a "Good morning." Instead, people who know each other quite well, such as family members or extremely close friends, will say to each other, "Did you sleep well?" first thing in the morning. A little later in the day, Koreans ask a simple "How are you?" instead.

Throughout the day, the Malays very often greet each other with "Peace be with you." Not out of nosiness but out of a simple desire to be friendly, the Malays also often ask people they meet on the street, "Where are you going?" The Chinese people who live in Malaysia will greet each other with "Have you taken your food?" which is equivalent to asking someone in the U.S., "How are you?" No matter how hungry someone is, the reply should always be, "Yes, thank you."

Activity

After sharing the information above, pair up the students and have them learn and practice the African/Swahili, Arab, Korean, Malay, and Chinese-Malaysian forms of verbal greeting. Discuss typical greetings in the U.S. and their difference from these other forms. Suggest that they try these new forms of greeting at home with their families. *(cross-cultural)*

Politeness Can Be Misunderstood

Polite language in one culture can be rude talk in another. A casual "Hi" to strangers may be taken not as a friendly gesture but as an invasion of privacy. One U.S. citizen who lived in London invited her neighbors in for coffee. While everyone was friendly, many were meeting their own long-time neighbors for the first time. In France, immediate neighbors may forever remain as "Monsieur" or "Madame." Although many Europeans are outwardly reserved, by U.S. standards, they do not hesitate to share restaurant tables with strangers. Yet, even then, the parties ignore each other, for to do otherwise would be considered an invasion of privacy. Many Europeans wait to talk until after they have been properly introduced, but then the talk usually stays off personal subjects. Such questions as, "How many children do you have?" or "What kind of work do you do?" usually are considered far too intimate for first-time meetings in countries like England and France.

Some Asians, on the other hand, can startle Westerners with questions that seem by U.S. standards very personal. "How old are you?" a Korean is quick to ask. Age establishes rank, and the older an individual, the more prestige that person has. The Korean, therefore, is only attempting to ascertain the other person's unofficial position. Filipinos are apt to ask, "How much money do you make?" simply as a sign of friendliness, not nosiness.

In an attempt to be polite and to make others feel good about themselves, Filipinos also often address people with ranks above their official social status. In other words, Colonels become "Generals," a beggar may be called "Sir," and a lowly employee is referred to as "Boss." Professional titles are usually attached to people's names whenever possible, so that Mr. Cruz becomes Attorney Cruz, or Architect Cruz, or Engineer Cruz (Roces and Roces, 1985).

"Thank you" can be perceived very differently in other languages. The Japanese feel it simply is not enough to express their appreciation with a mere "thanks," but often add *sumanai* (soo-mah-nah), which generally means, "I am sorry for all the trouble I have caused you." A U.S. student should not be surprised if a newly arrived Japanese child in their classroom says, "I'm sorry" instead of, or in addition to, "Thank you." He or she is expressing appreciation, but at the same time showing that he or she now realizes an obligation to return the favor.

With modesty understood differently among Asians, they often use their language for self-deprecation. Accepting a compliment is considered ungracious. Instead one might hear a Japanese respond, "I live in a hovel," "My children are not very smart," or "I am not worthy of receiving this award." All are common remarks which reflect the Asian cultures' propensity for modesty by U.S. standards.

Activities

1. Discuss standards of politeness with your class. What does it mean to be polite in the U.S.? What does it mean to be impolite? Have the students offer examples of rude questions one should not ask (i.e., Don't ask your friend's mother, "How much money do you make?" Don't ask your friend's grandmother, "How old are you?"). Explain to them what politeness and rudeness can mean in other countries like England, France, Korea, and the Philippines. *(interpretive)*

2. Explain to the students why a Japanese person might say "I'm sorry" instead of "Thank you." Let them practice Japanese politeness by spending an entire day saying "I'm sorry for all the trouble I have caused you" instead of a simple "Thank you." In addition, have them imitate Japanese humility by speaking modestly and responding to compliments with self-deprecation (i.e., "Oh, I am not worthy of this grade." "I am not very smart." "My handwriting is nothing special.") for the entire day. But make sure to explain to the students that these humble expressions are a form of politeness. Japanese people do not necessarily think so lowly of

themselves. It is a way the Japanese have to make others feel good and to avoid bragging. *(cross-cultural)*

Telling It Like It Is

For many in the U.S., directness in speech is an admired trait. "Get to the point. Quit beating around the bush," they tell each other. Yet such directness can be scorned in other cultures. Although many hundreds of different languages are spoken in sub-Saharan Africa, most people do not speak directly to the point, particularly when they are conversing with those who are not of the same generation. It is very important to be polite and not direct when talking with someone who is older. As a result, during these conversations between generations, people must often read between the lines and ask themselves what is really meant. Children never confront their parents with a direct "no," even though they may intensely disagree with their moms or dads. However, young people usually are very candid when talking among themselves. In Mexico, it is considered extremely rude to attempt to get down to business immediately. First, talk about the weather, ask about the family, discuss anything but the purpose that brings you together. Arabs, too, start with small talk, and the Japanese prefer to get to know you before business is ever discussed.

To some in the U.S., the Japanese speak in generalities. But to the Japanese, being dogmatic or arguing a point is a breach of etiquette, and conversations there often seem allusive and vague to those who do not understand the culture. Getting to the point is not important, even best avoided. What is important is making sure that the person to whom a Japanese is speaking is never forced to admit he might be wrong and thus *lose face.* The point is to maintain collective harmony, *wa* (wah), at any cost. The language style that reflects this value can lead Westerners *quite falsely* to assume that the Japanese are shy, unassertive, or evasive.

While on a visit to Tokyo, two of the authors experienced a Japanese way of saying no:

> We went to a hotel near the one where we were staying to inquire if we could have permission to use the swimming pool. The query was made to the desk clerk, who very politely replied, "Ah so, the lady and gentleman would like to use the swimming pool." "I think," said John, "he is telling us no."

In many Asian cultures, the speaker avoids giving a direct "no" in answer to a question that requires a negative response—again, to avoid conflict. Instead, a Japanese

Did You Know?

In many African cultures, a simple "no, thank you" is not enough to convince your hostess that you have really had enough to eat and do not want a second helping. With this simple answer, a hostess would pile additional food on your plate. It is necessary to repeat your point many times in many different ways in order to make your wishes understood. A U.S. citizen visiting in an African community might put it something like this: "Thank you very much, but I really have had too much to eat. I truly enjoyed the meal, but I cannot eat another bite. It is so nice of you to offer me more food, but I must not eat any more. I am so full."

person probably will reply indirectly, perhaps with "That can be very difficult," or "The matter will be looked into." A "yes" answer can also be vague. Rather than offering a positive reply, it usually means, simply, "Yes, I hear what you are saying."

Telling the truth takes different forms in many cultures. For the Japanese, there are two levels of honesty: *Tatemae* (tah-ta-my) is surface truth and reflects social politeness; *honne* (hoh-nay) represents what is really felt or believed. If a Japanese student in a U.S. classroom were asked if she would like to be in the school play, she might possibly answer that she will think about it or that it might be very difficult for her to find the time. Both replies indicate negative responses as well as truth at the *tatemae* level. At the *honne* level, the child might very well be thinking that she really wants to take part in the production but is not worthy of being in it. It is important for teachers with Japanese students to understand and recognize the dynamics of Japanese truth-telling so that they do not judge the students for evasiveness.

It might seem to someone in the U.S. that the Arabs, unlike the East Asians, use exaggeration, repetition, and self-praise when using their language. Arabs use their language as a verbal art form that has great emotional force for both the speaker and the listener. If a person from the U.S. were to visit an Arab country and hear verbal battles erupt into explosive arguments on a street corner, he or she might assume that a physical fight was about to take place. But then the heated discussion will suddenly end, and no violence has ensued. That is because, for many Arabs, words act as a substitute for actions.

To many Arabs, a simple "yes" or "no" to a question is not enough. The answer must be repeated in many different forms in order to make sure that the point has really been made. If a boy were to ask a girl if she would like to go to the movies with him, and she replied with a simple "no thanks," he would probably take it as a positive answer. In order to make her point clear, she would need to put her answer in several different ways, explaining that she definitely will not be able to attend the film with him.

Furthermore, in the Arab cultures, where a very high percentage of the people follow the Islam faith, there is a hesitancy to commit oneself to tomorrow. Everything is in the hands of God. When asked if an appointment is definite for a certain date, the Arabic speaker will reply, "We shall meet, Allah willing."

Activities

1. Explore with your students what it means to "tell it like it is." Is this something valued highly in the U.S.? What is more important: to get to the point or to talk around the subject? In what situations are students encouraged to get to the point and not beat around the bush? Is it considered a waste of time to talk about "irrelevant" subjects like the weather, family, or summer vacation in the U.S.? Why is "small talk" called *small* talk? Explain to them that in many cultures, such as some African tribes, Mexico, Japan, and Saudi Arabia, it can be considered rude to get straight to the point. *(interpretive)*

SIDEBAR

New Words from Japan

sumanai (generally) — "I am sorry for all the trouble I have caused you." Often added after the Japanese "thank you," *arigato* (ah-ree-gah-toh)

wa — harmony within the group. All-important concept in Japanese society.

kao (kow) — "face," as in "losing face"; a Japanese concept: being publicly shamed, embarrassed, or humiliated for violating the peace and harmony (*wa*) of the group.

tatemae — surface truth; what one says that reflects what society expects to be right or true.

honne — deeper truth; what one really feels or believes is right or true.

Did You Know?
Weather plays such an important role in the lives of the Inuits that they have many different words referring to "snow." Each has an important meaning, ranging from the conditions of the dog sled roads to the intensity of the storm.

Did You Know?
In U.S. culture, Friday the 13th is considered a bad luck day. In many Spanish-speaking cultures, the bad luck day is Tuesday the 13th. This is because the Spanish word for Tuesday, *martes* (*mahr*-tayss), comes from the word *Mars*, the Roman god of war.

2. Have the students practice some ways the Japanese might use to say "no"—that is, saying *no* without ever saying "no." Explain the reasons why many Japanese do not say "no" directly. Challenge them to go an entire day saying *no* in the Japanese way. *(cross-cultural)*

3. Discuss what it means to tell the truth in the U.S. How important is it? Explain the two different levels of truth in Japanese culture. Can they think of scenarios in which a Japanese student would employ *tatemae* or *honne* truth? See if they can come up with examples of incidents when they too operated with two levels of truth. *(interpretive, constructive)*

4. Share with the students the common Arab way of saying "yes" and "no," as well as the way of making future appointments. Have them role-play situations in which they act as an Arab might when saying "yes" or "no" to making an appointment. (Of course, some students may want to substitute "God" or "Fate" for "Allah.") *(cross-cultural)*

Words Reflect Values

The important role a specific word plays within a society often escapes those not truly in touch with that culture.

One of the authors experienced the following during a trip to Egypt:

> When I walked out of the airport with my seventeen-year-old daughter shortly after our arrival in Cairo, Egypt, a young man rushed up to me and eagerly proclaimed, "I shall give you two thousand camels for your daughter's hand." My daughter and I were a bit taken aback by the proposal, not only because of its implied intent, but also by the commodity being offered in exchange for my daughter's hand.

Camels, the visitors were soon to learn, still play a significant, if sometimes only a symbolic, role in the people's lives of the Middle East, where deserts cover large portions of the land. Even today, and certainly in the rather recent past, the camel provides a major means of transportation because of the animal's ability to travel for long periods of time without water. Contemporary Arabic, one of the principal languages of the Middle East, includes nearly six thousand words that refer to the camel, its parts, or equipment associated with the animal's use.

On the other hand, in the East African nation of Kenya, the Masai tribe computes its wealth in cattle. The animals are rarely traded or slaughtered, only collected in the same manner that people in many other areas of the world save their money. With cattle playing such an important role in this culture, no fewer than seventeen words of the Masai's language stand for what we in our part of the world simply call a "cow."

Yet some cultures don't even have words to label certain objects or ideas. The word *war* is one such term. One English language synonym book lists fifty-six alternatives for the word, but no expression for the term *war* even exists in the language of the Penan, a peaceful tribe in the Malaysian province of Sarawak. The word simply is not necessary in this particular culture. *Words—and, in this case, the lack of words—mirror the values and needs of a particular society.*

Activities

1. Discuss with your students the importance of camels, cattle, and peace in the Middle East, Kenya, and Sarawak, respectively. *(interpretive)*

2. Have the students name objects in the U.S. for which we have many, many words (the automobile, for example; or money). See how many words they can list that name or relate to each object. Can they think of something that would not exist if we did not have words for it? Would war be less possible if we didn't have a word for it? Discuss how the abundance or lack of words for certain things points to dominant values within U.S. culture. *(constructive)*

Lesson 3

How Sounds and Tones of Languages Carry Meaning

Languages relay meaning by the sounds and tones used in speaking them, and the tones used in speaking vary from one language to another. What sounds pleasing and normal to one cultural ear may be harsh or grating to another. Charles Berlitz tells us that languages are blessed with clicks, tones, guttural sounds, lisps, chirps, tweets, and twitters, all of which give different meanings to what is being said. There is even another sound, difficult to label, that is made by the speakers of Hebrew and Arabic. This special sound is made by a contraction of throat muscles and is difficult for English speakers to pronounce.

An Arab verbal argument can seem threatening and even dangerous to a Western ear. In turn, U.S.-English sounds like a series of unpleasant grunts to an Arab. The inflections used in the British way of speaking can sound condescending to the ear of a U.S.-English speaker. The lilted inflections of Norwegian and Swedish, caricatured most famously by the Swedish Chef on "The Muppet Show," sound as if these Scandinavians *sing* their language. When they caricature U.S.-English, they hold their noses and speak in a nasal monotone.

The tonal sounds of Chinese, in which the pitch does not change with regularity at the end of each sentence, can come across as dull or even angry to a Westerner. The Chinese change the levels of their voices with each word, thereby giving it a specific meaning based on the sound or tone. The same sound, pitched differently, can have a totally unrelated meaning. For example, a sound in Chinese that is identical to the English "my" can mean "sell" when asked like a question, but "buy" when expressed as an affirmative answer (Berlitz, 1982). This makes the verbal Chinese language very difficult for an English speaker to master, and can cause serious misunderstandings across cultural lines.

It has been estimated that there are 800 different languages spoken south of the Sahara desert on the African continent. Some say there are many more. These languages, in turn, are classified into five major groups. One of these major language groups is known as Bantu, and the best-known language within this group is Swahili, which has the largest number of speakers of any language in Africa. The Bantu tongues are spoken along the Equator and southward through the continent. With the exception of Swahili, which places stress accents over syllables, languages that come under the Bantu heading are also tonal. For example, the difference between a singular and plural form of a verb may simply be in the difference in tone.

Japanese and Korean are not tonal languages, but there are many words that sound alike while conveying different meanings. The word for "death" and the word for "four" sound alike in Japanese, Korean, and Chinese. So, among these three languages, "four" has come to signify an unlucky number, just as thirteen has in some English-speaking cultures. People in these East Asian countries avoid numbering a floor "four" in hotels, just as people in the U.S. tend to skip from the twelfth to the fourteenth floor in hotels. In Japan, the number "four" stays off license plates, and it is considered poor taste to give someone a gift that comes in four different sections.

The enthusiasm and excitement expressed in the English-speaking voices of U.S. residents can at times come across as anger to those from a culture where sound is more modulated. Not just what we say but how we say it can deliberately imply different meanings in many cultures, including our own. Problems arise when those of different cultures do not understand the implications of sounds and tones. While it is impossible to be aware of all the foreign meanings of sound and tone, we at least can be sensitive to the fact that they do exist and that our very voice pitch or tonal expression may come across quite differently from the true intent of what we are saying.

Activities

1. Experiment with various tones when speaking to the class. Say you are very pleased with their work but do it in a monotone. Then say it in an angry tone. Then try it in a sarcastic tone. Laugh when you say it. Say it as a question. Ask the class to interpret your sentence each time. They will come up with several meanings. Next say you are very upset with the level of discipline in the class but laugh and smile when you say it. Then say it in a flat tone with a blank face. Again ask the class how what you said came across to them each time. Explain to them that different cultures use different tones when speaking and that these tones are as important as what people say. *(interpretive)*

2. Have the students pair up and experiment saying things in different tones. Have the partner write down what he or she thinks the speaker means. Let them exchange roles and do the same. *(constructive, interpretive)*

3. If you have students from other cultures who can speak their native languages, have each say the same sentence (such as "I love studying other cultures.") in their own language, using the sounds and tones customarily used in that language. Have the other students respond to how the sentence sounds from culture to culture and identify the differences in tonality.
(cross-cultural, interpretive)

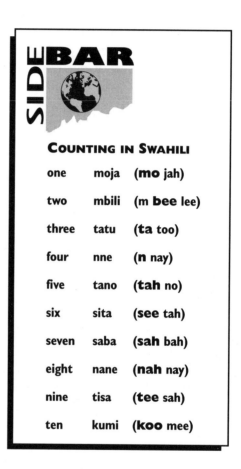

COUNTING IN SWAHILI

one	moja	(**mo** jah)
two	mbili	(m **bee** lee)
three	tatu	(**ta** too)
four	nne	(n nay)
five	tano	(**tah** no)
six	sita	(**see** tah)
seven	saba	(**sah** bah)
eight	nane	(**nah** nay)
nine	tisa	(**tee** sah)
ten	kumi	(**koo** mee)

Lesson 4

How Language Similarity Can Create Misunderstanding

Sharing a common language does not necessarily bring about a special understanding between cultures. People from England and the U.S. supposedly share the same language, but variations in words and the way in which each nationality uses them can create problems in communication. "We speak the same language! How dare they be so different!" each side often muses. English-English and U.S.-English have their idiosyncrasies. They are close, but yet so different.

Mutual frustrations can run high when attempting to communicate across cultures but in the same language. There is a simple reason for this: when two people share the same language, their expectations for successful communication are much higher than if they spoke two different languages. When these expectations are shattered, mutual contempt can result. The people in the U.S. and the English have a long history of poking fun at each other's customs and ways of speaking. Yet, just as two adjacent notes on the piano, when played together, are not always pleasing, those same two notes can be an integral part of a melodic composition, and the result delightful. Speakers of the two forms of English can also work their two ways of speaking into a harmonious relationship with the development of sensitivity and awareness of each other's differences.

The story on page 35 illustrates how difficult it is for people of different cultures to understand each other, even when they supposedly speak the same language. The story introduces the experience of a fifteen-year-old U.S. girl, Debbie Edwards, who has recently arrived in London, England, to visit her fourteen-year-old English cousin, Gloria Dean. Copy the story, and hand one copy to each student. Then read the story aloud with the class.

Did You Know?

People in England drive on the left side of the road. This goes back to the days when people traveled by horseback. They stayed to the left side of the road, just in case someone coming from the opposite direction proved to be an enemy. Swords were carried on the left side of the body and no one wanted that sword pressed up against an unfriendly rider who might be passing by.

Activities

1. After reading the story aloud with the class, discuss it. Why was Debbie so confused? Why did Gloria think Debbie was crazy? Were the students confused? How would they have felt in Debbie's shoes? What could Debbie or Gloria have done to make the experience less frustrating? *(cross-cultural, interpretive)*

2. You will find the correct definitions of the boldfaced British words from the story below. Have the students guess what each of the boldfaced terms means. Many of the expressions will be somewhat clear from their context in the story. Others will be a complete mystery. You may want to write several of the new words on the board every day for a week and take a few minutes each day to go over their definitions. At the end of the week, read the story again with the class and see if they know the meanings of all the words. *(cross-cultural)*

telly reader	TV anchorperson
Wellies	boots for wet weather
brolley	umbrella
M4	a main, limited access highway from London to Heathrow
flat	apartment on one floor
City of London	financial district of London
Jolly good	"Great!"
valises	suitcases
boot	trunk of car
petrol station	gas station
bonnet	hood of car
queue	line
thirty minutes	English way of measuring distance

elevenses	11 o'clock coffee time
maisonette	apartment on two floors
dual carriageway	divided highway
roundabout	circular intersection of several roads
block of flats	apartment building
chock-a-block	crowded with buildings
geyser	hot water heater
hob	top of the stove
joint	meat roast
cooker	stove or range
transferred charge	a collect telephone call
engaged	busy telephone line
jumpers	cardigan sweaters
proms	summer concerts held in Royal Albert Hall—seats are taken out of the main floor and people casually walk, or promenade, around the hall while the music plays
O levels	level in school reached by taking certain exams, equivalent to high school
A levels	level in school reached by taking certain exams, roughly equivalent to a year in junior college or high achievement in high school
tube	underground subway system
zebra	pedestrian crossing
subway	underground walkway
lift	elevator
moving stairs	escalator
"Way Out"	"Exit"
cha	slang for *tea*
scones	biscuit-like treat
coronet	ice cream cone
holiday	vacation
fringe	hair bangs

about what it's like to be a kid in your community. What would the U.S. student want the English visitor to know about his life? Have the "visitor" then ask the student to define all the slang terms she doesn't understand. The other students can help define them. This exercise should bring to the students' attention not only how slang can be a stumbling block in cross-cultural interaction but also how very difficult it can be to understand those who supposedly speak the same language. Discuss how much more difficult it would be to communicate with someone who speaks an entirely different language. Review what the students have learned up to now that would help them understand the use of language from another culture even without knowing the language. *(cross-cultural, constructive)*

3. Ask the students if they have ever had trouble understanding someone who also spoke English. Have they ever had trouble making themselves understood? Why? What happened? Perhaps they have met someone with a regional U.S. dialect or encountered someone using slang terms they have never heard. Role-play a situation in which one student is a visitor from England and the other has mastered one version of U.S. slang. Have the latter use slang to tell the visitor all

"Rain with sunny intervals," the **telly reader** had just announced. "I think we had better take our **Wellies** and **brolley**," Gloria said, as she and her American cousin, Debbie, were about to leave the apartment for a day of local sightseeing.

Debbie looked at her English cousin in complete confusion. What was she talking about? Problems had begun just moments after Debbie arrived at London's Heathrow Airport during the early morning hours of the previous day. Gloria had announced that her dad was waiting in the car just outside the terminal to drive them on the **M4** to the family's **flat** in St. John's Wood.

"But I thought you lived in the city of London," said Debbie.

"We don't live in the **city**," Gloria replied, "but we do live in London."

Mr. Dean seemed pleased to see Debbie. **"Jolly good,"** he had commented as the two girls came toward the car. "Here, Debbie, let me put your **valises** in the **boot**, and we will be on our way. I just have to stop at the **petrol station** to have them check under the **bonnet**. Let's hope there isn't a **queue**.

Then it is only **thirty minutes** to our home, and we will be there just in time for **elevenses**. Your parents visited us when we were still living in the **maisonette**."

Debbie was quite surprised to see the steering wheel on the right side of the car and that they travelled down the left side of the road. "Why are you on the wrong side of the road?" she asked her relatives. "My dear girl, we are on the *correct* side of the road. You in America are on the wrong side," her uncle teased.

As the car left the M4 and headed into the less busy **dual carriageway,** Gloria commented, "We live just beyond the **roundabout** in that **block of flats.** Our neighborhood is rather **chock-a-block,** but don't worry, we have plenty of room inside. I am so glad we moved because now we don't have to rely on the **geyser.** We have constant hot water."

Mrs. Dean greeted everyone at the door. "I put the water on the **hob,"** she told the girls, "and I believe I shall put the **joint** in the **cooker** in about an hour."

"I promised my family I'd call them collect right after I arrived," said Debbie. This time it was the Deans' turn to be perplexed.

"Oh, you mean you are supposed to telephone your parents and make it a **transferred charge,"** the British relatives laughingly replied. "Here, let us try for you." Moments later, Mr. Dean announced that the international lines were **engaged.**

But it was now the next morning, and in spite of jet lag, Debbie was ready to explore London. More instructions were coming from her aunt, however, and they were as confusing as the talk yesterday: "I think you girls had better take your **jumpers** along because, in spite of the fact that it is summer, the weather will probably be rather cool. And after the **proms** tonight, you definitely will need them."

"A prom in August?" queried Debbie. "But I didn't bring a prom dress! And who is going to be my date?"

Gloria looked at her U.S. cousin as if she had truly lost her mind, but she quickly changed the subject. "Are you going to be heading for the **O levels** or the **A levels** in school?" she asked as the girls hurried down the street towards what Gloria said was the **tube.** She informed Debbie that they had to cross the **zebra** and go through the **subway** to reach the tube station, but when inside they would catch the **lift** to get to the trains. It was better than the **moving stairs.**

When they got off the train at their destination, Gloria and Debbie exited through a door marked **"Way Out."** Debbie giggled at the sign, and Gloria looked at her strangely.

By mid-afternoon, Debbie's head was spinning. "Do we really speak the same language?" she thought to herself. It was then that Gloria sensed that her U.S. relative must be tired.

"Why don't we stop for some **cha** and **scones**," she suggested, "or maybe you would like a **coronet**." And with that she directed her cousin into a small restaurant. Much to Debbie's amazement, the hostess led the girls to a table for four where two strangers were already eating. The girls were seated, but the two other restaurant patrons did not even look up from their food and kept talking to each other. Debbie definitely felt uncomfortable sharing a table with two strangers.

At the end of the second day in London, Debbie, frustrated and confused, wondered if this vacation would be a success. Her relatives always referred to the **holiday** she was on, and this certainly was not the holiday season in Debbie's eyes. She had no idea what was being said half the time. London was exciting, but it certainly was tough to remember to look right instead of left when she crossed the street. She had almost been hit by a car several times that day. She did not know the names of foods, how to use the telephone, or why directions were given they way they were. When Gloria looked her straight in the eye and said she loved her **fringe,** Debbie became convinced that people on this island called England did not speak English.

Lesson 5

How Languages Depend On Each Other

If it is difficult to create harmony between two cultures that share the same language, imagine how much more difficult it can be to interact sensitively with those who speak a different language. Students need to learn that the difficulties are never insurmountable. One step in the process involves realizing how much their own language is already intersected with words from other cultures, and vice versa. Cultures constantly depend on each other for the development of their languages, and they borrow and reshape each others' words to meet their own needs. Words often credited as being firmly rooted in one culture may very well have had to travel the globe in order to find their way into common usage. As students look at how we import and transform foreign terms to fit our needs, and at how nations take our English words and change them to reflect their own, they will discover doors opening into other cultures.

There are nearly three thousand different languages spoken around the world. Add to these all the dialects, variations of specific languages, and there are believed to be ten thousand different forms of verbal communication. These languages developed not only out of the need for people to label components of their cultures, but sometimes because of the emergence of one form of speech out of another. Spanish, French, Italian, Romanasch (spoken in portions of Switzerland), Rumanian, Catalán (spoken in southwestern Spain), and Portuguese evolved from Latin. English is rooted in the tongue spoken by a Germanic tribe that for some unknown reason decided to forsake its native land in the northern corner of today's Germany for what is now known as England. The language on that newly invaded island became known as Anglo-Saxon, and it was powerful enough to send the original Celtic tongue retreating into Wales, Scotland, and Ireland as well as some offshore islands and a tiny portion of land on the southwest tip of contemporary England.

But in 1066, with the invasion of that same island by the Normans, a French-speaking group from northern France, the Anglo-Saxon tongue had competition. French became the language of the ruling class. It later, however, drifted down to the common people where it wove its way into early English and left its legacy in the form of a deeply enriched language. We owe most of our one-syllable words to the Anglo-Saxon vernacular, Charles Berlitz points out, and our more elegant or polysyllabic words to the French. English speakers have the option to smell, sweat, and eat (Anglo-Saxon origin) or to detect an odor, perspire, and dine (French origin) (Berlitz, 1982).

English did not simply emerge from a friendly blending of Anglo-Saxon and French, but absorbed words from many cultures. Some expressions, like *tofu*, the Japanese food product, arrived in our vocabulary unchanged, but other expressions traveled their way through several cultures before settling into the English language. During the great Arab Empire—which stretched from the eighth to the thirteenth centuries and spread across northern Africa into the Iberian peninsula of Europe and eastward to the borders of China—great achievements were reached in the fields of mathematics, medicine, geography, art, architecture, and agriculture, and new words evolved to meet these accomplishments. "Arabic was as much the universal language of culture, diplomacy and the sciences as Latin was to become in the later Middle Ages. Those who wanted to read Aristotle, use medical terms, solve a mathematical problem, or embark on an intellectual discourse, had to know Arabic." (Shabbas and Al-Qazzas, 1989).

Many words in English today are rooted in Arabic, and a number of these made their way into our language through Spanish. Quite a few words that begin with the letters *al* can be traced to this Middle Eastern language. Surprisingly, *adobe,* a word associated with the U.S. Southwest, really came from the Arabic word *"at-tub."* But some English words go back far beyond the Anglo-Saxon, French, and Arabic roots. The ancient Greeks also influenced the English language. Their word for "far," which was *tele*, attached itself to many English syllables (Berlitz, 1982). By the sixteenth century over fifty languages had contributed to the English vocabulary (Baugh and Cable, 1978).

It is interesting to consider that English narrowly missed being rejected as the accepted common language for the U.S. Although many of the early settlers brought the English tongue to our land, it was by no means the unanimous choice as the language for the newly established republic. With emotions running high against the mother country, many patriots argued that English should no longer be spoken here. Some opted for German. A vote finally was taken in the Continental Congress, and English won out by a solitary ballot (Berlitz, 1982).

Now three hundred million people use the English language, and only Chinese outranks English in the numbers of speakers. But English is more widespread than Chinese and has become the international language of business.

Languages do not lie dormant. New ones are born, and some completely disappear from the face of the earth. When Christopher Columbus arrived in the Western hemisphere, there were supposedly 1,000 different tongues spoken by the natives. Today, there are about 600, including the many Native American tribal languages found throughout South, Central, and North America. The Icelandic language, however, has defied the pattern and remained almost unchanged, at least in its written form. In *Mother Tongue: English and How It Got That Way,* Bill Bryson tells us that "if Leif Ericson appeared on the streets of Reykjavik, he could find his way around, allowing for certain difficulties over terms like airport and quarter-pound cheeseburger" (Bryson, 1990).

Words often slip easily across national boundaries to become an integral part of the local language. In Mexico, the Spanish is sprinkled with English terms that have made their way into common usage with few alterations. Property to rent, for example, will be advertised as *para renta* (**pah**-ra **ren**-tah). If Mexicans continued speaking the same Spanish used on the European continent, "for rent" would be *se alquila* (say ahl-**kee**-lah). In Puerto Rico, a parking space is *el parking* and a closet is *el closet.*

Complete languages, not simply phrases, exist side-by-side in many countries such as Belgium, a land splintered by French and Flemish. And hundreds of languages are spoken on the world's second largest island of New Guinea. Over a thousand different languages or dialects are used on the sub-continent of India. The continent of Africa is also divided by languages, making cross-cultural understanding among the people extremely difficult. Africa has a half-dozen imported languages, brought by the colonists who ruled over large portions of the African continent for many years, and more than 800 tribal tongues. Words from these tribal tongues are constantly seeping into Swahili, one of the major languages in sub-

Saharan Africa, thus changing the language and making it necessary to update dictionaries on a regular basis. A young woman from Tanzania in East Africa, where Swahili is spoken, came to the U.S. to do her graduate work at a Midwestern university. She expressed her concern to a U.S. classmate about returning to her homeland and having to learn many new words that would have slipped into her language while she was studying abroad. "Our language is always changing," she explained, "because many words from the hundreds of different tribal tongues are constantly being introduced into Swahili. The language is becoming more complicated every day. I shall have a lot to learn when I return home." Arabic words, or words of Arabic origin, also play a major role in the Swahili vocabulary. These roots date back many centuries to the days when men from the Arabian peninsula sailed across the Red Sea to trade with their African neighbors.

Quite often languages borrow from each other's vocabularies to produce a special effect. Residents on the island of Malta believe they add a touch of prestige to their buildings and residences by giving them English names such as Graceland, Daffodils, Sunrise, and Charm, while in Finland business entrepreneurs select French terms to promote an illusion of elegance. A bridal shop becomes Fiancée and a fashion boutique, Boutique du Boulevard (Haarmann, 1989). This is done in the U.S. too. Just think of all the names given to cars produced for a U.S. market: *Elantra, Le Sabre, Cabriolet, Coupe de Ville, Le Baron, Camaro, Ciera, Marquis, Calais, Bonneville, Grand Prix, Corvette.* These foreign and foreign-sounding names sell by evoking an image of luxury.

As the world continues to draw closer together socially and economically, our languages will depend even more upon each other. We shall have to borrow even more words to express new ideas, to share each other's prod-

cts, and to solve many of our problems. These new
ocabularies will increase at greater speeds as communi-
ation systems become more sophisticated and our eco-
omic systems more interrelated. Each of us will be more
n touch with the world, and with this stronger sense of
nterdependence our languages will continue to change,
row and, above all, become enriched by these exchanges.

Activities

. Copy the student worksheet on page 39 and have the
students match up the English words with their language of origin. *(interpretive)*

. Ask the students to think of words they commonly hear
or use that have come from or been made popular by certain ethnic groups or regions of the U.S. (*homey, dis,
dude, gnarly,* for example). Explain that this process of
sharing words in the multicultural U.S. is similar to the
ways cultures around the world share and swap words.
Languages, like cultures, depend on each other.
(interpretive)

. Ask the students to think of other words in English that
have come from another language. List them on the
board. What about names of streets or parks in your
area? Can the students think of any streets or parks
whose names come from a different language? Certain
regions of the U.S. (California, for example) will find
this more common than others. What about names of
states and cities? Many are Native American names.
We've been told that Chicago, for example, is a Native
American term for "stinky onion field." Explore the
translations and origins of these names. Explain to the
students that other cultures have adopted English words
as well. Discuss the information given above. Point out
the fact that the students already are closer to other cultures than they thought, because they already speak
words from other languages, see them every day on
signs, and hear them on TV. *(constructive)*

. Have students ask their parents and then their grandparents, or people of that generation, to think of words that
have entered the U.S. English vocabulary that did not
exist when they were children. Many, of course, will be
technologically related, but a large number may have
come from changes in mores and social norms. List
these terms on the board. What are their contemporary
equivalents? *(constructive)*

Worksheet

NAME _____

DATE _____

MATCH THE TERMS

Instructions: Many English words that you hear every day are not really English but instead come from languages around the world. See if you can match up the following English words with the language from which they really come.

perspire	Arabic
odor	Arabic
dine	Arabic
magazine	French
cotton	French
traffic	Arabic
admiral	French
sofa	Arabic
zero	Greek
alcohol	French
alcove	French
algebra	French
almanac	Arabic
adobe	French
telephone	Arabic
television	Arabic
boutique	Arabic
fiancée	Greek
croissant	Arabic
avenue	Arabic

Lesson 6

Body Language

Activity

Ask the students to observe a conversation between you and one student. The student participating will be told in advance what to do. You will appear to be very disgusted with the work the student has turned in. You continue to scold the student, telling him or her that he or she is not living up to expectations. The work is sloppy and incomplete. The student looks at you and smiles at all times.

Discussion: The students, of course, will have been told prior to the exercise that this is simply role-playing. But after the "scolding," ask the class what was wrong with the reaction of the student who was receiving the criticism. Discuss how the student was expected to react. What would a teacher think if a child smiled while being told his or her work was very bad? Then explain that in Thailand people often smile when they have made a mistake. The smile can be a way of saying, "I am sorry."
(cross-cultural, interpretive)

What Is Body Language?

It is reasonable to assume that early humans first communicated through body movements before they discovered how to use their vocal cords. This practical method of conveying messages has survived and matured through the ages to become what is now known as "body language." Linguists believe that all communities that use a spoken language also use many non-verbal gestures. These gestures may be used without or in conjunction with speech.

Some people believe body language is only a secondary means of communication used to supplement speech. Yet it is hardly secondary, for gestures convey more than just specific meanings; they are an expression of an entire cultural viewpoint. When a speaker uses body language as he speaks, the gesture will amplify, modify, confirm, or subvert what he is saying. When people cannot communicate in any other way, they resort to what is commonly called "sign language." The hearing impaired use "signing," a form of expression made up in great part of hand and arm motions representing words or thoughts, as their principle form of communication. Communications experts have estimated that humans are capable of producing 700,000 different physical signs or body movements.

There are thousands of hand gestures alone, all of which have meaning. Indeed, there are far more expressive body movements than forms of speaking and writing. Body language, therefore, should not be considered a subordinate or limited means of expression. As a cross-cultural resource, it offers a key to some of the fundamental values and assumptions held by a particular culture.

Silence is one aspect of behavior that has intrigued Westerners since they first came into contact with the "inscrutable" Japanese. Non-Asians consider silence a breakdown in communication and often try to fill the vacuum in the conversation with words. The Japanese, on the other hand, believe a pause to be an important part of the communication process; silence allows for consideration and analysis of what has gone before. In discussion, silence can be a method the Japanese use to avoid giving a negative response or jeopardizing the harmony of the meeting. Westerners would be making a mistake to assume communication has ended or to jump in and fill the silence; to do so may result in saying something inappropriate or unproductive. Teachers may note the Japanese use of silence in a conference with Japanese parents. If a parent falls silent for a few moments, the most sensitive response would be to wait the silence out until the parent resumes.

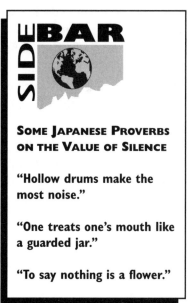

SOME JAPANESE PROVERBS ON THE VALUE OF SILENCE

"Hollow drums make the most noise."

"One treats one's mouth like a guarded jar."

"To say nothing is a flower."

Many forms of body language have ancient origins. The first description of bowing in Japan, for example, dates from A.D. 600. Walking with the head erect has signified authority, dignity, and detachment in many cultures for centuries. Another universal gesture is the clapping of hands in applause as a sign of approval, honor, or enjoyment. Remarkably few gestures can be labeled exclusively French, Mexican, or belonging to any other country. Since many cultures attach similar meanings to similar gestures, body language can be an effective way to communicate with others without needing to translate. "A picture"—in this case a visual body movement—"is worth a thousand words." Yet, always, one must use caution to be sure that the intended meaning for the gesture is correct in the circumstances or society in which it is used.

There is always a danger of being insulting or offensive by misusing or misunderstanding the meaning of a gesture. Just as body language can convey very positive and forceful messages if used correctly, a simple movement can be as unacceptable as the most rude verbal remark when used in a different context. Simply sitting down and crossing one's legs in the presence of someone in the Middle East can create the opportunity for an insult; this is because pointing or exposing the sole of the shoe in the direction of another is considered very rude in that region of the world.

Eye Contact

Most Western cultures consider direct eye contact absolutely necessary for effective one-on-one communication. U.S. parents often use "Look me straight in the eye" as a physiological lie detector test. Eye contact signifies rapt attention to the speaker, and any wavering of eye contact is interpreted as inattention, boredom, and evasiveness. Yet direct eye contact between two Japanese persons can indicate hostility. The Japanese practice lowering their eyes—considered a gesture of modesty and submission for many cultures, including, often, the U.S.—as a gesture of respect and humility by the female toward the male, by the student toward the teacher, and by one lower in the hierarchy toward a superior. In sub-Saharan Africa, too, many people lower their eyes as a sign of respect. In the Middle East, direct eye contact between a man and a woman who is not his wife or family member is considered provocative. It is avoided in traditional Muslim societies by veiling the women's eyes.

Winking in most Western cultures can be a flirtatious gesture, a sign not to take too seriously what is happening, or an indication of a shared secret. Yet in many cultures, the wink is regarded as impolite, off-color, and even insulting.

Raising one's eyebrows in the U.S. indicates that one is astonished or cynical. In Thailand raising the eyebrows can be a signal that you want someone, perhaps a waiter, to come toward you. Raising your eyebrows in the south of China can indicate that you are not pleased. Filipinos raise both eyebrows when they greet each other.

Hand Gestures

Motions such as waving goodbye or beckoning someone to come closer can mean something entirely different in other cultures. The U.S. goodbye wave, for example, is seen as a signal of "no" in parts of Europe and Latin America. Attracting the attention of a waiter in the U.S. is usually done by raising the hand with the index finger extended. But there are many countries where pointing a finger is impolite. In the U.S., we usually bend, or curl, the index finger to signal someone to approach, but this gesture is used only for calling animals in some cultures.

In the U.S., the "O.K." sign is made by forming a circle with the thumb and forefinger. Consider what it means elsewhere: In Latin America, it is very insulting; in France, it indicates that something is worthless; and in Japan, it signifies money or "I will take the bill."

Greetings

Most gestures involving body movements and positions are known as *kinesics*. This category includes manners and social rituals, such as the way one eats or greets others. Social greetings are very important because they establish the tone of the meeting. The standard way of greeting by a handshake is one of those gestures that means the same for all cultures that use it. The practice is said to have originated as a sign that the hand contained no weapon.

Although the intent and meaning of the handshake is universal, the method still can convey much about the individual initiating the shaking. A forceful, hearty shake with extreme movement is the sign of self-assurance and assertiveness in many cultures. Sometimes fingers are crushed and each person seems to make the handshake a contest of durability. This robust version is popular among North Americans and many Europeans who hate shaking a limp hand. In Islamic countries, men must not touch women unrelated to them, so handshaking between the sexes is out of the question, unless it is between family members. For men in many East Asian countries, handshaking is a practical alternative or addition to the bow.

The bow is the preferred means of greeting others in Japan, and to a slightly lesser extent, Korea. Some Korean companies require their employees to take bowing lessons in order to greet customers properly. The bow also can signify "goodbye," acknowledgement or acceptance, apology, and general respect. In this latter sense, bowing

Did You Know?

In a business meeting in France, if you wish to let the other person know that you are bored with the negotiations, you can stroke your cheek as if it were a beard with the back of your fingers.

conveys another cultural aspect: the recognition of hierarchy. Every Japanese either knows or figures out quickly his or her place on the social ladder in any given situation. Juniors with less status bow to seniors, youths bow to the elderly, shopkeepers bow to customers, and so on.

In India and Thailand, the traditional greeting gesture, known as the *namaste* (nah-**mahs**-tay) and *wai* (why), respectively, involves placing the hands in front of the body, chest high, in a praying position accompanied by a slight bow. The traditional Malay greeting, or *salam* (sa-**lahm),** resembles a handshake with both hands. The man offers both hands to his friend and lightly touches his friend's outstretched hands. Then he brings his hands to his chest.

Close acquaintances and family members in Europe, particularly in France, greet and often mark their departure with a kiss on both cheeks, even in public. Usually, the two people bring their right cheeks together, and then the left to avoid an embarrassing meeting of noses. They may actually touch the cheek with the lips but given the anatomical design of the face, which allows only one of the parties to make lip contact, and to reduce the degree of intimacy, sophisticated greeters limit the gesture to kissing the air. U.S. students are often amused to learn that men practice this form of greeting as much as women.

Considerable difference of opinion exists on the question of whether or not a Westerner should use one of these more alien forms of greeting or should stick to the handshake when greeting people from other cultures. Performing a bow or another Asian greeting requires grace and skill, which most Westerners either lack or have not practiced sufficiently to avoid appearing awkward. On the other hand, trying to use the native form of greeting demonstrates a sincere effort to understand another's culture and to abide by the local customs—something always appreciated. Expatriates who have lived in Japan or Korea for some time have learned to bow slightly with ease and polish. The solution to this dilemma is to try to seem as natural as possible, and any errors will be overlooked.

Activity

Greetings: Explain to the students that many cultures have very different ways of greeting each other. The following are examples of friendly greeting customs in Japan, Malaysia, and the Philippines. Have the students practice these forms of greeting. After practicing these gestures, ask the students to discuss what they believe these body movements indicate. For example, the Japanese bow will show respect; it is an important symbol in a culture where everyone has a definite place in the social hierarchy. The

Malay's form of greeting indicates heartfelt respect and warmth. The Indian greeting can also be considered a form of respect that goes further than the "glad to see you" handshake used by Westerners.
(cross-cultural, interpretive)

Japan
Ask each student to stand and face someone who is standing next to him or her. The boys should put their hands, palms down, on their thighs with their fingers pointing towards their knees. Tell the girls to link their thumbs, turn their hands so that one is over the other, and place these hands in front of them slightly below the waist. Now partners should bow towards each other, rounding their shoulders slightly. Their bodies should be bent at about a thirty-degree angle. If they are bowing to someone older, tell the younger to lower the head as a sign of respect. Also explain to the students that they must raise their eyes as they bow to see how low the other person is bowing and if that other individual is still continuing the bow. The bows may continue four or five times.

Ask the students to be seated. Then you will leave the room only to re-enter it immediately. Have the students rise, stand by their seats, and bow to you. You, in turn, bow to them but with your head held higher than theirs. Explain to the class that this is the way in which students always greet their teachers in Japanese classrooms.

Malaysia
Point out Malaysia on a world map. Explain to the students that there are three distinct cultural groups in Malaysia: Malay, Chinese, and Indian. The following are the forms of greeting each group uses. Have the students practice them.

Malay
Shaking hands is known as *salaming*. Men and women usually do not shake each others' hands, although this custom is being broken among the younger generation. Men shake hands with men, and women with women. However, it is done quite differently from the pattern found in the U.S. Each man stretches both hands forward and lightly touches the other's hands but does not shake them. Each then takes his own hand to his chest to indicate that he is greeting the other person from his heart. Women also use this gesture. But in small villages, they sometimes carry it a little further. After touching

SIDEBAR

NEW WORDS FOR GREETING GESTURES AROUND THE WORLD

namaste - traditional greeting gesture used in India

wai - traditional greeting gesture used in Thailand

In both the namaste and wai, the greeter places his hands in a praying position, chest high, and bows slightly.

salam - traditional greeting gesture used by Malays. This greeting is like a handshake with both hands. The greeter offers both hands and lightly touches the other's outstretched hands. Then he brings his hands to his chest.

mano po - traditional greeting gesture in the Philippines, used to indicate respect for an elder. The younger individual reaches for the elder's right hand and brings it to his (the younger's) forehead.

abrazo - a gesture used by Latin American men to reinforce the pleasure of a greeting. It is a bear-hug with a few claps on the back.

ly Muslim and the Indians often Hindu. Both these religions, to which the Chinese usually do not belong, have a strong sense of separation of the sexes.

Philippines

Explain to the students that in the Philippines young people have a very special gesture to indicate respect for an elder. Although it is not practiced everywhere, it is still considered the traditional greeting and is used in the small towns and villages. Ask the students to pair off and then decide who will be considered the elder and who will be the younger of the two. Have the younger individual reach for the elder's right hand and bring it up to the forehead of the former. The entire hand or just the knuckles can touch the forehead. This is known as *mano po* (mahn-oh **poh**) and is particularly appropriate between a godchild and the godparent.

Touching

Many Westerners consider touching another person a sign of sincerity and a demonstration of good feeling towards that person. Politicians and others who must make an impression in a matter of seconds when they greet someone often will place their left hand over the top of hands joined in a handshake to add an extra touch of sincerity to the encounter. Putting one's arm around another, giving him a squeeze, or patting him on the back is perceived as an expression of care. Giving someone the "high five" is a mutual indication of pleasure, excitement, or congratulation. The additional physical contact affirms whatever emotion is being expressed. Latin American men give one another an *abrazo* (ah-**brah**-sso), or bear-hug with a few claps on the back.

In the Middle East, males touch each other often; it is considered perfectly permissible as an expression of male bonding. It is not uncommon for two men to walk along a street holding hands. But let a man and woman walk along the same street holding hands and they will attract the shocked and disapproving stares of passers-by, and, if the incident takes place in Saudi Arabia, perhaps even incur arrest by the religious police. Most East Asians, particularly the Japanese, avoid casual touching in social situations, which explains their preference for the bow and their aversion to being hugged or patted on the back.

each others' hands, the women bring their own hands up to their faces in order to cover their noses and mouths.

Chinese

Chinese men may pat each other on the arm in greeting, as well as shake hands. Men and women shake hands with each other.

Indian

Men shake hands with men, women with women, but the different sexes do not customarily exchange handshakes. The more traditional form of greeting, however, is to put their hands in a prayer position and to bow their heads very slightly.

After the students have practiced the different forms of greeting in Malaysia, ask them if they have any ideas as to why these differences are found among the three groups. You can point out that Malays are usual-

Activities

1. The following are examples of body language and their meanings in countries around the world. As you share them with the students, be sure to illustrate each gesture and discuss the difference between what that gesture means in the culture named and what it means in the U.S. Have the students practice the gestures that are used in other cultures and are not used here. *(cross-cultural)*

Raising one's shoulders, a classic French shrug, means, "This is ridiculous."

In the Arab world, if one accepts another as a friend, he will place his two index fingers side by side as a sign that the friend is an equal.

To give a negative response in Greece, it is proper to jerk the head back, not shake it from side to side.

To signal "Come here" in Korea, cup the hand with the palm down and draw the fingers toward the palm.

A smile is not always a smile in every culture. The Japanese frequently use a smile or a half-smile to mask embarrassment, hide anger, vent frustration, and avoid confrontation. The Thais smile often and do so for many different reasons: to apologize for a mistake, to acknowledge an apology, to say "thank you," to avoid comment, and to reveal embarrassment. The French do not appreciate a smile, particularly from a stranger. Smiling at a salesperson when handed a package could be taken as a sign of insincerity in France.

In the Philippines, when cutting in between two people, hold the hands together in front and advance with a lowered head.

In Thailand, when people are sitting in a group, no one steps over the others when he gets up to leave. People will make room for him if he indicates that he must leave the group. Yet, he does not simply walk upright as he departs. Out of respect for the others, it is very important that he lower his body as he passes adults. To be perfectly correct, his head must never be above anyone else's head—which can be difficult to maneuver if he happens to be the tallest person in the room.

Making a fist and striking it against an open palm, a gesture used for emphasis in the West, is an extremely rude gesture in Singapore, Malaysia, and Russia.

The crossed finger sign, made by twisting the middle finger over and around the index finger, is said to have been a cryptic version of the sign of the cross. Instead of crossing themselves openly, a Christian could protect himself by making this concealed sign. Now, this gesture is used in the U.S. as a plea for good luck: "I'll keep my fingers crossed for you." Yet in Turkey, a Muslim country, kids often cross their fingers to signify the breaking of a friendship.

If you offer your pinkie finger to someone in the Arab country of Jordan, you have just asked that person to become your friend. But if you do this in the Arab country of Syria, you have indicated that the person is your enemy.

Finger counting: Most cultures utilize fingers for counting, but they do so in different ways. When counting in Europe, for example, one starts with the thumb not the index finger. In the West, we begin with a closed hand and then raise each finger as we count. But many East Asian cultures do it the opposite way. In Japan, one begins with an open hand and lowers each finger as one counts.

2. Role-Playing: Explain to the class that they will be assuming roles in two different cultures. Those who will be taking part in the role-playing will know in which culture they belong, but the class will have to guess. Those observing will also have to determine what message is being given strictly through the participants' body language. Select two students and brief them as follows:

Scene One

This is a gift exchange between two Japanese. The two parties greet each other with bows. Make certain that each participant knows the correct bowing procedure based on gender. The gift-giver presents the imaginary package to the receiver with both hands. The receiver accepts the gift with a bow and with both hands. The receiver then puts the package down and does not open it. No more gestures follow; the receiver will not open the gift or mouth a "thank you."

Do not discuss the scene with the class at this point.

Scene Two

This is a gift exchange between two residents of the United States. One comes into the room and waves "hello" in the emotive way many in the U.S. do it. The person entering the room hands a make-believe gift to the other individual with one hand. The receiver acts excited about receiving the gift and immediately tears the wrapping off the package and opens it. The receiver, through facial expressions, shows surprise, pleasure, and appreciation. He somehow makes it clear to the giver that he is really pleased and, through a gesture, thanks him—perhaps with a slap on the back or a handshake. Allow the two participating students to discuss between themselves how they can best portray these emotions.

Discussion: See if the students can determine what was happening in each scene. Can they guess which culture was portrayed in each scene? What significant differences in body language did they see in each culture, Japan and the U.S.?

Answer: Students should have noticed several differences. In the first scene between the two Japanese, each person bowed. The gift was handed and received with both hands. It should be pointed out that it is very rude to give or receive anything with one hand, even a business card, in Japan. Little recognition of the gift was made by the Japanese receiver. The gift was definitely not opened in front of the giver because in many Asian societies this is considered impolite for a number of reasons. Perhaps the gift will be a disappointment and the giver would be embarrassed. The gift is considered a very private matter and should be opened only when the receiver is alone. Excessive signs of appreciation in Korean society, for example, could be taken as putting a "finish" on the obligation and perhaps even ending the relationship between the two people. Expressing excitement, appreciation, and happiness through facial gestures is done in the United States, but is usually not shown in many Asian societies. The Japanese often reflect their happiness with a perfectly expressionless face. A smile may be used to express anger or frustration. *(cross-cultural, interpretive)*

3. Play Charades: Divide the class into two teams. Have a student from each team act out an emotion through body language. Perhaps they are very sad over losing a game or extremely happy about a grade. The class will try to guess the emotion, and the team who first guesses correctly scores a point. Play a few rounds. The important concept here is to have them show and understand how body language can express feelings. Why was it difficult or easy to guess the emotion? Explain that we in our own culture can readily recognize these gestures and their meanings because we share so many ways of expressing ourselves—and we learn these ways from our culture. But when this takes place *across* cultural lines, gestures often are misunderstood and misinterpreted. *(constructive, collaborative)*

4. Challenge the class to go an entire day, both at home and at school, without speaking. They must communicate only with signs and gestures (grunts are okay, too). You will need to obtain permission from their families and give each student a note that explains the experiment to their other teachers. Have the students keep a log for the day to record their feelings, their frustrations, and the ways they were able to devise to make themselves understood. The next day, discuss their experiences. What kinds of body language were successful in communicating? What kinds of things seem impossible to communicate without words? List on the board some common body language gestures used in the U.S. and that they used during the day. *(constructive, interpretive)*

5. Create a Body Language: Have the students divide into groups of five or six members, and ask them to create their own repertoires of body language. Have them act out a scenario before the class to see if the other students can understand what is being portrayed.

   Point out how difficult it is to understand body language across cultural lines. You might wish to discuss how a polite gesture in one culture can be an impolite one in another. For example, sneezing in a Chinese culture is considered an absolutely normal gesture and does not require an "excuse me." On the other hand, you do not blow your nose in front of other people in China. Belching at the end of a dinner is acceptable in a Chinese culture and is even encouraged as a sign that the meal was deeply appreciated. Discuss how people in the U.S. would react to such gestures. *(constructive, collaborative)*

   Suggestion: Combine this activity with Activity #5 under General Activities.

General Activities

Buenos dias   (**bway**-noss **dee**-ahss)   Spanish
Bonjour   (bohng-zhoor)   French
Hyvaa huomenta
(**hew**-vah **hoooa**-mayn-tah)   Finnish

1. The following is a list of the languages most spoken around the world. Mix them up, write them on the board, and see if the students can rank them in order of number of speakers. Be sure to point out the places on the map where the languages are spoken.
(cross-cultural)

   1. Mandarin
   2. English
   3. Hindi
   4. Spanish
   5. Russian
   6. Arabic
   7. Bengali
   8. Portuguese
   9. Malay-Indonesian
   10. Japanese
   11. French
   12. German

2. The following is "Good Morning" or the equivalent in ten European languages. Have the students make a sign that says "Good Morning" in each language. Hang the sign in the hallway or on your classroom door.
(cross-cultural, constructive)

God morgen   (goo mohrn)   Norwegian
Guten Morgen (**goo**-ten **mohr**-gen) German

(kah-lee-**meh**-rah)   Greek

Bongiorno   (boan-**joar**-noa)   Italian
Dzien dobry   (dzhehn **do**-bri)   Polish
Bom dia   (bohng **dee**-er)   Portuguese

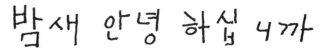

(**doh**-brah-yah **oo**-trah)   Russian

3. The following are customary greetings written in the Korean calligraphy. Have the students practice writing the Korean symbols, perhaps making a sign for the classroom. The Korean language, by the way, is considered the most efficient verbal and written language in the world. *(cross-cultural, constructive)*

"Did you sleep well?" (used first thing in the morning)

밤새 안녕 하십 니까

(pom say ahn-young hah-sim-ni-ka)

"How are you?" (used later in the day)

안 녕 하세요

(ahn-young hah-se-yoh)

4. The following is the equivalent of "Good Morning" written in Arabic. There are many forms of written Arabic, some more ornate than others. We have chosen a form that will be easier for U.S. students to learn. The students can practice writing the phrase in Arabic and attach in to the classroom sign.
(cross-cultural, constructive)

Sabah El Khair (sah-bah el ka-heer)

صباح الخير

5. Divide the class into two groups. Each group will meet to invent its own language. Although inventing an entire language is too difficult, they can make up words to substitute for certain common English words. (Example: "I saw a butterfly on the way to school today" could become "I mest a hogit on the way to grellup yebod.") The entire group must learn these words, so they will need to write up a vocabulary list in their new language and memorize it. Then, on another day, the students will pair up with one partner from each group. Each member of the pair will speak his or her group's language to his or her partner. They cannot translate their words back into English but must try to explain by using gestures, pointing to objects, miming, etc. Tell them the goal is not to confuse but to try to understand and to make oneself understood.

After the pairs have finished trying to communicate, discuss the ways students devised to come to an understanding of each other. Explore their feelings of frustration in trying to make themselves understood and in trying to interpret the other's language. You might want to point out that they have just experienced what it would be like if they visited another country. They also have experienced what it is like to be a foreign-born student with limited English when he or she begins school in the U.S. and attempts to communicate with English-speaking students. Perhaps the students will be more sensitive to the difficulties these newcomers face. *(collaborative, cross-cultural)*

Resources

Baugh, Albert C. and Thomas Cable. *A History of the English Language.* London: Routledge & Kegan Paul, 1978.

Berlitz, Charles. *Native Tongues.* New York: Grosset & Dunlap, 1982.

Bremmer, Jan and Herman Roodenburg, eds. *A Cultural History of Gestures.* Ithaca: Cornell University Press, 1991.

Bryson, Bill. *Mother Tongue: English and How It Got That Way.* New York: William Morrow, 1990.

Haarmann, Harald. *Symbolic Values of Foreign Language Use: From the Japanese Case to a General Sociolinguistic Perspective.* New York and Berlin: Mouton de Gruyter, 1989.

Hall, Edward T. *The Silent Language.* Garden City: Doubleday, 1959.

Harris, Philip R. and Robert T. Moran. *Managing Cultural Differences.* 2nd ed. Houston: Gulf Publishing Company, 1988.

Moeran, Brian. *Language and Popular Culture in Japan.* Manchester and New York: Manchester UP, 1989.

Patai, Raphael. *The Arab Mind.* Rev. ed. New York: Charles Scribner's Sons, 1983.

Poyatos, Fernando, ed. *Cross-Cultural Perspective in Nonverbal Communication,* Toronto: C. J. Hogrefe, Inc., 1988.

Roberts, John S. *Black Music of Two Worlds.* New York: Praeger, 1972.

Roces, Alfredo and Grace Roces. *Culture Shock: Philippines.* Singapore: Times Books International, 1985.

Rothwell, J. Dan. *Telling It Like It Isn't.* Englewood Cliffs, NJ: Prentice-Hall, 1982.

Shabbas, Audrey and Ayad Al-Qazzas. *The Arab World Notebook.* Project of Najda: Women Concerned About The Middle East. Berkeley, CA, 1989.

Chapter Two
Space

Images provided by © 1996 PhotoDisc, Inc.

Goals

This chapter explores several basic concepts of space and their implications for cross-cultural understanding. The information, stories, examples from various cultures, and student activities are designed to help your students achieve the following goals:

1. To see that members of cultures use and see the space around them quite differently from members of other cultures. Humans' use of space is determined by the culture in which they live.

2. To understand that how a culture perceives the world is often dependent on the kinds of spacial vistas (such as a jungle, a city full of skyscrapers, a wide open plain) to which it is accustomed.

3. To grasp the concept of territoriality; to see that humans, like animals, claim or perceive certain spaces as their own—even spaces as small as a telephone booth or a place in line. The perception of one's territory changes from culture to culture.

4. To become more conscious of how we use and feel about personal space as well as to see how personal space means different things to different cultures.

5. To learn how homes around the world reflect different approaches to the use of space.

6. To distinguish between the personal and public use of space and to understand how the layout of a city, a public space, reflects some important values and traditions of a culture.

7. To see the distinction between crowding and high density.

Cross-Cultural Attitudes and Skills

As students work towards these goals, they will develop the following cross-cultural attitudes and skills:

1. They will continue to become more aware of how culture shapes so much about them—their personalities, their perspectives, their perceptions. In so doing, they will continue to shed their prejudices against people from other cultures because they are beginning to see why people are they way they are and do the things they do.

2. They will continue to discover their differences from others as they learn that their use of space differs from others' use of space. At the same time they are realizing that no one way of using space is necessarily better than any other.

3. They will hone their critical and interpretive skills as they think more perceptively about the space around them.

4. They will expand their imaginative horizons as they develop clearer pictures of how people live around the world.

GENERAL INTRODUCTION

A culture's use of space is an important, often over-looked consideration in cross-cultural understanding. During the activity described in the previous chapter, students possibly burst into giggles or screeched, "ouch," as their heads collided during the Japanese bow. They probably had used the customary U.S. space allotment of approximately eighteen inches to greet and talk to close friends, only to discover that it was not enough room for the bow. The Japanese usually prefer a solid yard between themselves for the initial greeting and conversations. Experts call these distances that people keep between them *proxemics.*

Cultures have unwritten rules concerning how best to regard and use space. How far should one stand from others when having a conversation? What is considered a beautiful use of space in a garden or park? What is the most functional use of space in the home and in our cities? The answers to these questions will vary from culture to culture and from situation to situation within each culture. We must remember that not every member of a particular culture uses and perceives space in the same way. Still, we can find some dominant patterns in the role space plays for people in certain cultures.

The customs attached to the use of space are sometimes rooted in thousands of years of tradition. To those outside a culture, these spatial patterns can appear ridiculous, unfair, or completely impractical. With this view often comes a desire to "improve" the other culture. Consider the following actual case.

An "Improvement" Plan Gone Awry in India

On the Indian subcontinent, remnants of two cultural traditions, social hierarchy and the segregation of sexes, still shape the lifestyles of some of the Indian towns. Extended families live side-by-side along with members of their castes. Hindus, followers of the nation's dominant religion, believe cows to be sacred and therefore allow them to wander the towns at will.

A number of years ago, a group of Western city planning experts, including one from the United States, decided to introduce some "modern" ideas to the city of Chandigarh in southern India. The new plan called for the city to be divided into areas according to functions. Industry settled into one area, government buildings into another. A shopping center, which provided all the daily needs for nearby residents, was built into each of their neighborhoods. Houses were designed with bedrooms, living-dining room combinations, kitchens, and baths, all along the lines of Western dwellings, and windows were built into outside walls to allow the sun to seep into otherwise dark rooms. Cattle were banned from the street and home.

Well, the citizens of Chandigarh rejected all of these "improvements" and managed to work around the obstacles brought on by the new construction. They quickly pasted paper over the windows in order to maintain privacy and brought their cattle through the front door to be quartered illegally in the rear courtyard. One bedroom universally became an "entertaining" center for the guests. The women prepared meals on portable kerosene stoves placed conveniently on the veranda's floor, rather than in the kitchen, which was reserved exclusively as an eating area. Meals were taken in shifts based on the sex and age of the diners. Curtains were hung down the middle of the living room in order to convert it into a sleeping area on one side, a passageway to the "entertaining" zone on the other. Women tended to stay in their territory: the kitchen, sleeping space, rear veranda, courtyard, or bath. Although residents shopped in the neighborhood centers, they preferred their old stores, which had been scattered around the city, clustered by the types of merchandise they sold. This arrangement had allowed the shoppers

to compare prices on similar goods and bargain for the best deal. It also gave them an excuse to travel around the city and visit friends and relatives along the way.

The "new and improved" plan had failed because it ignored the culture's traditions, including the traditions of segregating the sexes and recognizing a hierarchy in gender and age. It also did not take into consideration the popular shopping patterns of the people. These cultural traditions governed the Indians' use of space in their homes and city. "The lesson to be learned," says R. S. Freed, "is that the way people visualize and use space is culturally conditioned and cannot be changed by the world's finest planners" (Freed, 1977).

Think how you would feel if suddenly you had to use your space differently. Could a person in the U.S. cook in the living room or sleep in the kitchen without feeling foolish and uneasy? Our use of space is something we rarely think about, and yet it is an integral part of our daily lives. We are so accustomed to the ways our culture dictates how to use space that we often feel anxious and disoriented, without even knowing why, when we visit cultures in which the use of space and the behavior associated with it differ from our own.

It is important to remember that differences in the use of space do exist and do matter when we attempt to interact with people from different cultures. Students should come away from these lessons with a general understanding of how the use of space can differ from culture to culture and how it can influence cross-cultural interactions. In doing so, they become more perceptive and insightful observers, as well as better-equipped participants in their increasingly multicultural world.

What Went Wrong?

These introductory activities are designed to introduce your students to the ways space can work as a stumbling block in cross-cultural understanding. Most students will not know the correct answer to the question posed in each activity, but that is not the point. Rather, the point is to initiate curiosity and discussion and to stir their interest in pursuing this topic.

Teacher's Instructions: Divide your class into groups of four or five students. Hand each group a copy of each of the following worksheets. Have each group work together to decide which answer best explains the behavior described in "What Went Wrong?" Then, as a class, each group will explain its reason for choosing the answer. After each group has spoken, reveal the correct answer and discuss it. An explanation to each one has been given below. Do the same with each "What Went Wrong?"

Some discussion questions include:

1. Why did your group choose this answer over the other answers? Were there clues given, did you simply eliminate the other answers, did you choose by instinct, or did you apply some assumptions you already had about the cultures mentioned? If you applied some assumptions, what did you already assume about the people from that culture?

2. How would you have felt in this situation?

3. What would you have done next?

4. What does this exercise show you about the different ways people from different cultures respond to the same situation?

Answers and Explanations

What Went Wrong? #1 = Answer #3

In Japan, the Kawamura family, like many other Japanese, did not confine their children to separate bedrooms, nor did the parents have a room of their own that was off-limits to the youngsters. Instead, everyone slept together in one area of the house. As Western influences infiltrate their society, some construction includes separate bedrooms for parents and children, but traditionally the Japanese family stays together throughout the night, particularly with children as young as the Kawamuras'. Bedrooms in Japanese homes may be used for storage or study areas, not necessarily for sleeping space. The Milwaukee apartment manager might easily have misinterpreted the Kawamuras' desire for a one-bedroom apartment as a need to save money. Or perhaps he figured that the Japanese are used to crowded conditions. Neither, of course, was true. But the manager worried that overcrowding would lower the standards of the apartment complex, so he rejected their application for a one-bedroom apartment. In this

case, the Japanese and the people from the U.S. completely misinterpreted the others' concept of space.

What Went Wrong? #2 = Answer #2

While Tammy Roth loved Hong Kong, she felt overwhelmed by the crowds along the sidewalks. She was left with strange sensations of uneasiness. The Chinese, on the other hand, appeared oblivious to the dense masses which streamed along the pavements. Hong Kong, like many East Asian cities, is known for its highly dense population. But high density does not necessarily result in crowding. Density is a physical phenomenon. Crowding is psychological. Tammy felt overwhelmingly crowded and claustrophobic because she was not used to such public closeness. What, to the Chinese, is simply high density was, for Tammy, overcrowding. We will explore the difference between density and crowding below.

What Went Wrong? #3 - Answer #1

When speaking with people from the U.S., Mohammed Abdulah chose to stand much closer to them than they liked. He simply was following the spatial patterns that are customary for people in his Middle Eastern culture. However, in cultures that allow more space for interaction among individuals, like the U.S., this closeness may be misinterpreted as pushy, overbearing, or flirtatious.

What Went Wrong? #4 = Answer #2

Germans usually leave their office doors closed, while people in the U.S. are inclined to leave them open unless engaged in private conversations, meetings, or work that requires an unusual amount of concentration. Putting your head through an open door in the U.S. in order to say, "Hi," is considered quite normal and friendly. In Germany, office doors are usually closed, so it would have been necessary for Dr. Barnes to open them in order to make her informal greeting. This definitely would be considered by the Germans as an invasion of privacy. Moreover, in Germany chairs are not objects that can be moved around within the office space, but are to be left where they are found. Dr. Barnes's good intentions violated the Germans' concept of unwritten spacial rules.

S t u d e n t
Worksheet

NAME _____

DATE _____

WHAT WENT WRONG? #1

Aki Kawamura, his wife, their eight-year-old son and six-year-old daughter moved from Tokyo, Japan, to Milwaukee, Wisconsin, where Mr. Kawamura was to head his company's subsidiary for five years. Shortly after arriving in this U.S. city, the couple began to search for a place to live. Much to their surprise, their rental application for a one-bedroom apartment in an upper-middle-class complex was turned down. The apartment manager told the Kawamuras that they would have to rent a three-bedroom apartment since they had two children of different sexes. The Kawamuras believed this to be completely unnecessary.

Why did the Kawamuras want a one-bedroom apartment for their four-person family? (Circle the answer that best explains the Kawamuras' behavior.)

1. They did not have very much money and could not afford a larger apartment in that expensive community.

2. The Kawamuras were used to very crowded conditions in Japan and did not mind being crowded into a small apartment.

3. The Kawamuras, like other Japanese families, often do not arrange their living spaces as those in the U.S. do. In a traditional Japanese home, especially with young children, there is one sleeping area in which the entire family sleeps together. They did not need so many bedrooms in the U.S.

4. The Kawamuras did not plan to keep their children in the U.S., so they didn't need a larger apartment. They only brought them for a short visit when they first moved to the U.S. Then they would send the kids back to Japan where they would live with their grandparents. Mr. and Mrs. Kawamura thought their children would be better off in Japanese schools.

NAME _____

DATE _____

WHAT WENT WRONG? #2

Thirteen-year-old Tammy Roth of Memphis, Tennessee, moved with her family to Hong Kong where her mother was to teach in a local university for several years. The family's apartment provided a spectacular view across the South China Sea and of the many ships that plied its waters. Hong Kong, with its many nationalities and rich culture, was an exciting place to live, and Tammy loved her new home. But as she walked along the busy sidewalks of Hong Kong, she became engulfed in waves of frustration and uneasiness. She enjoyed the people and loved the sense of adventure Hong Kong gave her. What, then, was making her feel uneasy?

Why did Tammy feel frustrated, strange, and uneasy on the streets of Hong Kong? (Circle the answer that best explains why Tammy felt the way she did.)

1. Tammy was lying to herself when she said she loved Hong Kong. Really, she was very homesick and wanted to return to the U.S.

2. As Tammy walked the busy streets of Hong Kong, she was surrounded by hundreds and hundreds of people. She wasn't used to being around so many people and to being shoved up so close to all of them. She felt crowded.

3. Tammy had a boyfriend back in Memphis who had just written her a letter to say that he was breaking up with her. Tammy loved Hong Kong, but she was very sad about losing her boyfriend.

4. As Tammy walked down the streets of Hong Kong, everyone stared at her because she looked so different. Without her realizing it, their staring was making her feel like an alien from Mars.

Student
Worksheet

NAME _____

DATE _____

WHAT WENT WRONG? #3

Mohammed Abdulah from the United Emirates arrived in a Chicago, Illinois, office to discuss the possibility of doing business with this U.S. corporation. He met many people, both men and women, in the U.S. office. When he left the office on the first day, the people from the U.S. began to talk about this visitor from the Middle East. "He appeared so pushy," said many of the men. "I think he was flirting with me," commented several of the women. Mr. Abdulah, on the other hand, felt the people from the U.S. were rather cold and unfriendly.

What could Mr. Abdulah have done to make the people from the U.S. think he was pushy and flirtatious? Why did Mr. Abdulah think the U.S. businesspeople he met were unfriendly? (Choose the answer that best explains why Mr. Abdulah and the the U.S. businesspeople thought the way they did.)

1. Mr. Abdulah stood very close to the others when he spoke because in his Middle Eastern culture, people stand closer together than people do in the U.S. The people from the U.S. would back away from him when they talked because they felt uncomfortable standing so close. Therefore, they thought he was pushy, and he thought they were cold.

2. Mr. Abdulah kept asking everyone in the office, one by one, if they wanted to meet him for dinner. He would not take "no" for an answer. But no one was available for dinner. Therefore, they thought Mr. Abdulah was pushy while he thought they were rude for turning down his invitation.

3. Mr. Abdulah kept calling everyone he met by the wrong name. He would come up to each of the people in the Chicago office, slap him or her on the back, and talk in a voice that was way too loud. Each time, the person from the U.S. would back away from him. Therefore, the people from the U.S. thought Mr. Abdulah was pushy and overbearing while he thought they were very cold.

4. This office was very serious and had strict rules about chatting during work hours. The U.S. staff was always working hard and had no time to show Mr. Abdulah around the office. Mr. Abdulah was not aware of these rules and kept popping into people's offices to say "Hi" or ask questions. The others would rarely say "Hi" in return. Therefore, Mr. Abdulah thought these people from the U.S. were very rude and unfriendly while they thought he was too pushy.

Worksheet

NAME _____

DATE _____

WHAT WENT WRONG? #4

Dr. Liz Barnes from Los Angeles, California, was living in Bonn, Germany, for several years in order to work with a group of local scientists on a special project. As she walked by some of her co-workers' doors, she occasionally popped her head into their offices just to say "Hi." She was offended when her friendly gesture was not met with a welcoming smile. But she was particularly puzzled when she went into their offices for meetings and discovered that they seemed to be displeased when she moved her chair in order to sit a little closer to some of the participants during the meeting.

Why didn't the Germans smile back at Dr. Barnes and why were they displeased when she moved her chair to sit closer to them? (Choose the answer that best explains the Germans' behavior.)

1. The Germans are very unfriendly people, and they do not like people from the United States.

2. By U.S. standards, Germans are more private. They usually keep their office doors closed, so when Dr. Barnes popped her head in to say "Hi," she had to open their door to do so. The Germans would have considered her action an invasion of their privacy. Also, in Germany, one does not move the chairs around. They are supposed to remain in the place where you found them.

3. Dr. Barnes's co-workers were jealous of Dr. Barnes because she had become very famous for her scientific research. No matter how much she tried to be friendly, they simply would not give her a chance.

4. Germans work very hard and have very little time to chitchat during the workday. Dr. Barnes was too casual for them.

Lesson I

Culture, Perception, and Space: What You See Is Not Always What You Get

"What you see," the saying tells us, "is what you get." But this is not exactly the case. What you see in the space around you may not always be what is actually there. *Our environments and our cultures influence the ways in which we perceive and view the space around us.* We tend to "see" the space around us in ways we need to observe it in order best to function within our society (Segall, 1979).

Sounds complicated? Not really. Consider an individual who has spent his entire life within the tightly woven foliage of a jungle. For him, there is no *need* to develop the ability to observe objects in the distance and to judge what size these objects might be if observed close-up. In fact, there is no opportunity for him to see anything beyond his very close surroundings. A story is often told about a man who was taken from the jungle, where he had always lived, to the wide-open plains. For the first time, his field of vision expanded, and far-off he could see little black specks. "Look," he said, "at the ants." But the specks were not ants. They were buffalo. This jungle dweller had no way of identifying objects on the distant horizon because his previous environment provided no far-reaching vistas.

Reality vs. Appearance

Western philosophers have pondered the question, "What is more real—what we see or what is there?" ever since Plato's time (circa 390 B.C.) in Ancient Greece. Plato wrote about this dilemma in his *Allegory of the Cave.* In this allegory, he describes a group of people who have been imprisoned in a cave their entire lives. They do not even know that there is a world of daylight outside the cave. Plato says that it would be natural for them to interpret the shadows cast on the wall from their fire as real objects. Thus, if these people were finally released from the cave into the world of sunlight, objects in the "real" world would not appear as realistic to them as the hazy shadings of black that had been cast mysteriously on the cave's walls.

Nearly two millennia later, in 1713, a British church bishop and philosopher named George Berkeley proposed that what we see and feel is determined by what we have experienced previously or been accustomed to seeing and feeling. In one of his writings, *Three Dialogues Between Hylas and Philonous,* two characters talk about how water can be both cold and warm at the same time. "Suppose," says the character Philonous, "now one of your hands was hot, the other cold, and that they are both at once put into the same vessel of water in an intermediate state: will not the water seem cold to one hand, and warm to the other?" (Segall, 1979).

Activity

Students can have fun with this very experiment as they discover that whether or not their hand actually feels hot or cold will depend on what that hand has experienced just prior to immersing it in the tepid water.

Fill a large bowl with water. Let it stand to adjust to room temperature. Have the students line up. Before each student gets to the bowl, have him or her hold an ice-pack with the right hand and a (non-electric) heating pad with the left hand for about thirty seconds. Then they may release the objects and place their hands in the water at the same time. How does the water feel to each hand?

When each of the students has had a chance to experience this phenomenon, discuss not only what they felt but also why the water felt a different temperature to each hand. Explain that how we feel and perceive the world around us often depends on what we are used to. *(interpretive)*

Discuss with them the stories about the jungle dweller and the cave dwellers, and explain the following:

What the experiment helps to illustrate is that how things appear to us and how we perceive them are just as important, if not more important, than buffaloes on the horizon or the sources of shadows or what the thermometer says. We need to learn that whatever reality is, it is our *perception* of reality that determines who we are—what we think, feel, and do. And it is our culture that plays a major role in shaping our perceptions. How we react and how we see the world around us depends upon our previous experiences within our own environments and cultures.

Lines and Angles

With the following activity, consider with your students the ways in which our environment influences how we look at lines and angles.

Activity

Draw the following figure on the board. Ask the students which line is longer. *(interpretive)*

Horizontal Vertical Illusion

Some students will see the vertical line as longer than the horizontal, but the lines are the same length. Explain the following:

Anthropologists have conducted experiments with people from different cultures to determine how their members perceive the line lengths of this same illusion. They discovered that people who live in wide-open spaces such as the Australian desert where no trees or poles impede a vast, extended view of the surroundings, have a tendency to look at the vertical line as longer than the horizontal one. They see the vertical line as extending away in space, just as their landscape does. Those of us who live in cities, towns, and wooded areas, on the other hand, are used to having our vistas obstructed by objects that stand perpendicular to the ground, such as tall buildings, telephone poles, and trees. Therefore we can more easily see that the vertical line is the same length as the horizontal because we don't tend to see it as extending away in space. Research shows that Westerners are only slightly susceptible to this illusion (Nanda, 1980).

Gardens and Space

In many cultures, space itself takes on different meanings. People of the Western world think of space as empty, something to be filled. East Asians, on the other hand, particularly the Japanese, see space itself as admirable, attractive, and full of meaning.

The gardens of these cultures often illustrate the difference. Brilliantly colored flower beds flow from shrubs to trees and back to buildings in the well-landscaped U.S. garden. More often than not, the goal is to highlight the buildings while softening the edges around them and providing color to please the Western eye. In contrast, a Japanese garden stands on its own; it quietly captures a visitor's attention and provides a focus for meditation with isolated, large boulders, delicate but important plantings, and large, empty spaces, which create a sense of quiet dignity. The empty space and the rocks and plants are placed strategically so as to complement each other.

Did You Know?

Some cultures can measure the space in which they live by sound rather than by visual and specific measurements, like yards and miles. The Inuits are an example. The sounds they hear allow them to understand what is happening around them (such as an approaching bear), even though they may not be able to see what is occurring. They have become so sensitive to these sounds that they can judge approximately how far away the origin of the noise is. This is known as *acoustic space*. We also can call it *sound space*.

In planning the Japanese garden, a designer utilizes the concept of *fuseki* (foo-say-kee), which governs the placement of the objects in the garden. The term comes from the favorite Japanese game of *Go* in which the artful placement of small uniform stone markers on a playing board accomplishes the goal of controlling the space of your opponent. Players place their markers with a plan in mind based on what they expect their opponents to do. Thus, in a more general sense, fuseki means planning ahead, but without any real knowledge of what future conditions will be. In the technique of Japanese gardening, certain elements such as a tree or stone, called *yakumono* (yah-koo-moh-no), become the focal points for the fuseki, or plan, of the garden. These key objects are placed first. Then the spaces between are filled in. There is no design blueprint. The garden designer's only guides are the sense of harmony with nature and the concept of fuseki (Nishihara, 1967).

Activity

Design and create a Japanese garden.

This is a relatively intensive project that requires some planning ahead. The students will be studying, designing, and actually creating, albeit in miniature, a Japanese garden. The best resources for learning about the layout and philosophy of Japanese gardens are books at the local library and your local Botanical Garden. You may want to bring some books to class and explain the garden design yourself, or you could assign this as a research project for the students.

We recommend that the students work in small groups of four or five. They will need a box the size of a large shoebox, some small gravel (available at an aquarium shop), some stones, and a few tiny plants (some weeds or twigs from a tree will be fine).

When the students have completed their miniature gardens, have them present their creations to the class and explain how they chose to design them. Discuss the differences between gardens in Japan and the U.S. Display the gardens in your classroom. *(constructive, collaborative)*

Space in the Japanese Hotel

The contrast between the typical Western hotel and the Japanese inn, known as a *ryokan* (dyoh-kahn), also demonstrates the cultural differences in the use of space. U.S. hotel rooms are always full of beds, chairs, tables, lamps, TVs, desks, and luggage racks. In the typical ryokan room, however, you will find only a low lacquered table surrounded by cushions and a small raised alcove with a scroll and simple floral arrangement. Unlike a room in a Western hotel, the ryokan room serves as a dining and sitting area before being converted into a bedroom each evening after the maids have rolled out thick, sponge-rubber pads over the *tatami* (ta-tah-mee) mats, which cover the floor. There are no luggage racks provided on which guests can scatter their belongings. All personal items are to be tucked away in the room's closets or cupboards.

Although Western-style hotels are common and popular in Japan, the ryokan still captures the hearts of local travelers and the imaginations of foreigners. The ryokan stands as a symbol of the Japanese conception of space, uncluttered and as free of cumbersome objects as the occasion allows.

The simplicity and absence of clutter in Asian lives can be traced to their philosophies, particularly Taoism (**dow**-ism), which stresses the coexistence of all opposites in the world: light and dark, good and bad, presence and absence. Taoism does not privilege one or the other. In Western thought, on the other hand, opposites are polarized and priority is often given to the former of the two terms. While Westerners tend to view empty space as a negative, something that should be filled, East Asians see the importance of having fullness and emptiness exist in harmony with one another. Privileging one brings chaos and upsets the natural balance in the cosmos.

Activity

Ask the class to name some pairs of opposites (light/dark, good/bad, etc.), and write them on the board. Then ask the students which one of the terms is better than the other. Why? Explain that in the Taoist philosophy, found in East Asia, neither of the terms is any better or worse than the other. The point is to have all opposites in the world live in harmony with one another. When one term is more important than the other, chaos and disharmony are brought to our lives. What do they think of this philosophy? How does it apply to the Japanese hotel, the ryokan, or the Japanese garden?

If they haven't suggested them, add the pairs "presence/absence" and "fullness/emptiness" to the list on the board. Which is the better term in their minds? How would an East Asian think about these terms? What have the students learned about space and the ways it is regarded in various cultures? *(interpretive, cross-cultural)*

Lesson 2

Marking Territories

Living creatures everywhere jealously guard their perceived territories from intruders. Even within their own herd or flock, animals will mark off and maintain a specific zone of space between each other. Just watch a flock of geese flying south for the winter or a cadre of ducks parading across a meadow, and notice how precisely spacing is maintained between each bird. Like animals, humans feel very strongly about their territories. Witness the tragic violence among diverse ethnic groups around the world who stubbornly fight over territories within former and current national boundaries.

How we define territory, particularly personal territory, often depends upon the culture in which we live. For many U.S. students, the school locker represents a hallowed area, and a bedroom or a portion of that room at home becomes sacrosanct. Students may not allow their lockers to be invaded without special permission, and they have been known to post "Do Not Enter" signs on bedroom doors. Yet, in Japanese schools, lockers are nonexistent because Japanese students, even in high school, do not change classes. Teachers come to them, so all books are kept at the desk and coats are hung on pegs at the back of the room. Since many families roll out their *futons* and sleep close together on the floor of one room, a private, walled-off space is often not available for a young person. But a special at-home desk, far different from anything a U.S. student possesses, does become personal territory in a Japanese home. Parents will invest many *yen* (the local currency) in these special study tables. They come equipped with three tall partitions across the sides and back to eliminate distractions, and often they contain a built-in clock and pencil sharpener.

As we stand in line for tickets to a rock concert or for a hamburger at a fast-food restaurant, we map out a temporary territory around us, that, if violated, raises our ire. How many times have you been angered when someone steps ahead of you in line or felt uncomfortable when the person behind you stands so close that he keeps nudging you forward? In England, there exists an even stronger regard for temporary territory when a *queue* (kew), or line, is formed. No one invades a bus queue or rushes ahead of another for an *underground* (subway) ticket. On the other hand, in some cultures such as the Polish, there is no sense of territorial invasion when people push and shove to reach

a ticket booth. What can appear a rude invasion of space in one culture can simply be a way of life in another.

For humans, territory can become a very complicated issue, especially because it is not always an actual area of physical space. Rather, human territory is more often than not an emotional boundary defined by one's state of mind and expressed by one's behavior. Because territory is an emotional boundary, it can shift and change according to the occasion. It can be relatively permanent or strictly temporary. Yet it usually arouses feelings of stubborn resistance against those who attempt to invade it. Even a territory as temporary as a public telephone booth can stir a sense of possession. A study was made to determine how willingly people gave up the public telephone if others were standing by to use it. The researchers discovered that people both here in the U.S. and in Germany *believed* that the users of the phone would hurry their calls if someone were waiting. But in *actuality* the talkers dug in their heels and lengthened their time in the booth (Ruback, Pape, Doriot, 1989). The "threat" of invasion only made them more stubborn.

It is important for students to realize that "territories" usually are not actual physical boundaries but emotional ones that are tied to behavioral patterns. The following research project will make this point clear for them.

Activity

A research project: How, When, and Where Do Humans Mark Their Territories?

After relating and discussing the information above, assign the students a research project in which they will devise experiments to observe how other people mark and claim possession of certain territories. In pairs, they will come up with a way of observing human behavior, even testing it, in a location of their choice. For example, a pair of students may devise an experiment in which one of them stands in a grocery store checkout line and inches closer and closer to the person in front of him or her. They will measure how many steps it took to make the person move away. (The students would need to obtain the store manager's permission for this experiment!) Another experiment would be to stand next to a phone booth, as if waiting for it, when someone is on the phone and count how many minutes the talker stays on the phone.

Then the students will need to measure the results statistically (after 3 steps, people will move forward 7 times out of 10, or something like that) as well as be able to write up the results with some qualitative conclusions. (Why do they think the people did what they did?) Have the students share their experiments and results with the class. *(constructive, collaborative)*

Lesson 3

Personal Space: If You Can Read This, You're Too Close

Everyone has a "comfort zone." Exactly how much personal space we need in order to avoid feeling uncomfortable or "invaded" is determined by our culture and situations that come up within a cultural context. U.S. residents, for example, usually allow just enough room for another person to squeeze through when talking to a close friend or family member. But these space requirements change, not only with the occasion but also with the individual with whom we are speaking or interacting.

Personal Space in Other Cultures

When Arabs speak with one another, they usually prefer to be within "smelling distance." Detecting an odor from the breath and body is an important aspect in personal conversations among Arabs. This can be accomplished only if the parties stand very close together, literally breathing on each other. Arabs are more comfortable standing closer together than people in the U.S. are; they believe there is an inherent connection between the way someone smells and his or her personality. When arranging an Arab marriage, the intermediaries may even request to take a whiff of the potential bride. If her smell is not to their liking, she will be out of the running (Hall, 1969).

The eyes, Arabs also believe, reveal the truth. They believe it is important to keep direct visual contact. A non-Arab U.S. resident may react to such closeness with "Get out of my face!" In addition, if the encounter takes place between members of the opposite sex, such closeness can mistakenly be interpreted as flirtatious.

Latinos also tend to stand very close together when talking with one another. A U.S. woman who lived in Mexico relates the following:

I remember very well the first party I attended. I spoke with a Mexican man who kept putting his face very close to mine. Instinctively, I backed up. He went forward. I backed up. He stepped closer, until finally I was in a corner. I unwittingly had embarrassed myself and my new friend by not understanding how far was too far, how close was too close.

There are members of some cultures who feel uncomfortable with closeness as defined by U.S. standards. Many Germans, for example, become annoyed when people from the U.S. move their chairs a little closer in order to have a more intimate conversation with them. While it is quite customary for people in the U.S. to leave office doors ajar (unless they are involved in a private conversation), the Germans prefer to have doors solidly closed (Hall, 1969).

Throughout the world, everyone unknowingly is programmed from childhood to maintain specific distances from one another under various circumstances within his or her culture. But problems arise when we attempt to interact with someone from another culture who has different standards and customs. There are several issues to consider: His or her standards for personal distance may vary from ours; the person's age, status, and gender also play roles in determining how far we should stand from them; how long we have known him or her plays a role as well; and distances may vary according to the situation.

Activity

The following student worksheet is a "Distance Log." Instruct the students that on the worksheet they are to keep a log of the distances they observe between them and others or between other individuals under various circumstances throughout one day, at school, at home, on TV, etc. Students will need to obtain and carry a measuring tape to be able to measure these distances. The worksheet contains spaces for the location, the situation, and the distance measured. Ask the students to draw some conclusions about what they have observed.

Discuss what the students have learned about personal space from their observations. Explain that the use of personal space will differ quite a bit in another culture. Share and discuss the information about the use of personal space by Arabs, Latinos and Germans. *(constructive)*

From *Windows to the World: Themes for Cross-Cultural Understanding.* Copyright © 1996 by Phyllis Kepler, Brooke Sarno Royse, and John Kepler

Student
Worksheet

NAME _____

DATE _____

DISTANCE LOG

Location	Situation	Distance
1._____		
2._____		
3._____		
4._____		
5._____		
6._____		
7._____		
8._____		

CONCLUSIONS:_____

_____

_____

_____

_____

Family Space: There's No Place Like Home

Activity

Have the students draw a picture of the floor plans of their homes as an interior designer would. The view should be from the ceiling of each floor. The picture will indicate where the doors and windows are, how the furniture is placed (with labels identifying each piece), and what each room is (i.e., kitchen, dining room). It would help if the students could obtain large pieces of graph paper for this purpose.

When they are finished with their drawings, tell them that this lesson will explore how homes are built around the world and how space is used within these homes. Students' drawings will be used to compare dwellings from their culture with dwellings from other cultures. The activities for this lesson will give them the opportunity to transform their own homes into East African, Afghan, and Japanese homes. *(constructive)*

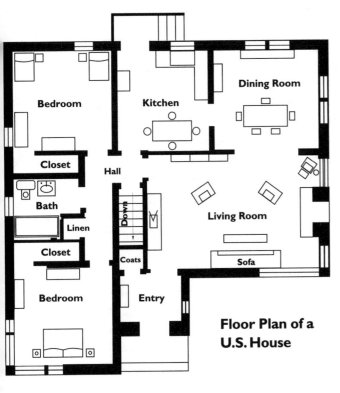

Floor Plan of a U.S. House

Homes Reflect Cultures

The ways in which families allocate space within the walls of their homes can reflect important social patterns in their society. Attitudes toward the segregation of men and

women, the importance of the individual or group, and other aspects of culture become significant in the planning of family space around the world.

What factors determine how a home is constructed? Many people believe that the environment and the climate are the main determining factors in how a home is built. But this is not necessarily true. Many farmhouses in Northern Europe, the Swiss mountains, and Southeast Asia share a common architectural feature: all are built on wooden posts. Yet the climate and topography of these areas are very different (Nishihara, 1967). The amount of money a family has to spend on a house is also not always the most important factor in deciding how a house will be constructed. Residents on the Philippine island of Cebu could build a cheaper home if they wanted to, but doing so would eliminate the socialization and fun that comes when friends and neighbors join in to help build the traditional structure. Available technology is not always a determining factor either. The French tried to introduce plumbing to the homes in North Africa and were met with stiff resistance from the women. As conservative Muslims who rarely left their homes, these women had relished their trips to the community well to meet and talk with other women. Once the water taps were disconnected and the well reopened, the women were happy (Rapoport, 1969). And even while the materials available may restrict what goes into a home, they do not necessarily dictate what will be used.

Although we cannot rule out climate, access to funds, technology, and availability of materials as factors that influence how a house will be built, these considerations tend to limit rather than define the construction. *It is cultural values that play an important role in deciding how to build the home and how to use the space within that home.*

The Swahili House

In the coastal cities of the East African country of Tanzania, life is shared with friends and neighbors, and nowhere is this so prevalent than in what is called the *Swahili House*. From the outside, these buildings appear to be one-family homes, but the front doors open into long hallways with several doors on each side, each of which leads to a one-room family unit. At the rear of the structure is a community kitchen where the women from the resident families cook together and into which the men rarely venture. Instead, the men sit outside to gossip and watch the world go by while the women prepare the meals.

To some in the U.S., such living conditions would seem entirely unsatisfactory—too crowded and probably due to poverty. But such is not the case. The Swahili

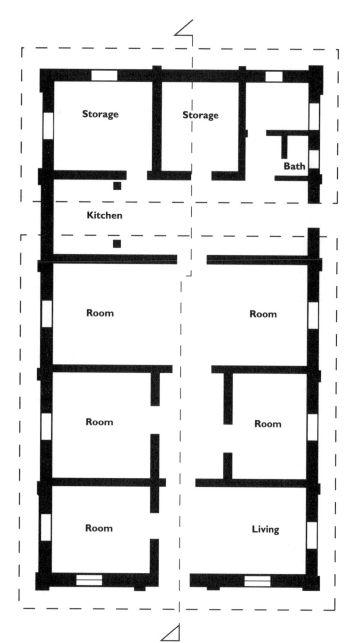

Floor Plan of a Swahili House

Did You Know?

In Sarawak, which lies on the island of Borneo but in actuality is a state of the mainland country of Malaysia, members of the Iban tribe live in *long houses.* As many as one hundred people live under one roof in apartments that open onto a long hall that runs through the middle of the building. The residents all gather in the hall to socialize.

House makes sense for a culture in which "your business is my business" and happiness comes in sharing (Condon and Yousef, 1979).

Activities

1. Discuss the following old Swahili proverb:

   "You should treat a guest like a guest for two days, but on the third day, give him a hoe, so he can work like one of the family."

   What does this proverb say about the culture that uses it? How do people in the U.S. tend to treat guests in their homes? Ask your students if any of them treats guests as the Swahili proverb suggests. *(interpretive)*

2. Study the floor plan of the Swahili House and discuss the information supplied about it. Do we have anything comparable in the U.S.? Ask your students if they would like to live in such a communal situation. *(interpretive)*

3. Now ask the students to plan their own Swahili House. Have them draw their plans on graph paper. Which families would they have live there? Have them label each area of the house. *(cross-cultural, constructive)*

German Homes

At the other end of the spectrum from the Swahili House is the German home, which lives up to Robert Frost's assertion that "good fences make good neighbors." Many German homes are apt to be enclosed by high hedges and rarely used for entertaining except for close friends and family members. Inside, heavy doors close off rooms, and draperies or curtains keep outsiders from looking in. Even coming to a front door may not give you a view inside, because often only the upper half of the door may be opened to a stranger (Smith and Fiber, 1979).

Activity

Discuss: What does "Good fences make good neighbors" mean? Is this a U.S. way of regarding neighbors?

How does life in the Swahili House probably differ from life in the German home? Where would you rather live? Which home is more like a typical home in the U.S.? *(interpretive)*

The Qala

Throughout the Islamic Middle East two traditions strongly influence many aspects of the cultures there. One is the

Put these words on a sign to hang in front of the classroom. Ask the students to think about how they would finish the statement. Have them make signs that finish the sentence, and hang them underneath this one.

Did You Know?

Across the windows and extending over the fronts of many of the older homes in the Muslim Middle East are beautifully carved wooden facades. They allow air and light to come in and people on the inside to look out, but they prevent anyone on the street from seeing in. This architectural feature aided *purdah* (pur-dah), a social custom associated with Muslim society in which women are kept in seclusion. In the near past, Muslim women were often restricted to their homes, so these window coverings allowed them to watch the world go by in privacy.

overwhelming hospitality offered to friend and stranger alike. The other is the custom of keeping women apart from men who are not members of their family. Muslims say that this tradition stems from the need to protect the local women. Exactly how the women are protected and the amount of freedom they experience is determined by the local laws and the interpretation of the Islamic religion in each particular area. In homes throughout the Middle East, men usually entertain their male guests in spaces as far removed as possible from the women's area in the home.

No other building in the entire Middle East so clearly demonstrates the importance of these cultural characteristics as the grand *Qala* (kah-la) in Afghanistan (*qala* means "fortress"). It was originally built as a fortified farm compound, but today it is strictly an enormous, walled dwelling for the extended family. Young adults are not pushed out the door and urged to make it on their own; instead, sons brings wives home to live with mom, dad and the siblings. Families grow, and large spaces quickly fill.

The typical qala is completely self-contained and protected from the outside world. It contains a mosque,

separate quarters for nuclear families, and space for animals. It is a multi-storied building with watchtowers that today are usually used as storage areas. The qala has few outside windows, the exception being those on the upper level and in the guest room, which perches high over the only entrance to the compound. To someone with a U.S. eye, these guest's quarters somewhat resemble the skyboxes in a U.S. sports arena. It is important to accommodate guests, but their quarters must be far enough away so that they will not mingle with the women of the family.

An alley-like corridor runs through the middle of the qala compound, but about three-quarters down a wall blocks the line of sight. In the small alleyways leading into each nuclear family unit, a similar wall impedes the view. It is behind these visual blocks that the women stay and the family gathers in multi-purpose rooms for talking, sleeping, and eating. During the hot summer months, the people move "upstairs" to another set of rooms to have access to open decks and to take advantage of the building's few windows (Szabo, 1991).

Activities

1. Study and discuss the picture of the qala and the information given about life there. What do the students think about such a living arrangement? Do any of your students live with an extended family? Take a poll of your class to see how many students have uncle, aunts, grandparents, and great-grandparents living with them. *(interpretive)*

The Qala House in Afghanistan

From *Windows to the World: Themes for Cross-Cultural Understanding.* Copyright © 1996 by Phyllis Kepler, Brooke Sarno Royse, and John Kepler

Did You Know?

Indonesia is a country made up of more than seventeen thousand islands and many different cultures. In some areas of this diverse region, you will find homes built on stilts and crowned with "saddleback" roofs. These roofs dramatically dip in the middle and then sweep up at the ends. These ends soar skyward with decorative finials at the very tips, which often take the shape of crossed horns, believed to represent buffalo horns. The buffalo is very important in many Southeast Asian cultures because it is on this animal, the people believe, that the dead will ride to the upper world. Other homes will have masterfully carved snakes or birds extending from the very tip of their pointed gables.

A Room in a Japanese House

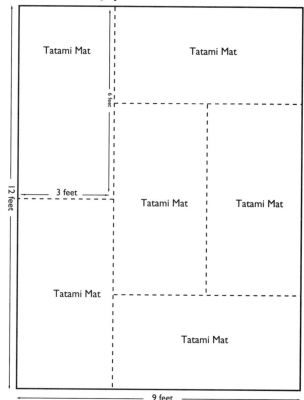

2. Ask the students to take a look at the drawings of their own homes and transform them into plans for a house to which *all* their relatives would come to live. Where would they add rooms? Where would they place the family members? Could guests come to stay? Where would the guests sleep? If you want to extend this activity, have the students conduct more detailed plans and write about them: When would everyone eat? Who would cook? What would the older people do in the home? What would the younger people be responsible for? How many bathrooms would there be? Who would get priority for using the bathrooms? Why?

Display the students' drawings and write-ups.
(cross-cultural, constructive)

The Traditional Japanese Home

Like the Swahili House and the Qala, the traditional Japanese home also is arranged quite differently from family space in U.S. homes. (Large apartment blocks and Western-style housing are creeping into Japanese housing patterns now.) In the U.S., homes are planned according to function—eating, sleeping, family recreation—and we name them accordingly. There are "dining rooms," "bedrooms," "family rooms," "living rooms," etc. The size of homes in the U.S. are identified by the number of bedrooms, individual rooms are measured in linear feet, and overall measurements are given in square feet.

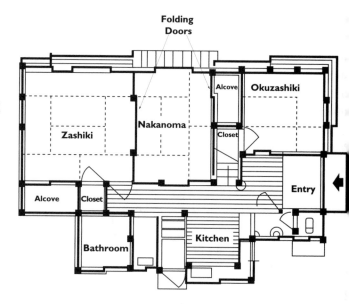

Floor Plan of a Traditional Japanese Home

In Japan, rooms are measured not by rulers or tape measures but by the number of fiber-woven *tatami* (ta-tah-mee) mats—roughly three-by-six feet in size—that fit on the floor. Rooms in traditional Japanese homes are far more flexible than those in U.S. homes. In fact, in the Japanese language, there is no word that exactly corresponds to the English word "room." The Japanese word *ma* (mah) comes the closest to the meaning of "room," but in actuality it is closer to the English word "place." In Japan, rooms are named by location rather than function: for example, there is the inner sitting room, *okuzashiki* (oh-koo-zah-shee-kee)*; the middle room, *nakanoma* (nah-kah-noh-ma); and the room farthest from the street, *zashiki* (zah-shee-kee). The use of these spaces varies according to need and time of day. Instead of having solid walls, the Japanese transform the space in the home throughout the day by sliding partitions, known as *fusuma* (foo-soo-ma), in and out of place. What begins the day as the area where the family eats, later becomes the area where they sleep (Nishihara, 1967).

U.S. bathrooms are very strange to the Japanese. Why, they wonder, would someone place something as unclean as a toilet in the same room as a bathtub? The unwritten rules of cleanliness are so carefully observed that the Japanese wash before climbing into the tub. Who, the Japanese reason, would want to sit in dirty water?

If you are fortunate enough to be given the place of honor when visiting a Japanese home, you will be seated in front of the sitting room's alcove. But you must never face this very special, raised, offset area where important family objects are exhibited. In a country where social hierarchy and protocol are all-important, space plays an important role in maintaining proper manners.

Activities

1. Observe and discuss how space is used in a traditional Japanese home, and compare it to the way it is used in U.S. homes. Does it make more sense to refer to a room according to its function ("dining room") or location? Why? Why wouldn't the Japanese refer to their rooms according to functions? *(interpretive)*

2. If the students have not already done so, have them measure the living room in their own home. Then see if they can calculate how many tatami mats (three-by-six feet each) would fit in the room. That is how a Japanese person might measure the room—in terms of the number of tatami mats. *(constructive)*

Did You Know?

The traditional family home in Korea includes a heating system known as *ondol* (ahn-dahl). Although central furnaces are found in newer construction, these old ondol systems keep the floors comfortably warm by sending hot smoke from the cooking area through ducts under the floor to the opposite end of the house and the dwelling's chimney. As in Japan, families in these traditional homes sleep on the floor. There the warm floors keep families very comfortable. Space is used interchangeably in these Korean homes. The main room may serve as a living and dining area during the day, but at night it is converted into a bedroom. Family members and guests sit on the floor and stretch out at night on a thin mattress known as a *yo* (yoh). An *eebul* (ay-bull), or thick quilt, covers them.

3. Have the students transform their floor plans into Japanese floor plans. They will need to take the walls out of their houses and replace them with sliding partitions. They will need to re-name each room according to its location. They should then list what activities will be conducted in various areas of the house and at what time of day. *(cross-cultural, constructive)*

U.S. Housing Can Be a Stumbling Block to Others

Housing in the United States, no matter how luxurious or technologically advanced, may be met with resistance by newly arrived immigrants to our country. While environmentally comfortable, U.S housing may prove to be culturally displeasing. When a person from the U.S. rented his midwestern home to a family from Saudi Arabia, some cross-cultural confusion resulted. The neighbors stopped by to call on the Saudi family, but no one answered the door. Typical of other U.S. houses, the home had an entryway with large doorways opening into the various rooms. But there were no doors behind which the Muslim women could hide. While the U.S. neighbors talked about the unfriendliness of the Saudis, the Saudis in turn worried about protecting the women from strangers' eyes. Again, space and its use turned out to be a stumbling block to healthy cross-cultural understanding and mutually enriching interaction.

Lesson 5

Public Space: A Crowd Is Not Always a Crowd

If all the people living in the mid-1990s were distributed evenly over the earth, there would be approximately ninety-three persons for each square mile. Each man, woman, and child would have several acres of land. Of course, people are not evenly distributed around the world. They are concentrated in urban areas and along coastlines, and scattered across deserts, mountains and jungles.

The number of persons living in any given unit of space gives us the population *density* of an area. The density for England, for example, is one hundred times that of Canada. It is popularly believed that if the density is low, as it would be if people were evenly distributed across the globe, there would be fewer social problems. High density is often cited as a root cause of poverty, crime, disease, economic stagnation, and even war. People are said to suffer because of "overcrowding." The more people crammed into a given space, goes the argument, the greater the tensions and stress. People feel restricted with so little space in which to move. No one has any privacy. It is no wonder that tensions erupt into violence. In other words, we tend to believe that high density and crowding go hand in hand.

But experts say this is not so. The concept of density is a physical one and does not vary by culture. The concept of crowding, however, is cultural and physical; it may vary from person to person and culture to culture. Having many people in one area does not necessarily bring feelings of frustration and claustrophobia. What triggers a feeling of crowdedness varies from culture to culture, even from individual to individual. A person in search of solitude in the wilderness can feel crowded by the appearance of another individual on the scene. For the U.S. girl (mentioned in the "What Went Wrong?" activities) who walked along the busy streets of Hong Kong, life in this East Asian city was "crowded." But for the Chinese, accustomed to high density and a culture that accepts closeness, the situation was not uncomfortable at all. Tokyo, with a density of about 844 people per square mile, has a far lower crime rate than major cities in the U.S. One of the female authors of this book was alone in Tokyo for a long time. She rode the subway late at night and then walked down a narrow dark street to her home with no fear of being mugged or robbed.

SIDEBAR

DENSITIES AROUND THE WORLD

Australia	5.4 people per square mile
Brazil	47 people per square mile
China	288 people per square mile
Denmark	305 people per square mile
Haiti	580 people per square mile
India	658 people per square mile
Iraq	104 people per square mile
Mali	17 people per square mile
Mexico	115 people per square mile
Mongolia	3 people per square mile
United States:	
New York	378 people per square mile
Ohio	264 people per square mile
Montana	6 people per square mile
Rhode Island	941 people per square mile
District of Columbia	9,792 people per square mile
Wisconsin	89 people per square mile

(Source: *The World Almanac*, 1990)

In early societies, people banded close together voluntarily. Archaeologists have discovered caves in which sixty or more Cro-Magnon humans lived for mutual protection and sociability. The density in the cave probably was high, even by today's standards. Whether or not early people lived in large groups or in isolation depended a lot on the type of animals they hunted. If the food source consisted of smaller, more widely dispersed game, as in the lifestyle of the Inuit, there was less pressure to form groups. But those in search of buffalo herds needed many people to capture their prey. A great change in the degree of density came with the introduction of agriculture, since farming could produce a surplus of food without the need to hunt (Freedman, 1972).

Today, what is crowding to one culture is simply togetherness for another. One of the first things a parent in the U.S. wants to know when his child comes home from school the first day is, "How many students are in your class?" When the number is over thirty, we complain the classroom is too crowded for healthy learning. Yet in East Asia, class size can reach seventy, and learning is not considered to be hindered at all.

What is meant by crowding can also vary within a culture, depending on the situation. Teens in the U.S. can eel crowded on a bus but perfectly at ease when jammed gainst other spectators at a rock concert. In Mexico, nembers of the opposite sex stand very close together vhen speaking. But when the rush hour comes, the definiion of acceptable closeness changes altogether. Subway ars are deemed too crowded for both sexes to share, so vomen go into one car, men into another.

The sense of being crowded all depends on what one s used to. Yet when we interact across cultural lines, it is mportant to keep in mind that high density is not synonynous with crowding or impoverished conditions. By eing able to make this distinction, students will be less ikely to make negative judgments about cultures with igher densities than their own.

Activities

. "Two is company. Three is a crowd." What does this saying mean? Why would this be so? *(interpretive)*

. Discuss the times your students feel crowded and the way this can vary according to circumstance (rock concert vs. a full busload). *(interpretive)*

. To illustrate the difference between high density and crowding, conduct the following experiment:

> Make a large square on the floor of the classroom with masking tape. Have ten students stand inside the boundaries of the square. Tell them that this illustrates *density.* There are ten people per "classroom square."
>
> Now take a rope and tie it around the ten students. How do they feel? Crowded, right? This illustrates crowding. The density has not changed. There is still a density of 10 people per classroom square but these 10 people are much more uncomfortable. In other words, crowding is an emotional reaction while density is simply physical and factual. *(constructive)*

Lesson 6

Public Space: Losing Your Way in City Spaces

Everyone has problems finding his or her way around a new city. This challenge is minimized in the U.S. because many major metropolitan areas have a similar design. Most U.S. cities are designed like a grid. Straight streets, perpendicular to each other, crisscross at intersections, making it possible to walk out of a building and stroll around the block. This design is known as the *grid pattern.*

Winston Churchill once said, "First we shape our buildings and then they shape us." Cities say so much about a culture, its people, and its values. In their architecture, they reflect what a culture believes to be attractive and functional. In their parks, they illustrate how the culture feels about nature. In their street layouts, they reflect

Chicago

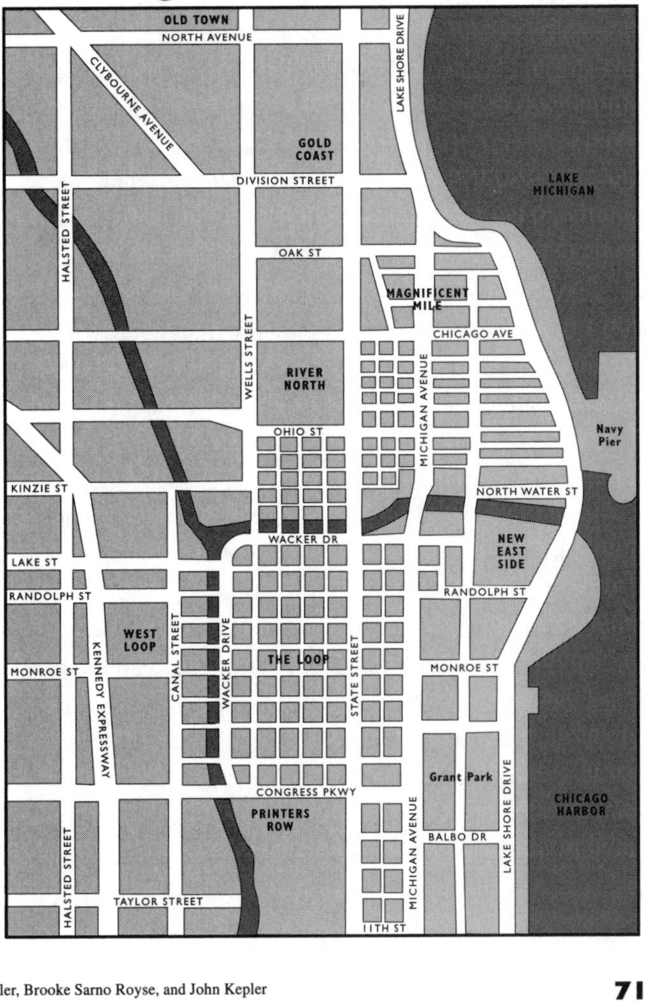

not only some important aspects of the culture's history but also some significant patterns of thinking. Humans may build cities, but cities, in turn, shape the mindsets and lifestyles of their inhabitants.

There are as many different kinds of cities as there are cultures around the world. Therefore, cities and their uses of space can present an enormous stumbling block in understanding and adjusting to another culture.

Outside the U.S., cities usually do not follow the grid pattern, for example. Imagine the difficulties people from the U.S. encounter when they attempt to find their way through a foreign city where not only are the names difficult to decipher but the street plan itself is so different that nothing seems to make sense.

London

To a person from the U.S., there seems to be neither rhyme nor reason to London's plan. No great boulevard sweeps through the city, and there is no "Main Street" to serve as an anchor, the way it does in so many U.S. towns. Rather, many streets follow medieval paths or end abruptly, because centuries ago a powerful estate owner said the road could go no further. One street may change names and street numbering several times. This is because London is really many villages that expanded and overlapped with neighboring towns to form a gigantic metropolitan area. Therefore, there is no "downtown" in London. Instead, each borough, formerly a village, has its own High Street, a busy shopping area that becomes a miniature "downtown." There are several major shopping districts throughout London, but the typical United States or Canadian downtown, consisting of stores and office towers, does not exist. Each former village has a character of its own, and London has become a patchwork quilt of fascinating neighborhoods and colorful, self-expressive people.

It would be incorrect to refer to the whole of London as the "City." The "City of London" is just one small area where it all began back in A.D. 43 when a determined group of Roman soldiers marched up from the south and settled along the Thames River at a spot narrow enough to build a bridge. They called their town Londinium, built a wall around it and settled in for several centuries. An invisible barrier of tradition and determination on the part of its people still separates this original area from the rest of London. The square mile City today is the financial and legal center of London.

DID YOU KNOW?
Space in department stores is used quite differently in some cultures. In England, the basement or ground floors are usually giant food stores. Roofs of department stores in Japan are often wonderful playgrounds where youngsters can enjoy rides and even fish while bargains are usually found on the top floor.

London

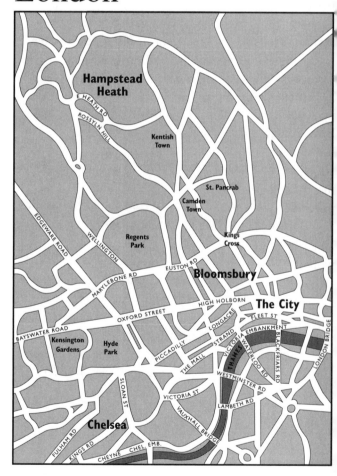

Tokyo

Tokyo

To a Westerner, Tokyo may represent one of the most bewildering spacial plans of all. Finding your way through Tokyo can be not only difficult but also frightening to the newcomer. It is impossible to walk around the block in that East Asian city. Streets do not run in a straight line but wind and twist in a pattern that is almost impossible to follow. It all dates back to the days when people built their homes in concentric rings around the castle of the feudal lords to whom they were the most loyal. These rings were eventually connected with twisting, winding roads that later became a hodge-podge of streets in modern-day Tokyo.

To make finding one's way even more difficult for foreigners in Tokyo, the streets are not always named, and houses are not numbered consecutively; they are numbered in the order in which they were built. Number one may be in the middle of the block, and fifty on the corner.

Tokyo presented quite a challenge when two of the authors worked there:

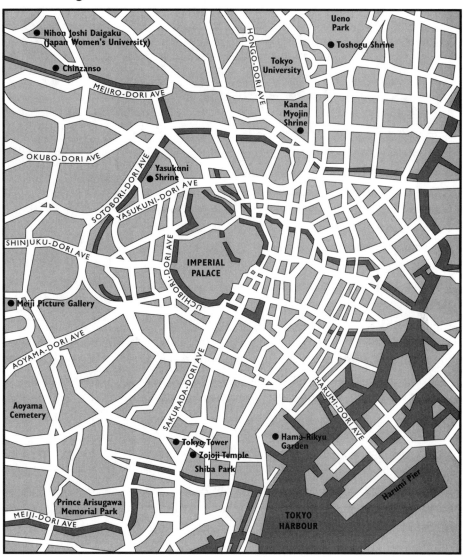

When we settled into the city with our two children, we were invited to the home of a friend who gave us directions that ran something like the following: Take the Chiyoda Line (subway) to the Akasaka stop. Then follow the signs to the Tokyo Broadcasting System. Pass McDonald's, Kentucky Fried Chicken, Shakey's Pizza, to the Korean Barbecue. Turn right, walk toward the Mikado, and go to the end of the street where it narrows into nothing more than steep steps up the side of the hill. At the top, turn right again, and we live in the concrete building right next door to the piano factory.

These directions revealed quite a bit about Japanese culture. They reflect the Japanese penchant for fast foods found in the U.S. (and all foreign foods, for that matter),

TV, entertainment (the Mikado nightclub), streets too narrow for cars, and neighborhoods that are not strictly residential. Unlike the United States, where zoning prohibits factories from being built next to a home, Tokyo is spotted with commercial buildings standing cheek to jowl with lovely homes. The visitors could not have made it without the help of the outstanding transportation system. Tokyo is crisscrossed, overlapped, and bisected by one of the world's best transportation systems—subways, trains, and buses that take you absolutely anywhere you want to go.

The layout of Tokyo mirrors some dominant attitudes and values of the Japanese people. The majority of Japanese people approach their work in a different manner from people in the U.S. In dominant Japanese thinking, ideas do not necessarily build, one on top of the other, until the goal is reached, as they tend to do in Western

Did You Know?

In European countries, floors are counted differently from floors in the U.S. The first floor is called the "ground floor" and our second floor is their "first floor."

Did You Know?

Finding your way through the African countryside is often made easy by the warm hospitality of the local people. If you are on foot, they often accompany you for at least a portion of your way, and then they turn you over to another individual, usually a complete stranger, who will feel it is his obligation to accompany you on the next portion of your journey. Directions are not given in distance nor even in the length of time it will take you to reach a site. Instead, people will tell you that you will travel down the road to "the first mango tree," and then you will follow the footpath to another natural or humanmade landmark.

thought. Instead, the Japanese may begin with an idea and then develop it with suggestions coming from many different directions. Similarly, conversations among the Japanese are not direct and to the point as they are in the U.S., where being able to "get down to business" as quickly as possible is an admired trait. In Japan, talking *around* the business at hand, first getting to know the other person with whom you will be working, is much more important than keeping a certain focus. To most Japanese, the direct approach is not the best approach, and their largest city, Tokyo, reflects this attitude: the streets and alleyways are not directed straight to a point but wander in many different directions, making the city a fascinating study in Japanese thought and culture.

Wandering through the spacial plans of another culture can be bewildering and frustrating. For a foreigner coming to the U.S., the grid plan, so simple and easy for those accustomed to it to follow, may not be easy to understand at all. So, while a city's use of space can be a stumbling block to the newcomer, it can, like any stumbling block, also be a key to understanding the culture. To the keen observer, the layout of a city can tell endless stories about a culture's history, values, and attitudes.

Activities

1. To familiarize the students with the map of Tokyo, choose two points on the map, and ask the students to give directions from one point of the city to the other. Repeat several times with two different points on the map. *(constructive)*

2. Discuss the ways London and Tokyo are laid out and the reasons for it. Have the class study the maps of London, Tokyo, and Chicago side by side. Consider the street plans, the locations of parks, etc. Which city looks more interesting? In which city does it seem like it would be more difficult to get around? Which city looks as if it might be more attractive? Discuss how a city's layout can say so much about some important

values and thinking patterns of a culture. If Tokyo's layout mirrors some dominant thinking patterns of the Japanese, what does the U.S. grid pattern say about they way people in the U.S. think? *(cross-cultural, interpretive)*

3. Go over the directions the authors were given to get to their friend's house in Tokyo. What can the students discover about Japanese culture simply from the directions and the way that they were given?

Ask the students to pretend that a friend is coming with his or her parents to visit from another country. They have never been to your town or city before. They are flying into your local airport and taking a taxi to the student's home. Have each student write down the directions he or she would give to the friends in order to get them from the airport to the student's front door.

Then discuss what a visitor could learn about U.S. culture simply from those directions.
(cross-cultural, interpretive)

Resources

Bond, Michael Harris. *Beyond the Chinese Face: Insights from Psychology.* Hong Kong: Oxford University Press, 1991.

Condon, John C., and Fathi Yousef. "Out of House and Home." *Toward Internationalism;* edited by Elise C. Smith and Louise Fiber. Rowley, MA: Newbury House, 1979.

Freed, R. S. "Space, Density and Cultural Conditioning." *Annals of the New York Academy of Sciences, Issues on Cross-Cultural Research;* edited by Leonore L. Adler; Vol. 285. 1977.

Freedman, Jonathan. *Crowding and Behavior.* New York: Viking, 1972.

Hall, Edward T. *The Hidden Dimension.* Garden City, NJ: Doubleday, 1969.

——. *The Silent Language.* Garden City, NJ: Doubleday, 1959.

Kent, Susan. *Analyzing Activity Areas: An Ethnoarchaeological Study of the Use of Space.* Albuquerque: University of New Mexico Press, 1984.

Keyfitz, Nathan. "Population Density and the Style of Social Life." *Crowding and Behavior;* edited by Chalsa M. Loo. New York: Arno Press (MSS Information Corporation), 1974.

Nanda, Serena. *Cultural Anthropology,* 3rd ed. Belmont, CA: Wadsworth, 1980.

Nishihara, Kiyoyuki. *Japanese Houses: Patterns for Living;* translated by Richard L. Gage. Tokyo: Japan Publications, 1967.

Rapoport, Amos. *House Form and Culture.* Englewood Cliffs, NJ: Prentice-Hall, 1969.

Ruback, R. Barry, Karen D. Pape, and Philip Doriot. "Waiting for a Phone: Intrusion on Callers Leads to Territorial Defense." *Social Psychology Quarterly,* 52:3. 1989.

Salmovar, Larry A., and Richard E. Porter, eds. *Intercultural Communication: A Reader.* Belmont, CA: Wadsworth, 1976.

Scheflen, Albert. *Human Territories and How We Behave in Space-Time.* Englewood Cliffs, NJ: Prentice-Hall, 1976.

Seamon, David, and Robert Mugerauer, eds. *Dwelling, Place and Environment: Towards a Phenomenology of Person and World.* Dordrecht: Martinus Nijhoff Publishers, 1985.

Segall, Marshall H. *Cross-Cultural Psychology: Human Behavior in Global Perspective.* Monterey, CA: Brooks/Cole Publishing (Wadsworth), 1979.

Segall, Marshall H., Donald T. Campbell, and Melville J. Herskovits. *The Influence of Culture on Visual Perception.* Indianapolis: Bobbs-Merrill, 1966.

Smith, Elise C., and Louise Fiber, eds. *Toward Internationalism: Readings in Cross-Cultural Communication.* Rowley, MA: Newbury House, 1979.

Szabo, Albert, and Thomas Barfield. *Afghanistan: An Atlas of Indigenous Domestic Architecture.* Austin: University of Texas Press, 1991.

Taylor, Sally Adamson. *Culture Shock: France.* Portland, OR: Graphic Arts Publishing Company, 1990.

Tefft, Stanton K. *Secrecy: A Cross-Cultural Perspective.* New York: Human Sciences Press, 1980.

Time

Goals

This chapter explores several basic concepts of time and their implications for cross-cultural understanding. The information, stories, examples from various cultures, and student activities are designed to help your students achieve the following goals:

1. To understand that time is a human invention imposed on nature to help us order, plan, and give meaning to our lives.

2. To learn about the many different ways we can measure time.

3. To see that cultures around the world use, interpret, talk about, and think about time quite differently from each other.

4. To understand that some cultures tend to look primarily to the past, some to the future, and still others to the present in order to explain what is important about their lives.

5. To grasp the concepts of cyclical and linear time and how certain cultures have adopted one or the other to explain the passage of time.

6. To learn about world time zones and to think about their own daily schedules in that context.

7. To understand that the way people follow the clock in the United States is different from the ways other cultures follow the clock.

8. To be introduced to a few of the many different calendars used around the world today and to understand that a calendar reflects some important values a culture holds.

Cross-Cultural Attitudes and Skills

As students work toward these goals, they will develop th following cross-cultural attitudes and skills:

1. They will continue to gain a view of themselves in a global context and understand that cultural differences can be a fascinating source of discovery about themselves and others. They will be stimulated to learn about how other people live around the world.

2. They will continue to develop their critical and interpretive skills as they turn a perceptive eye to the ways they think about and use time in United States culture.

3. They will continue to shed ethnocentric attitudes as they attempt to view their own cultural ways of doing things from the perspective of others.

4. Their participation in group activities will further deve op their interpersonal and interactive skills—essential skills for future, enriching cross-cultural encounters.

GENERAL INTRODUCTION

In many international hotels, airports, and shops, clocks display the time around the world. With one quick glance, one can see that it is time for bed in Seattle, breakfast in Paris, and tea in New Delhi. But what the clock fails to tel is how the people around the world are "interpreting" thei time. Therein lies a mammoth problem and a major stumbling block to cross-cultural understanding. For example, what is promptness to some is tardiness to others. "Keeping up with the times" may be essential to the people of one culture, yet scorned by millions in another. Even what is meant by "keeping up with the times" changes from culture to culture.

Throughout human history, people have puzzled over time. Through the ages, some thinkers have argued that time simply does not exist. Time is only in the minds of humans, whose sophisticated brain power makes it pos sible for them to define a past, present, and future. Animals do not think in these terms; only people do, and that, the experts argue, is proof that time is only in the human imagination. Time is a human invention, a way to order our lives in very specific ways.

Scientists have had trouble agreeing on exactly how to "tell time." Imagine the questions early thinkers had to ponder: When does a day begin? What is a week? What determines a month? How long is a year? No one got around even to thinking about a century until the 1500s. Although scientists and mathematicians over the years have created extremely sophisticated ways to tell time with infinitesimal margins of error, they have never been satisfied that the ultimate method has been reached. They persist in their unending search for "perfect time."

But the ordinary people around the world have not found it necessary to get on the same "time track." Many differences in time have developed, not simply because the world rotates in space, making it day on one side of the globe and night on the other, but because cultures' unwritten rules have made people use and interpret time in their own unique ways. The day does not begin at midnight for everyone, and more than forty different calendars currently are in existence. Even more intriguing than calendar differences and the precise time a day begins is the way in which time is used around the world. People are programmed from early childhood to shape and mold their time patterns according to the beliefs and philosophies of their cultures.

Yet, just like space, the rules for using time are forever changing within a culture. Just when you think you are beginning to understand how people use time, you discover that they have shifted into another pattern for a different occasion. Some of the most baffling and often amusing moments come when "keeping up with the times" invades old traditions, as two of the authors experienced firsthand:

We and our then six-year-old daughter straddled a trio of donkeys for a trip back in time to the ancient, now deserted city of Petra (the name in Greek means "rock") in southern Jordan. An Arab, his body draped in the traditional flowing white robe, his head swathed in the checkered shawl, held in place by a ring of thick cord, led us through a gorge so narrow we were able to reach out and touch each side of the soaring cliffs. Humans first came here in the early Stone Age, and Moses reportedly struck the rocks and sent water gushing forth. But it was the second century A.D. that left its mark on Petra and inspired adventurers to make the lonely trip back into the abandoned city. The people of this era carved magnificent, gigantic tombs into the pink sandstone cliffs, and one with spiraling columns and a majestic doorway reminded us of the great European cathe-

drals we had visited. The eerie silence that engulfed the ancient city and those spectacular monuments to a past era left us stunned and momentarily speechless.

Then suddenly the scene changed. Rock music blared through the valley, shaking the tombs with the intensity of an invading army's beat, or so it seemed to our confused group. Our gaze slowly shifted from the burial chambers to a nomad's tent, perched at the edge of the cliff high above the old city. The nomad family had discovered the portable radio and, with a few twists of its dial, contemporary music from the U.S. We were being honored by a rock serenade from home. And this unexpected clash of times brought us back quickly, if not rather harshly, into the late twentieth century.

After settling into an apartment in Madrid, Spain, one of the authors experienced living between two different time systems: one established by the local residents, and the other observed by people from the U.S. living in the community.

My apartment was on the top floor of a building about 50 percent occupied by families from the United States. Most were working for U.S. companies or the U. S. government and kept schedules similar to those back home. The native residents of the same building, including the *portero* (pohr-**tehr**-oh, the apartment's jack-of-all-trades), who resided with his family in a small apartment that had been built for him on the roof, kept Spanish time. Dinner for the Spaniards never began earlier than 10:00 in the evening and quite often continued until well after midnight. The voices of children and parents, the clash of dishes and cutlery, and the ring of pots and pans echoed through the building's stairwell, onto which my bedroom window opened. I usually retired rather early because I had to be up by 5:00 each morning in order to reach an early class, which I was teaching at the U.S. Air Force base outside Madrid. Classes were over shortly after noon, and, groggy from lack of sleep, I headed back to my apartment, anticipating a long nap during the local *siesta* (see-**est**-ah) hours. It was then that many of the Spanish residents pulled down their *persianas* (pehr-see-**ah**-nas), the outdoor, rolling shutters, and settled in for a rest. But for me, a rest was not to be. Instead, many of those from the U.S. in the building always chose exactly these hours to call on their neighbors, and

invariably, just as sleep was about to overtake me, this now exhausted expatriate, the doorbell rang. The sleepless cycle continued, as I tried desperately to adjust to the two time systems.

Such experiences are not uncommon for those who are living in a culture other than their own. A "perfectly normal" schedule back home can be completely out of sync with the new culture's time pattern. The physical and emotional toll for those attempting to adjust can be enormous, not only for people from the U.S. going abroad but for those coming to the U.S. as well. There are other time issues that plague those who interact across cultural lines. We will examine some of these problems in the following sections.

What Went Wrong?

These introductory activities are designed to introduce your students to the ways time can act as a stumbling block in cross-cultural understanding. Most students will not know the correct answer to the question posed in each activity, but that is not the point. The point is to initiate curiosity and discussion and to stir their interest in pursuing this topic.

Teacher's Instructions: Divide your class into groups of four or five students. Hand each group a copy of each of the following worksheets. Have each group work together to decide which answer best explains the behavior described in "What Went Wrong?" Then, as a class, each group will explain its reason for choosing the answer.

After each group has spoken, reveal the correct answer and discuss it. An explanation to each one has been given below. Do the same with each "What Went Wrong?"

Some discussion questions include:

1. Why did your group choose this answer over the other answers? Were there clues given, did you simply eliminate the other answers, did you choose by instinct, or did you apply some assumptions you already had about the cultures mentioned? If you applied some assumptions, what did you already assume about the people from that culture?

2. How would you have felt in this situation?

3. What would you have done next?

4. What does this exercise show you about the different ways people from different cultures respond to the same situation?

Answers and Explanations

WHAT WENT WRONG? #1 = Answer #2

Clock time is not always taken seriously in every part of the world. In many cultures, the time given for an event is thought to be simply a "general" indication as to when someone is expected to arrive. The Mexican hostess was very surprised to see the Edwardses arrive precisely at 9:30, for in Mexico it is customary to be as much as an hour late for a social engagement, even dinner.

WHAT WENT WRONG? #2 = Answer #1

The Germans, on the other hand, expect promptness. Tardiness of ten minutes is considered rude. While Britt Blomquist and her parents thought it was okay to be ten minutes late to their meeting with the school principal, they had broken the unwritten rules of acceptable appointment time in Germany and thus had caused the rector to become irritated.

WHAT WENT WRONG? #3 = Answer #4

The school principal in this incident was following a time pattern very different from what would commonly be found in a U.S. school. She was not being rude or inconsiderate. In some cultures, such as Egypt's, people use *polychronic* time. That is, they are comfortable doing more than one thing at a time. The opposite of this pattern is a *monochronic* time pattern, doing one thing at a time. Monochronic time is a common time pattern valued in business, government, education, and other areas in the United States. Cultures usually have both monochronic and polychronic people, but one pattern tends to be valued or used over the other. Polychronic people usually are very involved with other people. Human relationships are considered far more important than being punctual for an appointment. Friendships are taken very seriously and often last for a lifetime. These people will keep appointments, if possible, but do not feel deeply obligated to do so, particularly if a relative or friend needs them. They do not hesitate to change their plans or schedules if they think something else is more important. On the other hand, monochronic people take appointments and scheduling very seriously and try not to change schedules if at all possible. It is important not only to begin a meeting at the scheduled time, but to complete it at the appointed hour. Someone in the meeting might excuse herself with the following comment: "I hate to break this up, but I have another meeting I must attend." They may have friends for only a short time and then go on to develop new friendships under different circumstances. They consider privacy very important (Hall, 1990).

Student

Worksheet

NAME _____

DATE _____

WHAT WENT WRONG? #1:

The Edwards family of Pittsburgh moved to Guadalajara, Mexico, and were very pleased when they were invited to dinner at the home of some newly met Mexican friends. They had been told that dinner would be at 9:30 in the evening of the following day. The Edwardses thought that 9:30 was rather late to start dinner, but they arrived promptly at the appointed hour. They did not want to be late for their first social outing in this new land. The hostess let them in, but she seemed rather surprised to see them. She had indicated that several other families would be attending the dinner, but there was no one in sight. "Do we have the wrong day?" the Edwardses asked themselves. They were terribly embarrassed and did not know whether or not to make a quick exit. Mr. and Mrs. Edwards instead chatted uneasily with their hostess for more than an hour, and then finally commented that they should be on their way. The hostess, very perplexed, looked at her new friends from the U.S. with a puzzled expression. Just at that moment two other families entered the room. It appeared that the party was just about to get under way.

What did the Edwards family do wrong?
(Circle the answer that best explains the situation.)

1. The Edwards family arrived on the wrong day. When a Mexican host or hostess invites you to dinner for the evening of "the following day," he or she really means the day *after* tomorrow. The Edwardses did not understand the Mexican way of talking about a date. They arrived on the wrong evening, and the Mexican hostess was trying to make the best of an embarrassing situation.

2. The Edwardses were correct about the date of the dinner. All they did wrong was to arrive exactly "on time" by U.S. standards, which was too early by Mexican standards. In Mexico, it is customary to be as much as an hour late for a social event, even dinner. The Edwardses should not have said they were leaving as the other guests were just arriving for the dinner party. 9:30 P.M. is a normal time for a dinner party in Mexico.

3. The Edwardses had forgotten to set their watches back one hour to the correct time in Guadalajara. When it is 9:30 back in Pittsburgh, it is only 8:30 in Guadalajara. When their watches said 9:30, it was only 8:30 at the host's house. Therefore, the Edwardses arrived one hour early to the dinner party and surprised their Mexican hosts.

4. The Mexican friends had forgotten that they invited the Edwards family to dinner. Yes, they were having a late dinner party, but it was supposed to begin at 10:30 because the invited guests had gone to an early movie. The Edwardses did not do anything wrong. They simply embarrassed their new Mexican friends when they arrived at 9:30 and the hosts did not have enough food to feed them.

Student

Worksheet

NAME _____

DATE _____

WHAT WENT WRONG? #2:

Thirteen-year-old Britt Blomquist of Charlotte, North Carolina, had settled into her new home in Munich, Germany, where her parents were researching a book on the local architecture. Both Mr. and Mrs. Blomquist spoke German fluently and had trained their daughter to speak the language. Since Britt had no problem reading, writing, and understanding German, her parents decided to place her in a German school rather than in the Munich International School where English was spoken. This, they reasoned, would give her the opportunity to become better acquainted with the German people and their culture. The family was scheduled to have a meeting with the rector (principal) of the school Britt was to attend before she was to begin her studies. On the day of the meeting, the family was running a little behind schedule. They noticed that they probably would be about ten minutes late. That seemed to be so close to the appointed time that they were not very concerned about their tardiness. But when they arrived for their meeting, they immediately noticed that the rector appeared to be annoyed. They apologized rather casually for their late arrival, but this did not seem to relieve the tension.

What did the Blomquists do wrong? (Circle the answer that best explains the situation.)

1. While being ten minutes late is often acceptable in the United States, it is considered rude in Germany. The Blomquists irritated the rector when they were late for the meeting, and they annoyed him even more when they apologized so casually, as if their tardiness were no big deal. In Germany, one should arrive exactly "on time."

2. The Blomquists assumed that it would be perfectly fine to enroll Britt in a German school. But the rector of this particular German school did not think it was such a good idea. "What if her German is not good enough to communicate well in class?" he thought to himself. He was annoyed that the Blomquists just *assumed* they could place Britt in any school they wished.

3. The Blomquists were wrong about the time of the meeting. They arrived *an hour and ten minutes* late for the meeting, not just ten minutes late. The rector was a very busy man, so he was quite annoyed when the Blomquists were so late.

4. In Germany, it is customary to arrive half an hour late to a meeting. So, while the Blomquists thought they were late by ten minutes, they actually were *early* by twenty minutes, and this annoyed the rector who did not expect them to arrive so early.

NAME _____

DATE _____

WHAT WENT WRONG? #3:

Betty Jensen, a fifth-grade teacher in Syracuse, New York, had gone to Cairo, Egypt, for a visit. She decided she would like to visit a local school and received permission to do so. The principal invited Ms. Jensen into her office. But to Ms. Jensen's amazement, the principal had two mothers in her office, and she was having conferences with both of them about their children who were students in the school. She would talk to one for a time, and then the other. Then she would turn and talk to the woman from the U.S. Ms. Jensen was very confused. She could not understand why the principal would invite her into the office if a conference were going on not with just one mother, but two! Was the principal being very rude?

Why did the principal conduct her business in this way? (Circle the answer that best explains her behavior.)

1. Betty Jensen finally decided that the principal had just asked her into the office because she thought she had to. The principal was afraid that Ms. Jensen would be insulted if she weren't invited and then would go back to the United States and talk about how unfriendly the school in Egypt was.

2. The principal really did not want Ms. Jensen in her office and had thought she would not accept the invitation. She was very surprised when Ms. Jensen actually followed her into the room.

3. The principal was planning to finish the conference with the two mothers very quickly, and she thought Ms. Jensen should have the patience to wait.

4. The principal was following a time pattern that was very common in her country. It is known as *polychronic time,* which means that people do more than one thing at a time. In the United States, a principal would not consider having two parent conferences at the same time unless it concerned an incident in which the children of both parents were involved. Polychronic time people are not concerned about privacy, so the principal did not worry about Ms. Jensen's overhearing the conversation. Nor did she worry about the two mothers listening to information about the other's child.

Lesson I

How "Telling Time" Came to Be

Long ago, ancient humans grasped the concept of time by observing the sun rising and setting in a regular and predictable way, by watching the animals migrating during certain seasons every year, and by seeing the other cyclic aspects of nature all around them. By understanding these patterns, they could begin to plan ahead. Prehistoric engravings of the phases of the moon on bones dating back more than 28,000 years reveal the human fascination with the temporal nature of the universe.

Humans next divided life into uniform periods. They turned to the major recurrent and predictable influence in their lives, the sun, to subdivide time. The sundial became the first and most universally used clock. Its circular flat face was marked with lines around its circumference (much like hours on our modern-day clock faces), and a thin object would stick up from the center of the dial. As the sun traveled across the sky, the shadow cast by the object at the center would shift and move around the clock face as it pointed to a different time marker during the course of its daily movement. But how did one tell time at night or on a cloudy day? The solution was a clock not dependent upon the sun's movement: a water clock based on the theory that water (or another substance such as grains of sand) will drop through a narrow opening at a fixed and measurable rate.

Did You Know?

In the early fourteenth century the Chinese kept track of time through an incense clock. Heavily scented powders were placed in grooves that wound and twisted their way into a circle, forming an extremely complicated maze. The powders, it is believed, were placed in all the grooves and then the center of the circle was ignited. It took about twelve hours for the small flame to burn its way through the maze (Fraser, 1987).

No one is quite sure how the all-mechanical clock originated, but a key to its development was the discovery by Galileo of the principles of the pendulum, still used today in stately grandfather clocks. The remaining history of clock (and watch) development consists of efforts to beautify the timepiece and make it more accurate. The Swiss, whose culture places a high value on order and punctuality, are famous not only for the cuckoo clock but also for designing and making some of the most beautiful, intricate, and accurate clocks and watches in the world. Extreme accuracy, essential in many scientific procedures, is achieved today through atomic clocks that vary only one second in a thousand years.

Activities

The following activities are designed to get students thinking about time as a concept and the many different ways there are to use, tell, and think about time.

1. Make a sundial or "shadow clock." Take the class outside and choose a sunny location for the sundial. Draw a circle in the dirt and mark off "hours" with stones placed at even intervals around the circle. Place a stick in the ground at the center of the circle. At 1:00 (or whatever is convenient), note the place where the stick's shadow falls and name this mark "1:00." Have the class observe how the stick's shadow moves around the dial during the day. Discuss the advantages and disadvantages of this way of telling time. (*constructive*)

2. Make a water clock. Make a hole in the bottom of a tin can. Hold the can over a tall glass marked with lines at even intervals. Give each line a "time." Fill the can with water and see how long it takes for the water to drain out of the hole and rise to each line of the glass. Discuss the advantages and disadvantages of this kind of clock. (*constructive*)

3. Make a candle clock. Mark a candle with evenly spaced lines around it. Give each line a "time." Light the candle and observe how long it takes to burn to each line. Announce the candle "time" whenever a line is reached. Again, discuss this way of telling time.

   Have the class compare the sundial, water clock, and candle clock. Which is most accurate? In which situations would each work best? (*constructive*)

4. Ask the students to think of all the ways we measure and clock the time (oven-timers, stopwatches, digital watches, round clock faces, etc.). List them on the board. Which are easiest to use? Which are most accurate? What would life be like without clocks? *(interpretive)*

5. Make a classroom clock. Divide the class into groups of four or five students. Have each group invent and make a classroom clock face. It must still mark the standard hours we use but it can look as imaginative as they wish. Display the clock faces around the room. *(constructive, collaborative)*

6. Optional research project. Divide the class into groups of four or five students. Have each group choose a clock from history or another culture and prepare a report for the class. The local school or public librarian can help the students find books on clocks for their research. *(constructive, collaborative)*

Lesson 2

The Language of Time

Oh, a wonderful stream is the river of Time,
As it runs through the realm of tears,
With a faultless rhythm and a musical rhyme,
And a boundless sweep and a surge sublime,
As it blends with the ocean of years.

McGuffy Eclectic Reader, nineteenth-century U.S. textbook

For thousands of years, time has challenged the imaginations and sparked the creative spirits of people in many cultures. They have fought it, immortalized it, and romanticized it. The subject of time is woven through the works of the most celebrated Western poets. The early Psalmists, whose lyrical verses became one of the best-known chapters of the Bible's Old Testament, made an appeal: "Teach us to number our days, that we may arrive at wisdom of heart." The problem was that people could not agree on how to number the days nor exactly how to define wisdom (Fraser, 1987). Shakespeare's plays and sonnets often make time the metaphysical villain, destroying lives and lovers. By the mid-1800s, U.S. children were discovering poetic time in their *McGuffy Eclectic Readers*, one of the most widely read textbooks U.S. schools have ever known. And today, young people are still being introduced to time through verse as many parents across the U.S. tell their toddlers about clocks and hours through a popular nursery rhyme:

Hickory dickory dock,
The mouse ran up the clock,
The clock struck one,
The mouse ran down,
Hickory, dickory dock.

Did You Know?

The world has never come to an agreement as to how the days of the week should be numbered. Sunday is not always day one of the week. Those who speak Russian and Chinese believe that Monday is the first day (Berlitz, 1982). What constitutes a weekend certainly varies around the world. In the Muslim world the weekend often begins on Thursday afternoon and continues through Friday, the day of worship for followers of Islam. The first day of the week for people of this faith is thought to be Saturday. Followers of Buddhism worship on the full moon, and the first day of the week varies, depending on the culture of the country in which followers of this religion reside. Hindus have no special day of worship, although many go to temples on Tuesday and some close their shops on this day. In India, however, most shops close on Sunday, probably a carry-over from the days of the British occupation.

Time Is Serious Business—The United States

In the United States, time is not some vague theory but a very practical object that can be handled to one's advantage with a little good common sense. It can, in fact, be treated like most goods, bought, borrowed, and traded. Take your time, steal time, but please do not waste time. As if those suggestions were not enough to keep everyone functioning on the right time track, people in the U.S. have innumerable proverbs to remind them of how time should be used:

Time is money.
A stitch in time saves nine.
Never put off until tomorrow what you can do today.
Haste makes waste.
Time will tell.

Time in English is more than a simple way of keeping track of the hours and days. It actually is an event. It latches on to other words to become lunchtime, dinnertime, leisure time, bedtime. But not all languages elevate time to such status. The Japanese may say "It is time for lunch," but they do not have "lunchtime," unless they follow the common practice of using the U.S. term. They do, however, form whimsical combinations of Japanese and English words to raise time to its U.S. importance. In the U.S., for example, people refer to times for various sports as seasons—*baseball season, soccer season, hockey season*—and the Japanese have borrowed this concept to get *ryoko* (dyoh-koh) *season* (travel season) and *yasumi* (yah-soo-mee) *season* (holiday season). Then, of course, there is the Japanese *besuboru* (bay-soo-boh-roo) *season* (baseball season), to which millions of fans are devoted.

Did You Know?

Baseball in Japan, to which millions of fans are fanatically dedicated, was introduced to these island people in the late nineteenth century. Players originally played in kimonos and sandals. Today, the uniforms resemble those found on our side of the Pacific and are worn by high school, collegiate, and professional team members. Japanese fans cram the stadiums to watch their favorite teams and nibble on *sushi* (**soo**-shee, specially prepared raw fish with rice) and *hotto dogu* (hot-toh dog-oo, hot dogs).

For people in the United States, time is serious business. It is, in fact, so serious that it weaves its way into the U.S. legal system. The words "time is of the essence" are often included in a contract between two people. Briefly, it means that there is a time limit in which the job must be done. If not completed by the named date, full payment does not have to be made. Such time disputes sometimes end in long legal battles.

Activity

What is Time?—a class definition.

Ask students to complete the sentence "Time is . . ." on a piece of paper. Collect the papers. As you read the sentences out loud, work with the class to categorize the statements to develop a group definition, however long and multifaceted it may be. A convenient way to do this would be to make several columns on the board. As you read the first statement, place it in one of the columns. If the next statement seems to be in a similar category, place it in the same column. If it is different, place it in another. Continue to read and group the statements in the columns. When you are finished, assign to each column a title that

Did You Know?

People in the U.S. tend to use leisure time in a very organized manner, contrary to the style of many other cultures. If they play basketball or tennis, jog, or skate, they are often in pursuit of bettering themselves. They take this free time seriously. This is not the case in many other areas of the world. Leisure time in other cultures is the opportunity to sit in a cafe for hours to talk with friends or simply to stroll along a country path. In Germany, a culture where people follow the clock and are always on time, families can be seen relaxing on weekends by taking the time to stroll through the countryside and stop in country inns for leisurely meals. Almost all adult Germans get four to five weeks of paid vacation a year. U.S. adults are often lucky if they get two weeks of vacation from their jobs.

describes that category. Type up the entire class definition of time in the form of an outline, with the titles as headings and the statements as contents. Ask the students if this definition seems like a U.S. way of thinking about time. *(constructive, collaborative)*

Talking About Time in Other Cultures

Time is not interpreted the same in all cultures. In Mexico and Spain, *mañana* (mah-**nyah**-na) may literally translate as "tomorrow" but in actuality means "sometime in the future." Try to compel Greek people to conduct business as it is done in the U.S., with specific language that spells out exactly how long a meeting will last and work delegated to subcommittees, and one is met with strong resistance. Arabs, also, resist specifying definite times for arrivals and can be expected to answer, "It will be there on June 20, Allah willing." Only God knows, they reason, what is possible (Hall, 1959). In many African cultures, people hesitate to give an exact time for getting together. It is impossible to anticipate all the obstacles that could impede an on-time arrival, they reason. They also know that their friends will not mind waiting for them. A lunch date may be set any time between 1 P.M. and 3 P.M. Businesspeople with a specific lunch hour, however, must adhere to stricter schedules. The language of Japanese contracts can be a problem for people from the U.S. The Japanese contract has the language appropriate for the

moment, and if conditions and circumstances change in the future, the Japanese believe the contract should be changed. It is not "etched in stone," as those in the United States tend to believe.

From "hickory dickory dock" to "time is of the essence," people in the U.S. use their language to emphasize the importance they place on time. But not all cultures have this same interest in time, and their languages reflect the difference. Time to most North Americans is always moving onward—usually at a very fast clip. After all, clocks in the U.S. "run." But in Spanish-speaking nations, the clocks just "walk." For Native Americans, the clocks neither walk nor run; they simply tick. In his studies of Native American tribes, the anthropologist Edward T. Hall has not found a word for *time* in any of their many languages (Hall, 1983).

The Indians of the Asian subcontinent have still another view of time, and once again it shows up in their languages. They do not think of time as being dynamic and rushing ahead, and they are not so concerned, as those in the U.S. are, with exactly when an event took place. Hindustani, one of the fifteen official languages spoken in India today, has double meanings for adverbs associated with time. For example, the adverb *kal* (kahl) means both yesterday *and* tomorrow. *Parson* (**pahr**-sun) translates as the "day after tomorrow" and the "day before yesterday." *Atarson* (ah-**tahr**-sun) refers to three days ago *or* three days from now. Confusing? Not to the speakers of Hindustani. They know how to use these words so they make sense. The listener has to understand the circumstances under which these words are spoken or written and when and why they are being used in order to get the true meaning (Fraser, 1981).

For those from the U.S. traveling to other shores to visit, live, or do business, these differences in the language of time can be confusing. But consider young people from other countries, who suddenly find themselves settling into a classroom in the U.S. They must learn not only a new vocabulary but also how to use this new language to express the local attitudes toward time. Literal translations from their native tongue into English simply do not work.

Did You Know?

Students in Japan have very little free time and few opportunities to be on their own. They attend school not only from Monday through Friday but also for a half-day on Saturday. Many stay for after-school clubs and then head to a *juku* (joo-koo) or *yobiko* (yoh-bee-koh). *Juku* is a special school-after-school that is held in an instructor's home or at a large, national institution where students who need extra help in their academic subjects can get a boost. *Juku* becomes increasingly important as children progress through school, with junior high students taking as many as five different subjects in these supplementary sessions. These sessions also help students prepare for the high school entrance examination, which is a critical time in every Japanese student's educational life. As high school students, Japanese kids often attend *yobiko*, which are sophisticated cram schools, offering intense training for the dreaded university entrance examination.

3. Have students look again at the class definition of time. Of all the statements that comprise that definition, which ones would be most confusing to someone visiting the U.S. for the first time? Role-play a situation in which one student plays a visitor from another culture (have the class choose the culture) who is visiting your school for the day. The students can invent a scenario in which three of them are discussing a situation that involves speaking about time in a way(s) that is described in the definition. The visitor must point out all the moments when he or she is confused by what the U.S. kids are saying, and they, in turn, must explain what they mean. This kind of exercise highlights the many possible problems that can arise when newly arrived students from other cultures attempt to understand the most "ordinary" events of daily life in the U.S. How could your students be more helpful to them? *(cross-cultural, interpretive)*

Activities

1. Refer to a book of proverbs from your local library reference section. Look up those that have something to say about time. List some of the proverbs from the U.S. on the board. What do they say about the way those in the U.S. think about time? What value does time have? Then look up those proverbs that have to do with time from other cultures. Write them on the board. What do they say about the cultures that use them? Compare and contrast them with proverbs from the U.S. *(cross-cultural, interpretive)*

2. Discuss the ways Spanish-speakers, Native Americans, and some Indians speak (or don't speak) about time. If the clock "runs," what does that say about the way English-speakers think about time? If the clock "walks," what does that say about the way Spanish-speakers think about time? If there is no word for "time" in any Native American language, what does that say about the ways Native Americans think about time? What do the Indian adverbs say about the way Hindustani-speakers regard time? *(cross-cultural, interpretive)*

From *Windows to the World: Themes for Cross-Cultural Understanding*. Copyright © 1996 by Phyllis Kepler, Brooke Sarno Royse, and John Kepler

Lesson 3

The Perception of Time

Each culture around the world has its own view or perspective of time, and it can often be very misleading to the uninitiated.

There are two basic concepts concerning people's perception of time that must be kept in mind when interacting with those from other cultures:

Do people from a particular culture think of time as **cyclical** (traveling in a circle) or **linear** (running in a straight line)?

Which is most important to the people of a particular culture: **the past, the present, or the future?**

Subtly and without fanfare, these two ideas weave their way through cultures, greatly influencing people's responses to time. Let's take a look at how and why they came about.

The Wheel of Time: East Asia

Thousands and thousands of years ago when people first began to think about time, there was no clear dividing line between the past, the present, and the future. These early people learned from previous experiences, and they observed that the seasons appeared to roll around with regularity. The past squeezed into the present, and the future was simply the time that lay ahead when the growing season would begin again. Time seemed to run in circles. Long after these early observations, this concept of time became known as cyclical time, much like a wheel that rolls around and around without stopping.

The world's major religions helped to shape people's attitude toward time. Hinduism, for example, swept across the Indian subcontinent, engulfing every facet of human life, including the way in which people viewed time. The religion still plays a major role in Hindus' lives today. While deeds must be performed and schedules followed, the time span of one individual's life is of little consequence. People, Hindus believe, will be reborn again and again, a phenomenon known as *reincarnation,* until they finally are completely released from time altogether. The earth, too, will be re-created time and time again. The stories of creation within this religion are complex and differing. But it is generally believed that the four-headed god,

Brahma, was the creator of the world. His life span stretches, according to some estimates, over 155,520 trillion human years, then ends, only to begin again. With Brahma's death, the world, of course, disappears, but returns again with his rebirth (Fraser, 1987). In view of such overwhelming numbers, along with a belief that each individual's fate has been decided at birth, there is no sense of the urgency concerning time that is commonly found in Western Europe, the United States, and Canada.

From Hinduism sprang a reform movement, which developed into the religion known as Buddhism. While it contained its own stories of creation, there was still the basic belief of cyclical time in which people came back to earth again and again until they finally reached a timeless state known as Nirvana (Fraser, 1987). Buddhism spread eastward across Asia, deeply influencing the lives of the people and their attitudes toward time.

Activity

What does *cyclical time* mean? Ask one of your students to try to draw a picture of it on the board. This will be a very foreign concept to many of your students. If you have any Hindu or Buddhist students in your class, ask them to try to explain the concept. Have any of your students heard of reincarnation? Have them pretend to believe in the concept: What kind of person would they have been in a prior life? What kind of person will they be in their next life? A short essay might be a nice forum for thinking about these questions. *(interpretive)*

Looking to the Past: East Asia

China

In East Asia, history has been the dominating force of human life. Probably no other people in the world documented events and chronicled each invention and discovery as carefully as the Chinese, and they were doing it hundreds of years before Christ was born. In addition to their great reverence for the past, the Chinese also cherished stability. They introduced some rather revolutionary concepts—gunpowder, printing, and the magnetic compass—but these inventions did little to change the lifestyles of the people (Fraser, 1987). In contrast, such items in the hands of Europeans drastically influenced and changed Western cultures.

Surrounded by people whom they called "barbarians" and unfriendly mountains and deserts, as well as bordered on two sides by water, the Chinese turned inward. But their ideas and culture seeped into neighboring areas, the lands that today are Korea and Japan. While these countries developed distinct cultures of their own, they also inherited many of their ideas from China. Changes came slowly and methodically to these people of East Asia, and they tended to look back into history, as they still do today, for many of their beliefs and customs. Contemporary people of East Asia look more to the past than to the future and they constantly search for reasons for their present behavior in past events (Fairbank, 1989).

Japan
Each Sunday morning, hundreds of Tokyo teenagers—boom-boxes in hand and bedecked in blue jeans and sweat shirts emblazoned with English letters that spell out everything from names of U.S. universities to Mickey Mouse—descend on Yoyogi (Yoh-yoh-gee) Park in the heart of the city. They are about to take part in a weekly ritual of dancing to Western rock music. They may even be privileged to listen to live music, courtesy of local teenage rock groups. Many have made a brief stop on their way to the park for a treat at Dunkin' Donuts™ or McDonalds™.

At first glance, Tokyo may seem just like the United States. The streams of heavy traffic, the galaxy of flashing neon signs, and the messy parking problems—so severe that no one can buy a car until he has proof that he has a place to put it—lure first-time visitors to this city into believing it is not all that different from life in the United States. Many have been fooled, for even though Japan looks as modern as, if not more modern than, any country in the world, its reverence for old, old traditions has a great influence in Japanese culture.

A U.S. company discovered how old traditions and values lie just beneath this flashy, Westernized surface when it decided to introduce cake mixes to Japanese homemakers. Thinking like U.S. citizens, they promoted the product by telling Japanese women that using a cake mix was "as easy as" making rice. The promotion backfired. Rice, a daily staple on the tables of every Japanese citizen, is taken very seriously and has played an important role in the lives of the people for centuries. To trivialize rice preparation was to offend the homemaker (Cateora, 1990).

Watching the weekend gatherings in Yoyogi Park would lead any casual observer to believe that these teenagers are like teenagers in the U.S. But on Monday morning these weekend party animals exchange their trendy clothes for stark uniforms and head to school, prepared for personal inspections before entering the building. The girls' skirt lengths may be measured at the school door, and the boys' haircuts closely checked. They will begin their day by bowing to their teacher, reciting a polite "good morning" in chorus, and then settle down to a rigid

Did You Know?
The Japanese school year runs about four weeks longer than U.S. schools. The school year begins in April and ends the following mid-March. Summer vacation lasts for six weeks and is always filled with homework assignments. In addition to the summer break, students have two weeks off at New Year's, an extremely important holiday, and two weeks between the end and beginning of the school year.

class schedule, designed to prepare them for the battery of exams that lie ahead. If they are in junior high school, they eat, sleep, breathe, and agonize over the high school entrance exams that await them in the near future and which can literally decide their futures, for the "right" high school will help prepare them for the exams to the "right" university and ultimately to the best jobs. There is no turning back, no second chance.

The emphasis on education, respect, and conformity can be traced back into Japanese history. Although few Japanese today would admit to being followers of Confucius, the great philosopher who lived about four hundred years before Christ, his principles are deeply ingrained in their ways of thinking. They, like other East Asians, also see themselves in a historical perspective, always searching the past to explain today.

It is important to look at some of the past events on the islands of Japan in order to understand many of the customs of the Japanese people today. Japan, like China, isolated itself from the rest of the world, particularly during the Tokugawa period, a military regime that began in the early seventeenth century and ended in the mid-1800s when U.S. naval officer Matthew Calbraith Perry sailed into what is today Tokyo harbor and demanded that the nation open its doors to foreigners. The U.S. had ulterior motives. Their ships were now sailing to China, which earlier allowed foreigners in through demands of Europeans wishing to trade with that mammoth nation. Their ships needed to replenish supplies on their long journeys from the United States, and Japan was a convenient port. The U.S. also had whaling ships in the area that needed a port for supplies and repairs. Japan finally succumbed to Perry's demand and with this new contact with the outside world, changes were to come.

Did You Know?

The Japanese enjoy music, movies, and television shows from the United States, but they also like to attend their traditional theater known as *Kabuki* (kah-boo-kee), which dates back to the 1600s when it was founded by a woman dancer. An extravaganza of music, elaborate costumes and only male actors (who play both feminine and masculine roles), the play goes on for four hours, requiring patrons to bring a meal for sustenance. The orchestra sits right on the stage, a complicated platform with revolving parts and trap doors. A gangway stretches into the audience and is known as the "flower path." Once thought of as theater for only the common people, Kabuki today is a grand tradition of contemporary Japan which keeps old traditions alive in this East Asian nation.

The Japanese had been living under a strict code which demanded loyalty to those in social positions above. Everyone, in fact, had his or her place in Japanese society, located on a rigid staircase of hierarchy. In other words, there was always someone above you and someone below you, even among family members, and how each person was treated depended upon his or her rank. Social etiquette was so demanding that a person could be put to death instantly if a breech of conduct were made! Dress, speech, housing, and personal conduct were all based on a person's place on this social staircase. Rules were so rigid and detailed that they included a law prohibiting women from showing their teeth in front of men. The practice of females covering their mouths when they smiled or laughed began then and continues today.

Religion and history molded the perspectives of the people of East Asia, and as a result we can say that people of the East have a past orientation towards time. But as with all things cross-cultural, this is not true in all instances. Children, for example, must think of the future as they plan ahead for the all-important high school and university entrance examinations. And industries consider the future as they design new television sets, stereos, automobiles, computers, and other hi-tech products. But again it must be emphasized that while many East Asian nations have modernized, they have not Westernized, and many of their customs and traditions focus on the past. When it comes to education and business, people have their eyes on the future so they can plan ahead, but they function or act within a culture whose structure, customs, and traditions have origins deeply rooted in the past. We will explore this in more detail in the chapter on relationships.

Activities

1. Read the following scenario to your students:

Sixteen-year-old Tom Murphy of Seattle, Washington, was selected as an exchange student to Korea. He was to live with the Kim family in Chonju, a town in the southwest portion of the country. The Kims had a son Tom's age and a twenty-year-old daughter. When he arrived, Tom was amazed to learn that the Kim parents and the parents of a boy in the same town were discussing a possible marriage between their daughter and the other family's son. Neither young person appeared to object to the fact that their parents were arranging the marriage. "Why," Tom wondered, "wouldn't the Kims' daughter marry a man of her own choosing?"

Can your students answer Tom's question?

Answer: To Tom Murphy, the idea of having someone else select his wife was totally unacceptable. If his parents so much as hinted at the the "proper" girl for him to date, he would run the other way. While Korea has rushed rapidly into the modern world in many ways, especially technologically, beneath the surface lie old traditions and customs, tied to the past, which many Koreans still honor. Following one of those traditions, many parents choose whom their sons and daughters will marry. This custom is called an "arranged marriage." Arranged marriages are still common in Korea. The Kims' daughter was following this custom by respecting her parents' wishes for her. The mixture of past and present in East Asian cultures often confuses people from the West when they interact with East Asians. *(interpretive, cross-cultural)*

2. (This discussion is designed to have students face their preconceptions and stereotypes about the Japanese.) Discuss with your students any images they have of Japan and the Japanese people. Where do these images come from (TV, their parents, school, etc.)? What products in the U.S. are made in Japan? List them on the board. Do you think of Japan as being more technologically advanced than the U.S.? From the information given above, how are Japanese kids like U.S. kids? How are they different? Why would a Japanese person

be offended when offered a cake mix that is "as easy as" making rice? *(interpretive, cross-cultural)*

3. Discuss: What does it mean to look to the past? Does the U.S. look to the past in the same ways that the cultures of East Asia do? (Remind your students that looking to the past does not mean being "behind the times.") What old traditions are followed in the U.S.? Do any come from specific ethnic groups that make up the multicultural U.S.? List some of these traditions on the board. What would a visitor from another culture think of them? *(interpretive)*

4. Thinking like a person from a Western culture, make a time line on the board as such:

PAST   PRESENT   FUTURE

<————————I————————I————————>

China
Japan
Korea

As specific countries are mentioned in this lesson, list them under their time orientation. *(constructive)*

Looking to the Past: The Arab World

It is a fear of Westernization that has caused many of the Muslims in the Middle East to revert to old traditions, as two of the authors have observed firsthand:

We made our first trip into that part of the world in the early '60s. We have returned many times and have watched as the Muslim women appeared to be taking steps backwards in time. On our first trip to Egypt, we observed many local women dressed similarly to their counterparts in the United States. But on a trip in the '90s, we found many women covering their heads and wearing long skirts in the traditional Muslim fashion. Some were even covering their faces with veils, their hands with gloves, and their eyes with dark glasses, so that no part of the body would be exposed to passersby. For about a half century, women in that area had been dropping the veil and dressing in contemporary Western clothing, but now they were reverting to old traditions.

Wearing the veil is a tradition rather than a religious practice. Nothing in the *Quran* (or Koran, koo-**rahn**), the holy book of the Muslims, tells women to cover their faces. It originally was a social practice, picked up proba-

bly from their neighbors to the east in Persia (today called Iran) and made popular because it was a sign of prestige: women who wore the veil obviously did not work in the fields. However, there is no sharp division among the different facets of Arab life—religious, governmental, educational, and social. One flows into the other, so wearing the veil became associated with high morals and religious devotion. In very recent years, many Muslim women have looked towards the past and started wearing the conservative clothing again for a number of reasons. Some are truly Islamic traditionalists—although the Muslims themselves prefer to think of their movement as "revivalism" (Shabbas, 1989). Often, returning to the veil is a statement that says, "We are our own people, and we do not like what the West stands for, its low morals and lack of family traditions." Sometimes it is worn simply because others are doing it.

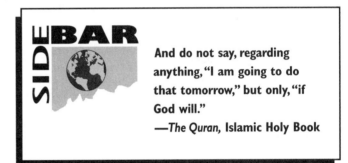

SIDEBAR

And do not say, regarding anything, "I am going to do that tomorrow," but only, "if God will."
—*The Quran*, Islamic Holy Book

One can find many examples throughout the Middle East of the area's emphasis on the past and its resistance to change. For instance, in Saudi Arabia, many people were reluctant to accept the telephone until the king read passages from the Quran over the lines. There still exists a ban on Saudi women serving as flight attendants on their nation's airline.

When one of the authors traveled extensively throughout the Arab world with her daughter, she had the opportunity to learn about some of the traditional roles of Arab women within the home:

I always felt very safe even though we were two females unaccompanied by men. Yet we did experience some attitudes towards women that were different from those found at home. One such experience occurred at a family home on the outskirts of Aman, Jordan. We had gone to talk to the children, mother, and father, all of whom spoke excellent English. The Jordanian mother spoke at length with me about her life in Jordan, how she spent five hours a day in the kitchen, and her concerns for her family. I asked if she resented spending all this time preparing meals and was told very emphatically, "Not at all." She asked us to stay for dinner. As the mealtime was announced, she quickly disappeared to the kitchen, only reappearing to serve the food. We ate in the dining room with the father. Needless to say, we felt embarrassed and uneasy with such an arrangement. But the hostess appeared quite content and happy with her role as cook and server rather than as table host.

The Jordanian woman was following an old tradition that has lingered on into the late twentieth century. Many women throughout the Middle East have assumed roles similar to those of their U.S. counterparts, yet those who hold to more traditional roles do not always resent their positions. They and the men in their culture believe that Muslim women are being protected by staying at home and wearing the veil in public.

Activities

1. Discuss with your students any images they have of Arabs, Muslims, and the Middle East. Where do these images come from? Do they think they are accurate or fair? Explain that not all people in the Middle East are Arabs and not all Arabs are Muslims.
(interpretive, cross-cultural)

2. Show your class a picture of a Muslim woman wearing a veil. Ask the students to try to explain why she is wearing the veil. Have they ever seen a veiled Muslim girl or woman? Have a Muslim student or an adult from your community discuss the wearing of the veil and other Islamic traditions with your class. *(interpretive)*

3. Discuss the difference between a tradition and a religious practice. Have the class name some traditions and religious practices found in the U.S., and list them on the board. Are there any that belong in both lists? *(interpretive)*

4. Discuss the situation in which the woman from the U.S. found herself when she ate dinner at the Jordanians' home. What would your students have done in the same situation? Sensitively and without judgment, have the students compare what they know about the roles of women in the U.S. and in the Muslim world.

   If they do make judgments, ask them if it is fair to judge other cultures by U.S. standards. In what instances *would it* be fair to judge? (If a culture were

practicing slavery?) This is a knotty question that has plagued philosophers, anthropologists, and ethicists alike for thousands of years. The basic rule, in most instances, is to judge other cultures only as they would judge themselves. To do so requires understanding why cultures think and act in the ways they do. *(interpretive, cross-cultural)*

NOTE: It is important to realize that all cultures care about the past, the present, *and* the future in some way. Yet anthropologists and other cross-cultural experts have observed that each culture will tend to emphasize one time orientation over another. We are focusing on specific time orientations so that students can understand how time works as a theme that cultures will express and perceive in different ways. In no way should students be encouraged to develop a one-dimensional image of a culture, as if it cared only about the past, the present, or the future. People in every culture have a sense of all three time orientations, while sometimes valuing one or two over the others.

The Line of Time: The Western World

The Western world tends to be focused on the future, a future that is always just down the linear track. Time for Europeans, Canadians, and people from the U.S. often runs, not in a circle, but in a straight line. It was the ancient Hebrews who first introduced this idea. For them time did not go round and round in a cyclical pattern but lay straight ahead into a future where God promised to protect them and establish them in the Promised Land. There are stories in the Bible's Old Testament about God's promises for the future, and the Christians carried on with these ideas of linear time and promises for the future in the New Testament of the Bible. The future to both Jews and Christians is full of promise; Judeo-Christian traditions provide an optimistic outlook on life.

Activities

1. Define the word *linear*. How is it different from *cyclical?* Draw a line on the board as such:

$$\longleftarrow\hspace{6cm}\longrightarrow$$

past   present   future

Is this what the passage of time looks like? Do any of your students picture the passage of time in other ways (i.e., a vertical line)? *(interpretive)*

SIDEBAR

To everything there is a season, and a time to every purpose under heaven:

A time to be born, and a time to die; a time to plant, and a time to pluck up that which is planted;

A time to kill, and a time to heal; a time to break down, and a time to build up;

A time to weep, and a time to laugh; a time to mourn, and a time to dance;

A time to cast away stones, and a time to gather stones together; a time to embrace, and a time to refrain from embracing;

A time to get, and a time to lose; a time to keep, and a time to cast away;

A time to rend, and a time to sew; a time to keep silence, and a time to speak;

A time to love, and a time to hate; a time of war, and a time of peace.

—Ecclesiastes 3:1–8, The Old Testament

2. Ask students to finish the following statements either in sentences or paragraphs and read them to the class. *(interpretive, constructive)*

The past is . . . . . .
The present is . . . . .
The future is . . . . . .

Looking to the Future: The U.S., England, and the Western World

The future has become extremely important to people in Western cultures. While people in the U.S., particularly children, sometimes concentrate on the present, we also frown upon "instant gratification." It is not uncommon for people to tell each other, "If you are only willing to wait, everything will work out."

Changes have often come rapidly and sometimes violently in Western cultures. Revolutions, wars, new ways of thinking, and inventions such as the steam engine and the automobile have brought about enormous changes, and people's lives have been transformed in a very short time. The rate of change has only quickened,

and new products and new ideas seem always to bring hope for a better tomorrow. Ask any U.S. child to complete the commercial slogan that plays throughout newspapers, radio, and TV: "new and _____." The young person will be quick to complete the phrase with "improved." "New" to most U.S. minds is better, and there is always tomorrow with a promise of a better day. Businesses in the United States focus on the future, but it usually is a short-term future of about five years. If profits cannot be made within that length of time, then it is best to drop the project and get on to something else.

The pace of change, however, is not the same throughout the Western world, and there are some historical reasons for these differences. The United States, a new country in comparison with Europe, expanded rather rapidly across the continent, and with the expansion came a quickly growing population as immigrants poured into the "land of promise." New products were required to meet the needs of all these new citizens. In England, on the other hand, the population's growth rate began to decline as the world slipped into the twentieth century. During World Wars I and II, England suffered extreme shortages of goods. Thus, "Show me I really need it before I make a change" became an unofficial, subconscious slogan of the English people. Today that attitude still exists. While changes do come to England, they come at a slower pace than in the United States. But once it is decided change is needed, the country often makes dramatic technological and commercial advances. For example, England provides an old traditional way to cross the Atlantic, the sleek ocean liner known as the *Queen Elizabeth II.* Yet England also has the newest and fastest means for getting between the European continent and North America, the *Concord*, a plane that cruises at 1,336 miles per hour to travel between London and New York in a little under four hours.

One of the authors experienced firsthand England's reluctance to change as well as its inclination to dramatically alter its lifestyle once it decides to accept a new idea.

In the 1960s I lived in London. In every borough (section of the city), there usually could be found a street called High on which the green grocer (fruit and vegetable market), fish monger (fish market), butcher, and baker were located. Scattered around the city were rather small versions of the U.S. supermarket, which the local people preferred to call "self-service stores." Most English shoppers preferred the smaller stores for limited, daily purchases because many of the homes had very small refrigerators or none at all. When I ventured into one of the self-service markets and bought six bottles of a soft drink along with a dozen other items, customers and cashiers were stunned. One child ran to her mother, tugged on her sleeve, and pointed towards me. "Look, look mummy," she cried excitedly. "Six bottles of Coca Cola!" And when I reached the checkout counter, an incredulous cashier counted all the items and exclaimed, "Having a party, luv?"

Then, in the early nineties, I returned to live in London again. This time the supermarket outsupered anything on my side of the Atlantic. Fruits and vegetables from all over the world, many of which I had never seen before, as well as exotic canned goods from everywhere lined the bins and shelves. Customers could step into a home economist's office for special recipes and menus, and forty-eight checkout counters stood ready to serve hundreds of shoppers at a time. The change was remarkable.

Activities

1. Write on the board, "New and _____!" and ask the students to fill in the blank. What does "new and improved" mean? Are new things always better things? Ask the students if they think the future will be better than today. If so, why? in what ways? Explain that this attitude is typical of the U.S. and it reflects the tendency in the U.S. to look forward into the future. Yet, as they have seen with East Asia and the Middle East, many cultures do not think the future is necessarily better than the past. It is important to realize that the U.S. is not necessarily "better" than other cultures simply because it looks to the future. How would an East Asian or a Muslim fill in the blank of "new and _____"? *(interpretive, cross-cultural)*

2. Make three columns on the board, titled "Past," "Present," "Future." Ask the students to name areas of their life or of U.S. society in which each time orientation is most important. List these in the appropriate columns. (Under "Future" might go education and business, under "Present" might go family and friends, etc.) Discuss their answers. What conclusions can they draw about the value of each time orientation in the U.S.? Does the future seem to be the most important overall?

   What is *most* important to your students—the past, the present, or the future? Why? (Young people tend to say that the present is most important, and this is understandable considering the issues they face at their age.) *(interpretive, constructive)*

3. After sharing the information about England and the U.S. woman's experience there, ask the students if they have ever experienced the attitude, "Show me I really need it before I make a change." Do any of their parents feel this way? Have they ever heard the motto, "If it isn't broken, don't fix it"? What does that mean? Why is Missouri called "The Show-Me State"? Like England, many people in the U.S. think that "new" does not equal "improved."

   Divide the class in half and stage a debate. One side will adopt the U.S. motto, "new and improved," and the other will adopt the English motto, "Show me I really need it before I make a change." As they argue for their own slogans, make sure they think of concrete examples to defend their points. At the end, summarize the philosophy of each side. The point is for them to understand that there are valid reasons for each cultural viewpoint. *(collaborative, cross-cultural)*

4. Continue to fill in the Cultural Orientation Line. Have the class vote on where to place the United States.

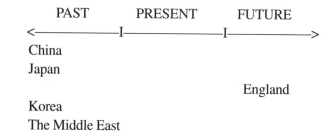

PAST	PRESENT	FUTURE
China		
Japan		
		England
Korea		
The Middle East		

There's No Time Like the Present (But the Past Should Not Be Forgotten): Mexico and Latin America

There is still a third overall way of looking at time and that is to focus on the present. People in Latin America value the present over the future, but they also take great interest in their past (Hall, 1990).

In all cultures, there are areas of life where people do not follow the predominant time pattern. Such is the case with students in many Latin American cultures. Many high school students are thinking about the future by having already chosen their careers and working toward them in school. They have selected a *curso* (**kur**-soh, "major"), something that usually is left for the college years in the United States. The past is highly venerated, and much of a family's perceived status is dependent on the name they bear and the ancestry they can claim. In a narrower sense, they also place more importance on their parents and grandparents than is common in the U.S. Generations far more often live together, and the past thus becomes more of a reality.

Generally, however, Latin Americans value the present over the future. Just like the Arabs, there is a hesitancy to commit to a definite future. The people in Mexico, for instance, often say to one another when contemplating an event, *si Dios quiere* (see **dee**-os kee-**ehr**-eh) ("God willing") (Heusinkveld, 1993). It is interesting to consider why the Mexicans, as well as many other Latinos, might follow this present-orientation. Cultures constantly mold, influence, and leave their marks on each other. Occupied for hundreds of years by Spain, the natives of many Latin American countries were forced to serve the conquerors. Daily survival must have been a high priority with little time for thoughts of the future. Could this have become the driving force toward a present orientation, which later generations inherited? Another reason that might be considered is the cultural background of the conqueror. The Spaniards, too, had come from a nation only recently released from occupation. The Arab Empire had extended to the Iberian peninsula—present-day Spain and Portugal—and the Arabs had finally retreated from these occupied lands in 1492. Could the Arabs possibly have passed their attitudes toward time ("We shall be there, Allah willing") on to the Spaniards who, in turn, carried it to the Americas? These are intriguing ideas to consider.

Activities

1. Discuss: What does it mean to think only in terms of the present? Is this attitude entirely foreign? Can your students think of any sayings, proverbs, or even bumper stickers found in the U.S. that emphasize the value of today? ("Live for today," "Today is the first day of the rest of your life," "There's no time like the present," "Don't put off until tomorrow what you can do today.") Explain that, even though they may not have these expressions, many Latin American cultures hold this general attitude. Is there something appealing in this attitude? *(interpretive)*

2. Ask the students to pair up, think of, and role-play scenarios in which someone from another culture with another time orientation settles in the U.S. and has a hard time adjusting to certain time orientations here. For example, how might a person with a present orientation respond to a long term-paper assignment in a U.S. school? How might a person with a past orientation feel about being forced to replace a food staple such as rice with pasta, just because pasta is "in"? How could the students help the newcomer to adjust to the clash in time orientations?

Discuss: Should students from other cultures *always* conform to U.S. ways of thinking? Are there other ways in which to meet all the needs of students from various cultural backgrounds? *(constructive, cross-cultural)*

3. Finish filling in your Cultural Orientation Line:

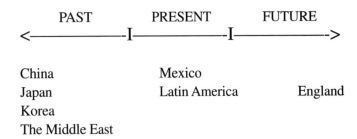

PAST	PRESENT	FUTURE

<————————-I—————————-I—————————>

China	Mexico	
Japan	Latin America	England
Korea		
The Middle East		

4. Optional. Ask students to rent the film *Dead Poet's Society*. Produced in the late 1980s, this movie pits two cultural perspectives against each other. One is the tradition of thinking ahead, always preparing for the future—taken to a suffocating extreme by the parents and educators in a New England prep school. The other is embodied in the philosophy with which the literature teacher attempts to inspire his students: *Carpe Diem*, "Seize the Day." The students are caught in the middle of this conflict as they attempt to negotiate between these two, seemingly opposing philosophical forces. The movie does contain some painful, tragic consequences, but older students will be equipped to handle the disturbing, thought-provoking content. Use your discretion in generating discussion of what can result when two time orientations clash. *(interpretive)*

Lesson 4

Clock Time

What Time Is It?

People throughout history have devised their own means of keeping track of the hours through a system often based on cultural or personal interests, and while some methods have been rather ingenious, they have not been completely accurate. Throughout Europe for many centuries, church bells kept the surrounding town conscious of the time of day. In the eighteenth century, a European botanist by the name of Carolus Linnaeus came up with the idea of recording time based on the daily opening and closing of flower petals. His invention became known as the flower clock.

As early as the second century B.C., the Chinese had decided the day began and ended at midnight and was divided into twelve equal parts, thus making their "hours" equal to a present-day two-hour period. Always conscious of nature and a desire to live in harmony with it, the Chinese named these "hours" after animals. Our 5 P.M. to 7 P.M. was their period known as the hare, and 7 P.M. to 9 P.M. was the bear time. Midnight cut into the middle of the rat hour, 11 P.M. to 1 A.M. (Fraser, 1987).

For many centuries, people around the world had problems synchronizing their time with others. While it might be 3 P.M. in one town, a neighboring village might consider it thirty minutes or an hour later or earlier. Imagine the confusion in traveling or doing business in the modern world if such a system were still to exist!

Although time patterns had settled down by the mid-nineteenth century, people realized there was still a lot to be done to bring together baffling and unconnected time systems around the world. Clocks had to be put in order, and the sun, as it already was in many cultures, would be the source from which time would be based. But the sun does not travel at a steady pace. It sometimes speeds ahead, at other times falls back, and while these differences are infinitesimal, over a long period they could make sun time inaccurate. In the nineteenth century, scientists skirted around the problem by creating mean sun, a steady but make-believe sun, which in reality was only slightly different from the real thing, which then became known as the apparent sun.

Then they decided to select a spot on earth where clock-time would begin, and the Royal Greenwich (**Grenich**) Observatory, just a short distance south of London, England, was chosen. Scientists designated twenty-four time zones that circled the globe, beginning at Greenwich, and the line that stretched from the North to South Poles and ran through Greenwich became known as the *prime meridian.* The time at Greenwich took on special significance and a distinctive name: *Greenwich mean time. Greenwich,* of course, referred to the town, and *mean time* referred to a "corrected" sun time. As travelers journeyed eastward into each new time zone, they lost an hour. As they wandered westward, they gained an hour. But at what point did east dissolve into west and west into east and times clash with each other? An imaginary line was drawn from north to south through the Pacific and became known as the international date line. As a person crossed this line heading westward, he lost an entire day. At one moment it would be 1 P.M. Tuesday, and the next moment, it was 1 P.M. Wednesday. But a traveler moving in the opposite direction gained a day.

Did You Know?

Some Swahili-speaking people of Africa keep a "clock-time" that is very different from that found in the U.S. They believe that the day begins not at midnight but at the time the sun rises. Since many of them live on the Equator, the sun comes up at approximately the same time every day throughout the year. To them, one o'clock in the morning is by Western watches 7 A.M. Two o'clock in the morning, Swahili time, is 8 A.M. Western time. In other words, there is a six-hour time difference. Those Swahili-speakers who live in large metropolitan areas follow the Western method of keeping time.

From *Windows to the World: Themes for Cross-Cultural Understanding.* Copyright © 1996 by Phyllis Kepler, Brooke Sarno Royse, and John Kepler.

Did You Know?

A more efficient way of telling time is used by the military and international airports, among other institutions. It is the 24-hour clock. Instead of using A.M. and P.M. to designate the hours before and after noon and midnight, the 24-hour clock runs from 0:00, which is midnight, to 23:59, which is 11:59 P.M. So, 1 A.M. is simply 1:00, 6 A.M. is 6:00, 12 noon is 12:00, 2 P.M. is 14:00, 7 P.M. is 19:00, and 11 P.M. is 23:00.

Did You Know?

While most people around the world have accepted the ideas of one-hour time zones and days beginning at midnight, there are some cultures that have not. Visitors to these lands sometimes run into problems. Many people in Malaysia, for example, consider about 6:30 of each evening as the beginning of a new day. If you are visiting in that country and are asked to come to dinner at 7 P.M. Friday, you had best check to make certain your host does not really mean 7:00 in the evening of Thursday by non-Malaysian time standards (Craig, 1984). Then there are cultures that do not observe the "hourly" difference in time zones. Traveling from Pakistan to India, for instance, an individual enters a new time zone with only a half-hour's difference rather than the traditional one-hour variation.

Activities

1. Illustrate how the earth revolves both on its axis and around the sun to explain how it can be day in one part of the world and night in another. Take a spherical object like a soccer ball and hold it a fixed distance from a lamp. Choose one spot on the ball as your location. Slowly turn the ball on its imaginary axis and at the same time walk the ball around the lamp. *(interpretive)*

2. Refer to a world almanac for an illustration of the time lines that circle the globe. Copy it and hand one to each student. Then make copies of the following two worksheets for your students, and have them complete the activities described. *(constructive, cross-cultural)*

NAME _____

DATE _____

What Time Is It?

Study the drawing of the time lines that circle the globe. At the top of each line is an hour (1:00 A.M., 3:00 P.M., etc.) that tells you what time it is in certain places around the world. Fill in the hours in the worksheet below.

City	Time
Chicago, Illinois, USA	
London, England	
Beijing, China	
Los Angeles, California, USA	
Rio de Janeiro, Brazil	
Johannesburg, South Africa	
Moscow, Russia	
Auckland, New Zealand	

Student
Worksheet

NAME _____

DATE _____

Study the drawing of the global time zones again. In the chart below, fill in the name of your city or town. Mark it on the map. In the spaces provided under "Your Activity," describe what you would be doing at the hours marked on the chart ("eating lunch," "sleeping," etc.). Then, find out what time it would be in the four cities named at the top of the chart and fill in the blanks. Can you imagine what kids in these cities might be doing at the same hour when you are sleeping or eating lunch or doing your homework?

Your town _____

Time	Your Activity	Time in London	Time in Beijing	Time in Rio de Janeiro	Time in Moscow
1:00 A.M.					
7:00 A.M.					
10:00 A.M.					
12:00 NOON					
4:00 P.M.					
6:00 P.M.					
9:00 P.M.					

What's the Rush?

Most of the world may tell time by a clock, but time is not always regarded the same in every culture. For some, like the Germans, the clock is to be adhered to strictly. For others, like Arabs, Latin Americans, and some Africans, being punctual is not a top priority. After all, the latter groups reason, people are not machines. They do not have to operate as precisely as a clock. It is far more important to finish a conversation with a friend than abruptly to break it off because of an appointment. To most people in the U.S., being kept waiting is an insult, at least after five or ten minutes. But for people in many Arab, Latin, and African cultures, waiting is an acceptable practice. Patience regarding time is one of the most difficult traits for a person from the Western world to develop when interacting with people who have a different concept of being "on time."

Activity

Discuss: What does it mean to be "on time" in the U.S.? How late is "late"? Ask the students to think of situations in which they must never be late. How about times when it is okay to be five minutes late? Ten minutes late? One hour late? How do they feel if someone is thirty minutes late to meet them? Are there certain hours of the day when they absolutely must be doing a certain activity? Can they draw some conclusions about how people in the U.S. feel about being "on time"? What do they think about the Arab, Latin American, and African attitudes about being "on time" and about waiting? *(interpretive, cross-cultural)*

The "Tilted Clock"

There is also the problem with a "tilted clock," which many people from the U.S. encounter in some cultures around the world. While lunch in the U.S. is usually considered to be around twelve-noon (straight up on the clock) and dinner around 6:00 in the evening (straight down), the practice is not always followed in all cultures. In many Latin countries, like Mexico and Spain, for example, lunch does not begin until 2:00 or later in the afternoon and dinner at 10:00 in the evening or even midnight. Social events are scheduled for much later in the evening than in the United States, and a sense of urgency is nonexistent. To people in these cultures, it is *our* clock that is "tilted."

Activity

On the following worksheet is a true story about a family from the U.S. who lived in Mexico City and immediately fell into several time traps. Divide the class into groups of four or five. Copy the worksheet on page 103 and hand it to each group. Have the students read the story in their

groups and work together as they follow the instructions. When the groups have completed the worksheet, have them share their answers with the class. After the discussion, explain to your students the following:

Teenage parties in Mexico are a far cry from typical get-togethers in the United States. Parents, grandparents, aunts, uncles, cousins, friends of parents, as well as the teenage crowd, are all invited to the festivities, which always begin way past the customary U.S. party-time and

SIDEBAR

People in many African cultures are *event-oriented* while people in the U.S. and other Western cultures tend to be *time-oriented*. For event-oriented people in Africa, what is happening is far more important than the time. Time, they reason, is limitless. "We always have time to help a friend," they are quick to tell a visitor to their cultures. Recipes, for example, do not come in cookbooks nor are they written down as a convenience to others. Instead, women will go to a friend's home to demonstrate how to make a dish, no matter how complicated and lengthy the preparations might be. Conversations with friends and relatives are not cut short in order to reach an appointment on time, nor would anyone use an excuse of "not having enough time" to assist an ill family member.

go well into the morning hours. Adult supervision is not even a consideration because the entire family is present. The Mexicans are very family-oriented and respect the wishes of parents. The Mexican boy did not object to Amy's curfew because to do so would have been disrespectful to her parents. Instead, he dutifully brought her home after only a little less than an hour at the party, but then returned to celebrate until the early morning hours with all his family and friends. He arrived an hour late to pick up Amy not because he was rude but because in many cases it is perfectly acceptable to be late for social events in Mexico. The Teagues soon learned that, by U.S. standards, clocks in Mexico are tilted. That is, everything begins and ends much later than on our side of the border. In Mexican culture, it would have been quite reasonable and logical for the Teagues to have allowed their daughter to begin the evening at 10:00 or 11:00 and stay at the party until 3:00 or 4:00 in the morning. *(collaborative, cross-cultural)*

Student

Worksheet

NAME _____

DATE _____

What Went Wrong?

The Teague family of Boise, Idaho, had settled into their new home in Mexico City with their two children, Brian, 17, and Amy, 15. The brother and sister were attending an international school in the city where local students, as well as those from all over the world, were enrolled. One of the Mexican boys invited Amy to his eighteenth birthday party. The Teague parents said she could go but she must follow her usual U.S. curfew, which meant being home by midnight. Amy argued that her date was not picking her up until 10:00 P.M. Couldn't she stay out a bit later? she asked. Mr. and Mrs. Teague said "No." They were very surprised that a boy would come at that late hour. The Mexican friend, however, failed to arrive at 10:00 and in fact did not appear until nearly 11:00. The Teagues were still determined that their daughter be home at the designated time.

The Mexican boy agreed immediately and did not appear to be the least bit upset by the request. The two left for the party, and right on schedule the Mexican boy had Amy home at midnight. He thanked her and said he would be leaving to return to the party. Amy was upset and embarrassed. She explained to her parents that this was ridiculous. Why had she not been allowed to stay out much later since they had such a late start? Her parents argued that it was not their fault that the boy had been so late. They said that 10:00 P.M. was not an appropriate time to begin a date, and no matter when it started, they did not want their daughter out past midnight.

This short story contains several clues about the different attitude towards time in Mexican culture. In the chart below are two columns. On the left are some clues about Mexican culture that the Teagues did not understand because they were thinking like people from the U.S. Can you guess what each clue can tell you about some of the ways Mexicans think and act? Discuss each clue with your group and what it might mean, and then fill in the space in the column on the right.

Clue	What the Clue Tells You About Mexican Culture
1. Amy's date said he would pick her up at 10:00 P.M.	
2. Amy's date did not arrive until 11:00 P.M.	
3. The Mexican boy agreed immediately to Amy's parents' request that he bring her home by midnight.	
4. The Mexican boy brought Amy home by midnight.	
5. The Mexican boy returned to the party after midnight.	

     Think about the following question and discuss it with your group:
     Should the parents have backed down and allowed their daughter to stay out past midnight, or should they have stuck to the rules they believed to be the right ones?

Did You Know?

People divide their day in Indonesia into four segments. From the time the day begins at midnight and until eleven in the morning is known as *pagi* (**pah**-gee). *Siang* (see-**ahng**) runs from eleven in the morning until three in the afternoon when it becomes *sore* (soh-**ray**) until six-forty-five in the evening. The day then settles into *malam* (ma-**lahm**). When someone wants to indicate an extreme in time, they repeat the words. For example, *pagi-pagi* means "very early" and *malam-malam* means "very late" (Draine, 1990).

Did You Know?

In the Philippines, the time must be repeated on several occasions when you ask someone to dinner at your home; otherwise he or she probably will not show up. If asked only once, in spite of answering "yes" to the invitation, the expected guest will not take you seriously. You must follow up with a telephone call or ask another person, who also will be attending, to tell the individual that he or she really is expected (Roces and Roces, 1985).

Can You Hear or Smell the Time?

A clock can be more than a mechanical device that tells a person when to get up, go to school, attend a meeting, or have a meal. There also are clocks of the senses. Certain sounds and odors tell people it is time for action. The smell of coffee perking in a U.S. home announces it is time for breakfast. The dramatic, haunting call of the *muezzin* (moh-ah-zin) as he intones the *adhan* (ahz-**ahn**), the call to prayer, from the top of the graceful minarets of the mosques in the Middle East tells people five times a day that it is time to pray. The shrill, piercing whistle of the sweet potato man cuts through the early evening air of Mexico City to announce the time for a special treat, and the melodious tones of bells during the daylight hours alert residents to the coming of the garbage collector. In Iran,

the early-morning aroma of flat breads being baked in deep oven ground pits summons shoppers to the local bakery to get their day's supply as the breads are hung out on poles in the open air, waiting to be sold.

Activity

Discuss: Other than looking at the clock, how else do we know what time it is? Are there sounds that tell you what time it is? smells? List these on the board. *(interpretive)*

Jet Lag

Our biological clocks often exert a greater influence over us than our mechanical time pieces. A system known as *circadian rhythms*, based on a twenty-four hour cycle, have great control over our bodies. One of the most important factors in the circadian rhythm is its influence in telling us we are sleepy each evening. Why do we not want to go to bed at noon, three o'clock, or even six in the early evening? Our circadian rhythms have programmed us into a pattern that makes us sleepy at a later hour and wakes us after so many hours of rest. One of the greatest problems in interacting cross-culturally comes when this circadian rhythm is interrupted. It is known as *jet lag*. People formerly traveled across oceans to foreign lands by ship, gradually easing into different time zones. But today they board jets that deliver them to the other side of the world in short order. It is nighttime back home, but the middle of the day in their new location. Their bodies, based on the circadian rhythms, do not know this, and the travelers are extremely tired and sleepy. One unofficial estimate is that it takes one day of adjustment for every hour that is different from the home base. In other words, if you travel to Tokyo and it is fourteen hours ahead of your time back home, it will take you two weeks to adjust completely to the new time. You will be awake in the middle of the night and dead tired, frantically wishing to fall into bed, in the middle of the afternoon. While under the spell of jet lag, people find it difficult to operate at full power, think clearly, and interact with others successfully. Scientists have recently located the gene that governs our biological clocks, thus leading the way toward inventing a drug that could make jet lag obsolete.

Activities

1. Ask the students to make a log of their circadian rhythms. Have them carry with them a sheet of paper throughout one day. Whenever they feel hungry, thirsty, sleepy, peppy, irritable, etc., they should jot down on the paper the time and the feeling. In class the following day, survey the students to see if there were certain

Did You Know?

The first *muezzin*, the official who calls the Muslims to prayer five times a day and to worship on Friday, was an Ethiopian named Bilal, who had a beautiful voice. Although Bilal's ancestry was rooted in this African nation, he actually was born in the late sixth century in Mecca, the holy city of the Muslims. Bilal was a slave who was tortured by his master for declaring his belief in Islam. He supposedly was chosen by Muhammad, the founder of Islam, to call out, "Come to prayer! Come to prayer! Come to salvation! Come to salvation! God is most great! God is most great! There is no god but God." Today, the calls come throughout the Muslim world just before sunrise, immediately after noon, in the late afternoon, just after the sun has set, and the final prayer, two hours after the previous one. Many office buildings have special areas curtained off where people may go to pray, and many shops, particularly in Saudi Arabia, close at prayer time (Hoberman, 1989).

There are no ministers or priests in Islam. Instead, men gain the title of *ulama* (oh-**lahm**-ah) for their in-depth knowledge of the religion, their influence on the community, and their religious leadership. But a clergy is avoided in order to maintain the religion's firm belief in equality and the desire that no one should stand between humans and God.

times of day when the majority of students felt the same way. Tallying the responses on the board will help. *(constructive)*

2. Have the students refer to the illustration of world time zones. Choose several foreign cities, and see if the students can figure out how many days it would take them to recover from jet lag if they traveled by plane to get there. (There is a more official and complicated formula, but this formula comes close enough: one day for every hour of time difference.) *(constructive)*

Lesson 5

Calendars Around the World

When we look at a typical calendar in the classroom, we see that certain days have been identified as holidays. These may be important dates in a country's history (the Fourth of July), religious events (Yom Kippur, Easter), the anniversary of the birth or death of a famous person or persons (George Washington's Birthday, Martin Luther King, Jr.'s Birthday, Veterans' Day), or an occasion to remember loved ones (Mother's Day). If we were to examine the calendars in other countries, we would see that some of the holidays are the same as ours, but there are others that are unique to those cultures or groups. Creating a holiday, with time off from work and special festivities, has been a means throughout history to commemorate deserving persons or events. By observing who and what are so honored, we can learn much about those who are doing the honoring.

Many of these special days are connected with a specific religion. This is not surprising since the reason humans developed ways to segment time into regular intervals often was because of the need to set specific dates for religious celebrations. The giant circle of stone blocks in England, Stonehenge, is believed to have been constructed to enable its builders to ascertain appropriate times for their worship from astronomical observations. More than six hundred other similar but more simple wood and stone structures dedicated to the same purpose have been discovered in Europe and the Americas.

Throughout history, each civilization developed calendars to meet its own needs. The reasons for dividing time into intervals and how these intervals were determined varied with each culture. Since days, months, and years are repetitious, humans have taken their cues from natural forces such as the seasons and especially the movements of the sun, moon, and stars, which also repeat and can be measured to establish cycles. The scientists and astronomers around the world, however, subdivided the cycles into many different patterns, and, as a result, calendars have been very diverse over the centuries.

At least one group, the Native American tribes, did not create a single integrated system of designating days and longer periods that could be called a true calendar. Instead, intervals of time were counted independently of one another. For example, a bundle of sticks often was used to represent a period of days; one stick would be withdrawn to note the passage of each twenty-four-hour period.

The standard calendar used almost universally around the world today (and on your school wall) is the Gregorian Calendar named after Pope Gregory XIII and dating back to A.D 1582. Despite is ecclesiastical origin, it is the definitive calendar of international business and diplomacy. Some cultures also use other ethnically and religiously oriented calendars. The largest unbroken chain of time measurement is believed to be the Chinese Calendar which was introduced in 2953 B.C. Other calendars among those still in active use are the Islamic Calendar, the Jewish Calendar, and the Hindu Calendar. Below is some information about these calendars and their holidays, which can provide some insight into the cultural heritage of those who use them.

Chinese Calendar

The traditional Chinese Calendar is important because of its longevity and the number of Chinese throughout the world who still follow its interpretation of the celestial constellations. One reason that this calendar has survived nearly five millennia is that it was considered a sacred document until the middle of the twentieth century. Although minor adjustments have been made in the astronomical calculations, its essential structure today is just as it was when first introduced.

The Chinese Zodiac

The Chinese zodiac is also unique. In most cultures, the zodiac is a twelve-part division of the year based on the paths of the sun, moon, and principal planets. Each division or sign is named after a major star constellation: Aries, the Ram; Leo, the Lion; and so on. It is credited by many to impart certain characteristics to those born within one of these signs.

The official calendar of the People's Republic of China (Gregorian) has very few holidays. The name of one, The International Working Women's Day, gives us an idea of the nature of the rest. Probably the major holiday of the classic calendar is the Chinese New Year, which has a moveable date. Visits are made to friends and relatives, debts are settled, red envelopes containing lucky money are presented to children, and firecrackers are exploded to drive the demons away.

Islamic Calendar

Over two billion Muslims refer to this calendar in their personal lives, and many nations have recognized it officially as an authorized method for observing time, particularly with respect to religious events. Among the countries which have authorized its use officially are Saudi Arabia and Yemen. Most Muslim countries, such as Egypt, Turkey, and Syria, have sanctioned both the Gregorian and the Islamic versions. Among the holidays in the Islamic calendar year are New Year's Day, the Ascension of Muhammad, and Ramadan—all occurring on different dates each year and thus called "moveable" holidays. Days begin at sunset, so the night portion of a day precedes the daylight.

One particularly important and unique Muslim holiday is *Ramadan* (**Rah**-mah-dan). It actually is a whole month during which believers observe a holy fast. From sunrise until the stars can be seen, Muslims are not allowed to eat or drink anything except water. After sundown, food and drink are permitted and families will get together to eat and restore their energy. The end of Ramadan, to which Muslims eagerly look forward, is the three-day holiday of *Id al-Fitr* (Id ahl-**fit**-re).

Jewish Calendar

The present Jewish calendar is based on the sun to determine the year and on the moon to determine the months. It is complicated by religious requirements that dictate that certain events must occur on specific days. The New Year, for example, must not fall on a Sunday, Wednesday, or Friday. Passover must precede the New Year by 163 days. Still, with all the adjustments that must be made to comply with ritual, the calendar is used today in Israel for all civil and religious purposes. Sixteen holy days are identified on the calendar, the best known being *Rosh Hashana* (New Year), *Yom Kippur* (Day of Atonement), *Hanukkah* (Festival of Lights), and *Pesach* (Passover). On the first day of Rosh Hashana, a ram's horn, the *shofar* (**shoh**-fahr), is blown in the synagogue to signal God's sovereignty over men and women. The family meal on this first night will feature apples dipped into honey to signify the coming of a "good and sweet year." On the second night, a new fruit is eaten. The date for this holiday is moveable, and it occurs around the beginning of September.

Indian Calendars

India, with its many subcultures and different languages, has given birth to a great number of calendars, but they fall into two basic types: a civil calendar and religious calendars of the Hindus. The former has only six holidays, one of which is the celebration of the birthday of Mahatma Gandhi, India's most famous leader and hero. The many regional Hindu calendars make up the shortage with a number of fasts, feasts, festivals, and other celebrations. The abundance of regional calendars caused great confusion until India became independent in 1947 and attempts at unification began. There were some common features in the regional versions based on the *Kali Yunga*, the country's first calendar developed around 2000 B.C. The months correspond exactly to the signs of the zodiac. The festivals are inspired by Hindu mythology and its trinity of gods: Brahma, the Creator; Vishnu, the Preserver; and Shiva, the Destroyer.

Activities

1. Copy the worksheet on page 108 and give it to the students to complete. *(constructive, cross-cultural)*

2. Discuss the Islamic holiday of Ramadan. If you have any Muslim students in your class, ask them to explain what they do during Ramadan. What should teachers and students be aware of during this time? (For example, P.E. teachers should be particularly sensitive to the fact that physical activity will be hard for Muslim students who are fasting.) *(interpretive, cross-cultural)*

3. Are there special cultural holidays that students in your class observe? If so, mark them on your classroom calendar, and when they occur, have the students who celebrate them announce the occasion to the class and

Did You Know?

Each year, on November 2, Mexicans observe one of their most important holidays, *El Dia de los Muertos* (Ehl **dee**-a day lohs **mwehr**-tohs), "The Day of the Dead," to honor deceased friends and relatives. In a macabre but festive spirit, families show respect for their ancestors by putting flowers and food on the grave sites. Hundreds of vendors erect booths outside the churches and cemeteries to sell bright red candy, skulls, stark white skeletons, bread specially baked and decorated for the holidays, masks and other paraphernalia of the devil. On this day, the spirits of the deceased are said to return to earth, and families celebrate rather than mourn the reunion.

explain how they celebrate them. On some, like Id al-Fitr, you might have the students organize a special party or meal for the class or the entire school. *(cross-cultural, constructive)*

4. Obtain a drawing of the Western zodiac, and have your class compare it with the Chinese zodiac. *(cross-cultural, interpretive)*

5. List some U.S. holidays on the board, and have the class categorize them according to what they celebrate: a hero or heroine's birthday, a religious occasion, a political event, etc. Explain that calendars can tell stories about the cultures that use them simply by the holidays they celebrate. Assign a short essay with the following topic: If the U.S. were to add another holiday to the calendar, what would the students suggest? Why? How would it be celebrated? *(constructive)*

Student
Worksheet

NAME _____

DATE _____

Match the Holidays

Match the holidays listed in the left-hand column with the
calendar of the cultures or countries that celebrate them on
the right.

Holiday	Culture or Country
Rosh Hashana	People's Republic of China Calendar
A holiday when red envelopes with lucky money are given to children	Islamic Calendar
Ramadan	U.S. Calendar
Yom Kippur	Indian Calendar
International Working Women's Day	Jewish Calendar
Ascension of Muhammad	Chinese Calendar
Veterans' Day	Jewish Calendar
Mahatma Ghandi's Birthday	Islamic Calendar
Id al-Fitr	Jewish Calendar
Hanukkah	Islamic Calendar

Resources

Berlitz, Charles. *Native Tongues.* New York: Grosset & Dunlap, 1982.

Cateora, Philip R. *International Marketing,* 7th ed. Boston: Irwin, 1990.

Craig, JoAnn. *Culture Shock: Singapore and Malaysia.* Singapore: Times Books International, 1984.

Draine, Cathie, and Barbara Hall. *Culture Shock: Indonesia,* rev. ed. Portland: Graphic Arts Center, 1990.

Fairbank, John K., Edwin O. Reischauer, and Albert M. Craig. *East Asia: Tradition and Transformation,* rev. ed. Boston: Houghton Mifflin, 1989.

Fraser, J. T. *Time: The Familiar Stranger.* Amherst: University of Massachusetts Press, 1987.

——. *The Voices of Time.* Amherst: University of Massachusetts Press, 1981.

Hall, Edwin T. *The Dance of Life.* Garden City: Anchor Press/Doubleday, 1983.

——. *The Silent Language.* Garden City: Doubleday, 1959.

——. *Understanding Cultural Differences: Germans, French and Americans.* Yarmouth, ME: Intercultural Press, 1990.

Heusinkveld, Paula Rae. *The Mexicans: An Inside View of a Changing Society.* Worthington, OH: Renaissance Publications, 1993.

Hoberman, Barry. "The First Muezzin." *The Arab World Notebook,* edited by Audrey Shabbas and Ayad Al-Qazzaz. Berkeley: Najad: Women Concerned About the Middle East, 1989.

Lamb, David. *The Africans: Encounters from the Sudan to the Cape.* London: Bodley Head, 1982.

Roces, Alfredo and Grace Roces. *Culture Shock: Philippines.* Singapore: Times Books International, 1985.

Shabbas, Audrey. "An Introduction to Islam." *The Arab World Notebook,* edited by Audrey Shabbas and Ayad Al-Qazzaz. Berkeley: Najad: Women Concerned About the Middle East, 1989.

Whiting, Robert. *The Chrysanthemum and the Bat.* Tokyo: Permanent Press, 1977.

Relationships

Goals

This chapter explores several interesting angles on relationships and their implications for cross-cultural understanding. The information, stories, examples from various cultures, and student activities are designed to help your students achieve the following goals:

1. To understand that relationships of all kinds are formed, maintained, and valued in different ways in different cultures.

2. To see that people make friends and express friendships in many ways around the world. Trying to make friends with someone from another culture can be both rewarding and frustrating.

3. To learn that people date, marry, and divorce for different reasons and in different ways in various cultures.

4. To grasp the concept of "arranged marriages" and to understand the important role family plays when young people date and marry in some cultures.

5. To understand that there is no such thing as a "typical" family and that cultures form families and express their feelings for family members through various means.

6. To grasp the concept of "extended families" and how their living arrangements compare to other kinds of family structures.

7. To begin to consider the social and cultural forces (such as economic level or parents' working styles) that influence how a family lives and fits together.

8. To see that children may be reared in different ways and with different goals.

9. To begin to think about the roles of women in cultures around the world and how much freedom and equality they may or may not have.

10. To have the opportunity to observe and ponder their own ways of forming relationships in the light of what they are learning about how it may be done in other cultures.

Cross-Cultural Attitudes and Skills

As students work toward these goals, they will develop the following cross-cultural attitudes and skills:

1. They will develop the ability to see that their own attitudes and behaviors are taught and perpetuated by the culture in which they live.

2. They will continue to achieve a perspective on their own cultural attitudes in the context of other cultural attitudes.

3. They will develop keener and deeper insights into *why* they hold certain opinions and have certain goals for their lives.

4. They will continue to hone their interpretive and critical thinking skills as they participate in extensive discussion of issues regarding relationships that they may not yet have thought about or may simply have taken for granted.

5. They will be more hesitant to judge other cultures wrongly or unfairly for having different values and customs.

GENERAL INTRODUCTION

People around the world have different ways of expressing friendships, dating, marrying, and living in families. It all depends on the values, customs, and other social forces of the culture in which they live. The differences can confuse us and make us judge people from other cultures wrongly. Yet they also can enrich our lives as we grow to understand and accept the fascinating and vast variety of ways relationships are expressed, formed, and honored from culture to culture around the world.

Relationships in the United States seem to change quite rapidly. The ways in which we make friends, meet members of the opposite sex, practice gender roles, decide to marry or form families, and extend hospitality to others are very different today from just a generation ago. As we look across cultural borders, we discover that relationships are changing there as well. Relationships in other cultures are not easy to understand in the first place. The fact that they are constantly evolving, too, makes them a complex and dynamic challenge to cross-cultural understanding.

The changes in these relationships are coming about as a result of many dynamic and interacting forces at play around the world. Among them are the recent industrialization of a particular economy, the instant and far-reaching communication systems now available, new opportunities for mass education, and the emergence of women in the workplace and political arenas. These factors eventually have an influence on changing the social patterns within a culture. Moreover, as large numbers of immigrants move into different cultures, they bring with them rules of behavior regarding relationships from their own lands into a new country where patterns are also shifting. The United States is not the only nation opening its doors to immigrants. Throughout the world, people are crossing national borders to begin new lives. As the immigrant's own changing culture rubs against the evolving culture in his or her new land, it is not unlike two land masses deep in the earth sliding against each other to cause surface tremors or even an earthquake. Friction between different cultural groups can disrupt the cultural landscape to create a whole new social geography.

The cultural adjustment for individuals can be unsettling and difficult. For example, roles within the family may change completely for many immigrants. Father may slip from his role as chief wage earner and prestigious patriarch in the home country to only one of many family members who contributes to the financial pot in the new culture; he may no longer be the power head of this intimate group (Banks, 1993).

Since relationships are always evolving, as are gender roles, it is nearly impossible to describe the "typical" way to make friends, date, or get married in any particular culture. Indeed, as we know so well in the U.S., there is no such thing as a "typical" or "normal" family. Yet there are some general characteristics of relationships that we can pinpoint from one culture to another, and that is what we have attempted to do in this chapter. The main point that students should glean from this set of lessons is that relationships are formed, valued, and maintained in different and fascinating ways in various cultures. Studying these differences should shed some new light on their own assumptions about friendships, hospitality, dating, marriage, and family.

NOTE: You will find many proverbs from cultures around the world in the sidebars of this chapter. As an activity, you could discuss some of these proverbs with the stu-

dents, have the students compare and contrast their meanings, and have the students write their own proverbs having to do with relationships. You also could copy the proverbs onto signs to display around the classroom during this series of lessons on relationships.

What Went Wrong?

These introductory activities are designed to get your students thinking about the ways relationships can act as a stumbling block in cross-cultural understanding. Most students will not know the correct answer to the question posed in each activity, but that is not the point. The point is to initiate curiosity and discussion and to stir their interest in pursuing this topic.

Teacher's Instructions: Divide your class into groups of four or five students. Hand each group a copy of each of the following worksheets. Have each group work together to decide which answer best explains the behavior described in "What Went Wrong?" Then, as a class, each group will explain its reason for choosing the answer. After each group has spoken, reveal the correct answer and discuss it. An explanation to each one has been given below. Do the same with each "What Went Wrong?"

Some discussion questions we suggest include:

1. Why did your group choose this answer over the other answers? Were there clues given, did you simply eliminate the other answers, did you choose by instinct, or did you apply some assumptions you already had about the cultures mentioned? If you applied some assumptions, what did you already assume about the people from that culture?

2. How would you have felt in this situation?

3. What would you have done next?

4. What does this exercise show you about the various ways people from different cultures respond to the same situation?

Answers and Explanations

WHAT WENT WRONG? #1 = Answer #3

Jeff Vavak had been very surprised when his Saudi friend said he did not know where he would go to college or what he would study because his family had not decided. To a person from the U.S., this would not be a question for the family to settle unless, perhaps, financial issues were involved. A young person in the U.S. is expected to select his or her own college under the guidance of a school counselor and parents, and then definitely make up his or her own mind as to the career to pursue. Parents who interfere too forcefully are usually considered domineering and unreasonable. In Saudi Arabia, however, it is not the individual's wishes but the extended family's desires that are important. Marriages are still arranged by the two families, although the young people usually have the option to reject their parents' selections. A first cousin is thought to be a good match, one of the reasons being that property would then stay within the family. Decisions on such matters as education and career choices seem to be logical extensions of the family's important role in each of its members' lives.

WHAT WENT WRONG? #2 = Answer #4

The three women from the U.S. who were walking in their neighborhood saw their new neighbor, a German woman, working in her yard. When the U.S. women approached and the neighbor turned her back on them, the group thought the German was unfriendly and even impolite. But friendships in Germany are different from those in the U.S. Germans are not necessarily and automatically "friends" with their neighbors. The German woman also probably felt that she should not invade the privacy of these walkers by intruding on their conversation with a casual "hello." She turned her back as a gesture of *politeness* and so as not to intrude on the conversation of the other women.

WHAT WENT WRONG? #3 = Answer #1

Pat Tully had been told by his Mexican friend that "my house is your house." But that very popular saying in Mexico is not quite the equivalent of "make yourself at home" in the United States. Mexicans value hospitality, generosity, and friendliness. They are very quick to extend the hospitality of their home to people they have only recently met. But this hospitality is on a much more formal basis by U.S. standards. Teenagers would not invade the refrigerator nor casually slip their shoes off and prop their feet up on the coffee table. A certain dignity should be maintained, particularly in front of any older people present.

WHAT WENT WRONG #4 = Answer #1

Grace was rather astonished that someone would think that a telephone call meant you wanted the person at the other end of the line "to do something for you." Sally probably thought she was being friendly to the newcomer from Africa. But in Grace's country, family and tribal relationships are so strong that everyone automatically shares in another person's life and often helps to rear the children of relatives and friends. This is never considered a favor or looked upon as "doing something." In Africa, an individual is usually surrounded by family members, and Grace missed having someone with whom she could simply chat. She was calling her new friend to do no more than that: talk.

Student

Worksheet

NAME _____

DATE _____

WHAT WENT WRONG? #1

Sixteen-year-old Jeff Vavak moved with his family from Fargo, North Dakota, to Damman, Saudi Arabia, where Jeff's father worked for an oil company. Jeff met the son of one of the Saudi employees with whom Mr. Vavak worked, and the two boys became good friends. "Where do you think you will go to college and what do you want to be?" Jeff asked his Saudi friend. He was startled when he heard the answer. "My family has not decided yet," said his friend.

Why did Jeff's Saudi friend say that his family had not decided where he would go to college and what career he would follow? (Circle the answer that best explains his answer.)

1. The Saudi boy's parents, like many Muslim parents, were very strict and had strong opinions. They would not let him make any decisions for himself.

2. The Saudi boy's father worked for the oil company and his mother was a professor. They wanted their son to follow in their footsteps, but they were having trouble deciding whether he should be a businessman or a professor. The boy was waiting for his parents to make up their minds.

3. In Saudi Arabia, parents and other family members are the ones who help decide what schools their children should attend, what jobs they should take, and even whom they should marry. The children can disagree with their family's wishes, but more often than not, they respect their family's decisions and obey them.

4. The Saudi boy's grades were not very high and his parents were not happy about that. They would not let him even *think* about college or a career until he improved his grades.

From *Windows to the World: Themes for Cross-Cultural Understanding.* Copyright © 1996 by Phyllis Kepler, Brooke Sarno Royse, and John Kepler

Student
Worksheet

NAME _____

DATE _____

WHAT WENT WRONG? #2

Three U.S. women who lived in New Jersey met each morning for a three-mile walk. One day as they headed down the road, they noticed a new neighbor working in her front yard. "That's the family who just arrived from Germany," one of the walkers said. "Oh, we should invite her over for coffee," commented a second member of the group. But as they came close to the new neighbor, she turned her back on the threesome and appeared not to want to speak to them. The U.S. neighbors began to chat at once. "Did you see that?" asked one. "She certainly was impolite," said another. "She obviously doesn't want to meet us," remarked the third. The three decided the new neighbor was very rude.

Why did the German woman turn her back on her U.S. neighbors? (Circle the answer that best explains her action.)

1. Germans are rude.

2. The German woman did not speak English very well, and she was afraid to try to speak with her neighbors. She turned her back on them to avoid an embarrassing situation.

3. Germans are hard workers. The German woman was busy working in her garden and did not want to stop her work to make chitchat with her nosy neighbors.

4. The German woman was actually trying to be polite by turning her back because she did not want to intrude on what looked to her like a private conversation between the three women. Moreover, for Germans, just because you are neighbors with someone does not mean you are automatically "friends" with them. Many people from the U.S. think that if someone is your neighbor, he or she is your "friend." The German woman did not assume that she had to act as if she were friends with the other women.

Student
Worksheet

NAME _____

DATE _____

WHAT WENT WRONG? #3

*"Mi casa es su casa (My house is your house)," said
Pedro Gonzales to his new friend, Pat Tully, who had
moved to Mexico City from Boston, Massachusetts. Pat
really liked Pedro and had found him, as well as his family, very warm and friendly. Pat knew his friend really
meant what he said. One day when Pat was visiting in
Pedro's home, he helped himself to a cola that was sitting
on the kitchen counter. Pedro walked into the room just as
Pat began to take his first sip. From the expression on his
Mexican friend's face, Pat could tell that something was
wrong. "But didn't he say that I should make myself at
home?" Pat thought to himself.*

Why did Pedro act as if Pat had done something wrong by
helping himself to the cola? (Circle the answer that best
explains Pedro's expression.)

1. "My house is your house" in Mexico does not exactly
   mean, "Make yourself at home." Pedro and his family,
   like most Mexicans, were very generous and friendly
   toward Pat, but their form of hospitality is different
   from that found in the U.S. Pat was being too casual
   by helping himself to the cola. Pedro probably would
   have preferred it if he offered the cola to Pat first.

2. Pedro really wanted Pat to make himself at home, but
   he had bought that cola for his mother, so he was
   shocked that Pat had taken it for himself.

3. Colas are very expensive in Mexico, so each day
   Pedro's family would split the soda among themselves
   as a treat after dinner. He simply could not believe that
   Pat was rude enough to take the whole bottle for
   himself.

4. Pedro wanted Pat to make himself at home, but that did
   not include eating and drinking whatever he wanted.
   "My house is your house" simply means that a guest is
   welcome to come over whenever he or she wants.

Student

Student

Worksheet

NAME_____

DATE _____

WHAT WENT WRONG? #4

Grace Karimi had come to the U.S. from Uganda for graduate study at a large university. She had met many U.S. students in her class and had found them to be very friendly. Several of them had given her their telephone numbers. One day, Grace, feeling rather lonely and home-sick, decided to call Sally, one of these new friends. When Sally answered the telephone, she said, "Oh hi, Grace. What can I do for you?" Grace was disappointed and hurt by Sally's response.

Why was Grace hurt by Sally's question? (Circle the answer that best explains her reasons.)

1. Grace did not expect Sally "to do anything for her." Instead, Grace just wanted to chat with a friend.

2. Grace expected Sally to invite her out to dinner. She thought that her friendliness in class indicated that she wanted to entertain her.

3. Sally's response appeared to be very aloof and remote. Sally did not give a direct reply and probably was trying to avoid really becoming involved with a foreign student. All the friendliness had simply been on the surface and was not sincere.

4. Grace was really just "testing the waters." She had heard that U.S. citizens were often very friendly and outgoing but didn't really make good friends. They will act as if they want to help you, but then they never follow through.

Lesson I

Friendships

"A friend in need is a friend indeed." "Don't be a fair-weather friend." "A dog is man's best friend." "Diamonds are a girl's best friend." Definitions of friendship in the U.S. can range from the profound to the trivial, and yet the concept of friendship is one that many of us feel is vital to our lives. Indeed, for U.S. kids, the building of friendships may be all-important, outranking family and school during periods of social development. Whom they choose for friends—and how—greatly influences their personalities and values, and the loss of a friendship may be their first real experience of heartbreak.

How people make, maintain, and express friendships is not the same from person to person, nor from culture to culture. What may be a deep friendship in the U.S. may be shallow to someone from another culture. In this lesson, students will learn a bit about how people in Mexico, France, and Korea feel about friendships, and about how U.S. friendships appear to people from other cultures.

Friendship in Mexico

Activities

1. Seventeen-year-old Brad Kepler wrote the essay on page 120 for his English class in a U.S. high school. In it he reflects back to nine years earlier when he lived with his parents in Mexico City.

   Copy the story on page 120 and distribute it to your students. Read the story together. After you have discussed the story, assign a short essay on the topic of an experience in which the student learned the true meaning of friendship.

   After the students have written the essays, divide the class into small groups and have each group stage a read-around, in which each student reads another group member's essay. When each is finished reading, he or she passes the paper to the person on the right to read, and so on until all the papers in the group have been read. Then have each group devise a group definition of "friendship" in the following way. One student will be the recorder. The group will discuss each essay and find one major point about friendship contained in each one. The recorder will record the conclusions in a list. The list will then be the group's definition of friendship.

Have each group share its findings with the class. Point out similarities and contrasts between the groups, if there are any. In addition, you might want to see if there are any special viewpoints from members of specific ethnic groups and explore the cultural backgrounds for these perspectives. *(constructive, collaborative)*

The U.S. boy in the story had discovered one of the most valued traditions of the Mexican culture: No matter how much or little someone has, he or she is eager to share it with a friend. Material things are not as important as people themselves, and hospitality and generosity are given top priority. An exchange student from the U.S. wrote on her final exam that the most important thing she learned about Mexico during her stay there was "a sense of helping others." She had improved as a person by living and getting to know what friendships meant in that country (Heusinkveld, 1993). We learned in the previous chapter that Mexicans do not tend to break off conversations with friends simply because they have another appointment. After all, people are more important than punctuality, and they are not expected to function like clocks.

Mexican lives are filled with spontaneity. "To be without passion, in sadness and joy, is to be less than complete as a human being" says John Condon as he describes the Mexicans in *Interact: Guidelines for Mexicans and North Americans* (1980). North Americans, according to Condon, tend to be logical and practical where Mexicans are emotional. He describes Mexican friendships as deeply rooted and crammed with affection and strong feelings of closeness—ties so close, in fact, that good friends often call each other "brother" or "sister" rather than by name (Condon, 1980).

2. In light of your discussion of the story about Chucho, the group definition of friendship, and the information above, ask the students to compare friendships in Mexico and the U.S. If you have Mexican American or other Latino students in your class, have them share their points of view. *(cross-cultural, interpretive)*

Keep Your Eyes upon the Doughnut and Not upon the Hole

Twelve sugar-coated doughnuts forever changed my life one early June morning as I sat at the breakfast table in a tiny Mexico City flat. They taught me how people could get by with very little and still bring happiness to others.

My parents had moved to Mexico to do research on the culture. In order for my parents to get the real feel for the country, they chose to settle into the dead center of Mexico City. Our apartment had three bedrooms, a tiny kitchen, and a far-from-luxurious living room.

In our new neighborhood, I met a boy named Chucho, who lived across the street. Chucho came from a family of twelve: four brothers, five sisters, and two parents. They lived in an apartment that had a total of three rooms. Chucho's father was a false-teeth maker, and he made them right there in his apartment. One of the rooms was used as his laboratory.

Chucho was my only friend in Mexico City. We did everything together. We played soccer—or "football," as they called it—in the road and on the sidewalks. If it were raining and we could not play football, we would sit in his house and watch his dad make teeth. The job brought very little income to the family, but they sure did get by.

My moment of realization came that summer morning as I sat at Chucho's breakfast table. His dad had gone out and bought a dozen doughnuts for the family. The only problem was, he did not know that I would be there. Automatically, my eight years of junior etiquette training went into gear, and I excused myself with the intention of running home. But the father insisted I stay. As they began to eat, they noticed that I had no food. But there were only twelve doughnuts, and I now made thirteen at the table. Without a word from either parent, each person tore off a piece of his doughnut and handed it to me. I have never forgotten that. All I could think of at the moment was how people who spent probably a good day's pay for this treat gave me, a boy they hardly knew, their food. I have never felt so wanted in my entire life. No friend has ever treated me so kindly.

Ever since that trip, money never really mattered to me. Sure, it is not a bad thing to have. But you can learn more without it than you can with it, I believe. You can learn that a real friend shares, and in sharing a real happiness is achieved. My mom had often jokingly said to me, "Brad, keep your eyes upon the doughnut and not upon the hole." I think I know now what she meant. Keep your eyes on the really important things in life and forget about the superficial stuff that can trap you in a web of discontent. Those twelve Mexican doughnuts showed me the way.

Friendship in the United States

People from other cultures often accuse people from the U.S. of forming shallow friendships. "You Americans," many foreign-born people have said to the authors, "are very friendly, but you don't make good friends." They list several reasons for their opinions. In the U.S., they have observed, people are quick to tell you how you must get together soon, but then never follow through. And, they say, people in the U.S. tend to sugar-coat their answers when asked to give a personal opinion about a problem. This can be very confusing since, in so many other instances, people in the U.S. tend to "tell it like it is." Finally, foreigners are puzzled by the reluctance of people in the U.S. to share confidential financial information with close friends, or to lend money in time of need.

A young Belgian woman who had recently moved to the United States told us that people in the U.S. are great "telephone friends." In her eyes, we appeared to spend more time talking over the telephone with our friends than actually doing something with them. "I didn't chat a lot on the phone back home," she explained. "But I did go to the market [grocery] with my close friend each day."

Many newcomers to the U.S. comment on the tendency in the United States to change friends or make new ones rather quickly. This in part is due to the mobility of society in the U.S. People do not stay put. According to Atlas Van Lines, the average U.S. person moves 11 times during his or her lifetime. In a recent typical year, more than 43 million people—that's one out of five—changed residences. In some cultures people not only grow up and stay in the same house or neighborhood all their lives, they often leave their homes to the next generation. But in the United States, old friends often become "long-distance friends" with whom we keep in touch with holiday cards and an occasional telephone call.

Very confusing to someone from another culture is the casual use of the term *friend* in the U.S. One observer—a woman who is able to compare U.S. and French cultures first-hand, having been reared in France and now living in the U.S.—notes that the word *friend* in the U.S. is often used for "acquaintance," "buddy," "chum," "team-mate," "playmate," and "co-worker" (Carroll, 1987). (Students will think of other terms, such as "dude," "homey," or whatever the latest popular and regional slang offers.) In many European cultures, a long period of time is involved before people refer to each other as "a friend" and use first names. In France, for example, children usually do not select a friend without their parents' approval. Invitations to birthday parties are issued only to those youngsters whose mothers know each other and sanction the friendships.

While a definite reserve characterizes friendships in many European countries, attitudes sometimes vary from village to city and from country to country. The small towns and countryside in Europe may appear to be friendlier than the cities, just as in the United States. In Austrian villages, residents greet passing strangers with *Grüss Gott*

PROVERBS: FRIENDSHIP

A good friend is often better than a brother. —Yiddish

We know our friends in time of need. —Dutch

Tell me who your friends are and I'll tell you who you are. —Philippine

He's a friend that speaks well of us behind our backs. —English

There is no better mirror than an old friend. —Japanese

Correct your friend secretly and praise him publicly. —Czech

He who seeks to have many friends never has any. —Italian

True friendship is like a single soul split to fill two bodies. —Mexican

(greuss got), which literally translates as "God's greeting" but really means, "How do you do." In the cities, however, people walk by without acknowledging one another.

Outside influences are often responsible for U.S. friendships. While people in the U.S. may select their friends because of personal reasons, they usually are brought together in the first place because of some type of organizational unit: the neighborhood, school, a sport's team, church or synagogue, a hobby, or perhaps a club. Close family ties usually do not play as important a role in U.S. friendships as they do in some other cultures. Work and school, however, often act as catalysts for forming lasting relationship in the U.S. and elsewhere. In many European countries, for instance, students at the secondary school level remain together not only throughout the day but also for several years. Unlike large U.S. high schools where each person moves into a different group with each change of subject, many European students continue throughout the day and their entire secondary school career with the same group of students. These long periods of time together give students the opportunity to know each other very well and to develop deep friendships within the classroom. In U.S. high schools, however, students are more apt to make their friends outside the classroom through extra-curricular activities or social engagements.

Activities

1. Ask the students to write a paragraph about their best friend. How did the student choose that friend? Why did he or she choose that friend? Discuss some of their responses. Are there any patterns that emerge? Is it true that many in the U.S. choose their friends because of some outside influence? *(constructive, interpretive)*

2. Discuss: What do you call your friends? (List some of the terms on the board) Why do you use these terms? Do you think it is true that these terms are less personal than the word *friend,* as the French woman says? Do we use terms like these to be more casual and less intimate with our friends? Or are terms like these signs of affection? *(interpretive)*

3. Refer to the proverbs on friendship listed in the sidebar on page 121. Discuss those that intrigue your students. Can the students think of any sayings or proverbs about friendship in the U.S.? Do they know any sayings from their own ethnic backgrounds? What do these proverbs tell you about the value of friendship in particular cultures? *(cross-cultural, interpretive)*

Friendship in France

Friendships have a much deeper meaning in France than in the U.S., the French-born writer Raymonde Carroll explains. The French also tend to assume responsibilities toward their friends that those in the U.S. do not. "Let me know if there is anything I can do to help," people in the U.S. might say to each other when problems arise. But the French, Carroll says, simply step in and take action when they see a need. Rather than asking, "Would you like for me to look after the children tomorrow afternoon?" a French woman might say, "I shall take your children tomorrow, so you can rest." To a person from the U.S., the French approach may appear bossy (Carroll, 1987).

Carroll tells us that the French do not hesitate to telephone their friends time and time again to repeat their problems, a practice some in the U.S. might consider pushy or maybe a little boring. According to Carroll, people in the U.S. are more apt to give upbeat, encouraging comments when friends talk about their difficulties while the French provide very practical and detailed instructions on how to handle the dilemma. In addition to this different way of solving problems among friends, the French conversational style can result in misunderstandings when people from that culture interact with those from the United States. For instance, when talking with one another, many French often interrupt and comment before sentences are finished, not because they are insensitive or argumentative, but simply because they are sincerely interested in what is being said (Carroll, 1987). In the United States, this conversational style can appear rude.

The French attitude toward repaying kind deeds, according to Carroll, is quite different from the attitude in the U.S. about returning favors. In a letter sent to advice columnist Abigail Van Buren ("Dear Abby"), a woman expressed a common U.S. viewpoint. She wrote that she enjoyed entertaining friends for weekends at her summer cottage. Most of the friends then returned the favor by inviting her to their houses. One friend, however, had never returned an invitation, so the woman decided not to invite her to her cottage again. "Whenever I see her, she hints to be asked," wrote the woman. "What do I say? We value all our friends, but friendship should not be a one-way street." The letter was signed "Waiting to Be Asked" (*Chicago Tribune*, December 26, 1993).

Many in the U.S. want friendships to be two-way streets; they expect to be paid in kind. A dinner in a friend's home is usually returned by an invitation to dinner in the other person's home. But the French, Carroll explains, do not feel this is necessary. Perhaps one friend simply does not like to cook. She may accept many, many dinner invitations to her friend's house without ever feeling bad that she has never made dinner for her friend. She can repay the favor in another way, if she wishes, perhaps by a gift or tickets to the theater. In other words, according to Carroll's observations, the French do not keep a running tally when it comes to being kind to one's friends (Carroll, 1987).

Activities

1. Have the students keep a "friendliness log" for a day. Every time they witness or experience an act of friendliness, they should record it in the log. Who did it? How did they express it? What was the response? Discuss these logs. How do people in the U.S. express friendliness? What do your students think someone from another culture would think about us if they observed the same acts of friendliness? *(constructive, interpretive)*

2. Discuss: Are friendships in the U.S. shallow or superficial? How easy is it to lose a friend? Why do you break off a friendship? *(interpretive)*

3. Discuss: How many times have you moved? Do you keep your friends when you move? What makes it difficult to form deep friendships in the U.S.? If you have a student who has recently arrived from another culture, ask him or her to give his or her opinions on this question. *(interpretive)*

4. Relate the Dear Abby letter to the class. Ask the students to pretend they are "Dear Abby" and write a response to "Waiting to Be Asked." Read some of the responses with your class and draw some conclusions about their attitudes on this matter. How do your students feel about repaying kind deeds? Ask: If a friend bought you a pack of gum, would you do something in return? What? Compare some of their attitudes to the French attitude about returning favors.
(constructive, cross-cultural)

Korean Friendships

It often is difficult to sense the subtle cultural differences in friendships. Imagine the confusion immigrant children experience during their first days in U.S. schools. When their culture is grounded in traditions far different from those found in the U.S., frustration and hurt feelings can result as they attempt to make friends in their new school.

The authors interviewed a group of Korean American children who recently had settled in the U.S. We asked them how they felt about their new lives in the U.S. and how they were getting along and making friends with other kids in their new school. Two kids, thirteen-year-old Michelle and eleven-year-old Brian, told us they had Americanized their names shortly after arriving in the U.S. from Korea. Back in their homeland, they had been known as Eunjo Choi and Sangnan Choi, but the other kids teased them about their names, so the two Koreans changed them to Michelle and Brian.

To understand some of the problems Korean youngsters might face in the U.S., it is first necessary to understand some basic concepts found in their culture. For instance, in Korea it is extremely important to keep the *kibun* (kee-bun) in order; that is, to maintain a good mood not only within yourself but also among those with whom you are interacting. Actually, it is more than mood that is involved. Self-esteem, reputation, and saving face are all tied to kibun. Children are brought up to respect others' feelings and to do everything in their power to avoid upsetting their friends. Koreans feel that "the wise man is . . . one who can make things appear in such a way that all will feel at peace, comfortable and secure" (Crane, 1968). People in Korea avoid giving each other bad news in the morning and instead postpone it until the end of the day, the end of the week, or preferably forever (Howe, 1988). With this strong need to maintain harmony, Koreans do not simply greet each other with a casual "Hi, how's it going?" but instead ask, "Are you in peace?"

Greatly influenced by the ancient philosopher Confucius, the Koreans have a deep respect for their elders, including parents, teachers, and even school friends who are a year older than themselves. Michelle explained it this way:

We never used our teacher's name back home. We just called her "teacher." Names are hardly ever used in Korea. If we were to call an older child at school by his or her name, we could really be in trouble. Instead, we must say "older brother" or "older sister." We were really surprised to hear kids call each other by names and funny terms like "dude" here in America. Back in Korea, adults don't address others by name either, unless they know each other very, very well. Even then close friends add *ssi* (shee) to the given name. It would be like your saying "Mr. Tom" when you addressed your friend. When talking to a woman, someone would say "madam" or just "sister." It's important to know if someone is older than you, so you know exactly how to treat the person. That's why people often ask each other how old they are; something we found that American adults don't do.

The influence of Buddhism brings out the humility in the Korean people, and yet Shamanism, the beliefs linked closely to the spirit world, brings out a "no-holds-barred" attitude in the Korean personality. In his study of Korean culture, Ronald Morse has found that, just like the food, strong and robust, the people themselves can be strong and earthy. Koreans can be easily excited or upset

Did You Know?
"You must not step on even the shadow of your teacher," goes a popular Korean saying. According to old traditions, students are supposed to show great respect by walking around their teacher's shadow if cast across their pathways.

when their feelings are hurt, while resentment and anger can trigger deep emotions known as *hahn* (hahn) (Morse, 1987).

With these background notes in mind, one can begin to see some of the problems that arose for Michelle and Brian as they met U. S. kids for the first time. They were not only surprised by the casual use of names and lack of respect for elders, but also put off and even angered by many remarks made by the U. S. children when they first met. They were often taken for Chinese or Japanese by U. S. kids who either knew nothing about their homeland or who lumped all Asians into the same category. The Korean kids were extremely hurt when classmates began to tease them by calling them "Chinks," a derogatory term sometimes used in association with the Chinese, and accused them of being "dirty." Boys on the school bus teased Brian and told him he should go out with a girl, something never considered or talked about by boys his age back home. Brian, angered and frustrated, physically hit back and told the other boys not to bother him or his sister anymore. "We can protect ourselves," Brian told an adult who spoke to him about his problems. "We Koreans know Tae-kwan-do."

Michelle found it strange that children here "talked about each other" all the time and sprinkled their conversations with such expressions as "I hate her" or "I like her." She felt there was so much fighting among friends in the U.S., and yet people here always had a "best friend." It was hard, she found, to break through all these problems and to make friends with students in the U.S. "If someone from your country were to come to my school in Korea," said Michelle, "she would have friends right away. Friendships are happier in Korea, and friends we make in the elementary grades often remain our friends for life. We will do anything for our friends, and adults will give money to their friends who need it."

It is important for students to hear and understand the experiences of kids who move to the U.S. from other cultures. Their perspectives shed new light on how U.S. kids behave and treat each other. Do students quickly stereotype newcomers, or do they make an honest effort to understand the differences that exist between themselves and their new classmates? The following exercises may bring some new insights.

Activities

1. Discuss the Korean concept of *kibun*. If you have any Korean or Korean American students, ask them to help explain the concept. Do we in the U.S. have a similar concept? See if the class can go an entire day practicing *kibun*. *(cross-cultural, constructive)*

2. Discuss Michelle and Brian's experience in their U.S. school. Do kids in the U.S. treat each other and newcomers that way? If your students were in Michelle's or Brian's shoes, how would they feel? *(cross-cultural)*

3. Ask the students to share some experiences they've had when kids are mean to each other. Why do they treat each other this way? What would make them be nicer to each other? *(interpretive, constructive)*

4. Have the students write a brief essay about an experience they have had making friends with someone who is culturally different from them. Was it frustrating for any reason? Did they learn something new from their friend? *(constructive)*

5. Have the class organize an interview with a group of students or an adult who moved to the U.S. from another culture or various cultures. In the interview, the class would ask about the nature of friendships in the interviewees' native country or countries, as well as what the interviewees think about friendship in the U.S. The class will need to compose appropriate questions, organize them, select the questioners, etc. (Teams of students could work together composing questions from their group.) To make this a more extensive project, the class could videotape the interview and get involved with all aspects of production, including editing, and then show the videotape to other classes. *(cross-cultural, collaborative)*

Lesson 2

Dating, Courtship, Marriage, and Divorce

Dating in the U.S.

In the United States, individuals usually have much freedom to choose a mate, and the way they date and form lasting relationships is much more casual, by U.S. standards, than in many other cultures around the world. People in the U.S. have opportunities to meet through direct contacts—through friends, at parties, in clubs and sports, and on the job. Having met, the relationship can flower with or without the knowledge, assistance, or approval of any family member. But if they decide to make the relationship formal by a traditional marriage, the customs and ceremonies are often family-oriented, so much so that it seems as if the service, the bridal showers, and the reception are more for the relatives and friends than the bride and groom.

Since it is difficult to generalize about dating styles in the U.S., it might be more insightful simply to explore your students' cultural attitudes towards dating and romantic relationships with the following activities.

Activities

1. Discuss your students' opinions on dating. At what age should kids begin dating? Do they need their parents' permission? What roles do they think their parents or family members will play when they decide to date someone seriously? What is the purpose of a date? *(interpretive)*

2. Have each student select and interview a couple who have been together for a long time, married or otherwise. How long did they date? How did they know they were "right" for each other? Ask some of the students to report their findings to the class. Have dating styles changed over the years? *(constructive)*

3. Ask the students to write a paragraph or two describing their ideal date. What would they do? Where would they go? How would they behave? When you read their papers, note any common themes and opinions and share them with the class. These could be considered common cultural attitudes about dating styles in the U.S. *(constructive)*

SIDEBAR

PROVERBS: LOVE AND MARRIAGE

You can tell lovers from their faces.
—**African (Ovambo)**

Love is blind. —**English**

Propose marriage through your ears, not through your eyes [go by a girl's reputation not her looks]. —**Arab**

When one is passionately in love he becomes stupid.
—**Japanese**

Marriages are made in heaven. —**English**

With obstacles, love grows. —**German**

Marriages are not as they are made, but as they turn out. —**Italian**

Before you are married keep both your eyes open; after you are married shut one. —**Jamaican**

Think before you marry, for it is a knot you cannot untie. —**Portuguese**

Love comes after marriage. —**Icelandic**

4. Discuss: What is romance? Is it important? Where do students find images of romance and romantic relationships? Cut out several print advertisements from magazines that depict romance in some way and show them to the class. What do these media images teach us about U.S. ideas of romance? *(interpretive)*

5. Discuss: Would any of your students date someone from another cultural background? Why or why not? How would their families feel? *(constructive)*

What Do You Look for in a Mate?

Obviously, not everyone looks for the same thing in a life-long mate. And in other cultures, what a woman or man wants in a partner can be quite different from what people in the U.S. want. Below are some results from a study of how Japanese women rated various marriage conditions as compared with the ratings by U.S. women.

Important Conditions of a Successful Marriage, How Japanese and U.S. Women Ranked Them:

Conditions for a Successful Marriage	Rank given by Japanese Women	U.S. Women
Being able to talk together about feelings	1 (73%)	3 (84%)
Being in love	2 (68%)	1 (87%)
Financial security	3 (66%)	10 (63%)
Having husband understand what I do every day	4 (59%)	8 (67%)
Having children	5 (52%)	11 (48%)
Having similar ideas on how to raise children (tied)	5 (52%)	6 (73%)
Husband being faithful	6 (46%)	2 (85%)
Both being able to see the humorous side of things	7 (38%)	5 (76%)
Having similar ideas on how to handle money	8 (34%)	7 (71%)
Liking the same kind of life, activities and friends	9 (31%)	9 (64%)
Keeping romance alive	10 (29%)	4 (78%)
Having similar backgrounds	11 (19%)	12 (34%)

*The numbers in parentheses show what percentage of women responded that this condition was important for marriage. The percentages indicate that there were big differences in how the women felt about each condition. Even though both Japanese and U.S. women ranked "Liking the same kind of life, activities, and friends" as #9, for example, only 31% of the Japanese women surveyed thought that this condition was important while 64% of the U.S. women thought it was important (adapted from Iwao, 1993).

According to this survey, the Japanese women placed more emphasis on the practical aspects of being married than the U.S. women did. The goals the Japanese ranked highly are probably the things that a Japanese family would consider important when their sons and daughters choose a bride or groom. The U.S. women, on the other hand, tend to be more interested in the romantic aspects of marriage.

Activities

1. Copy the chart for your students, and study it together. Have the class conduct the same survey among themselves, with the same categories. How would your students rank the conditions for themselves? It might be interesting to compare the boys' responses to the girls'. *(constructive, interpretive)*

2. Why do people get married in the U.S.? Discuss the differences between the Japanese and U.S. attitudes about marriage goals. *(constructive, cross-cultural)*

3. Ask the students to write a paragraph or two on these questions: What kind of person do you eventually want to spend your life with? Describe him or her. Why? *(constructive)*

Arranged Marriages: The Role of Family in Courtship and Marriage

In most Asian and Middle Eastern cultures, the family often plays a very important role when young people date and choose a lifelong partner. Sometimes, it is as simple as having an aunt or uncle say she or he knows the perfect partner for the niece or nephew. Sometimes, the family chooses the mate for the young person and he or she obeys the family's wishes. At other times, the family uses a third person to help select the mate. The last two are examples of "arranged marriages."

After the family has chosen the mate, their role does not end there. Then there are the events that lead up to the marriage, and the family is in charge every step of the way. In the Arab world, they need to set up the "dowry." A dowry consists of gifts, material items, and money that the groom and his family promise to give the bride before they marry or if the husband divorces the wife or dies before she does. Then they need to meet with the family of the bride- or groom-to-be, fill out and sign the marriage contract, decide where and with whom the new couple will live, and plan the festivities on the wedding day.

Traditional courtship and marriage customs, like other aspects of everyday life, are quietly changing in most cultures as time goes by. In the U.S. today, more and more couples are dropping the standard "I dos" and writing their own vows, in part to express their independence from traditional ways. In 1950, China passed a Marriage Law that says that family cannot interfere in the selection of a bride or groom. Many cultures have adopted customs from other cultures in the courtship and marriage process. Indeed, using a foreign custom can add a note of prestige to the festivities. A Japanese bride, for instance, may wear a traditional *kimono* for one part of the wedding events, and then put on a white satin dress, as Western brides do, for another occasion. The halls for the reception may be decorated in different styles, from a traditional East Asian theme to a "wild, wild West" motif.

Nevertheless, tradition is still quite important in many cultures. Some feel that if the family is involved in the courtship and marriage, the married couple will have a stronger and more lasting marriage with less chance of divorce.

Courtship and Marriage in Viet Nam

The selection of a spouse in Viet Nam is an important event, and the family is involved throughout the process. If the parents do not actually select the mate for their son or daughter, at least they must approve of her or him. U.S.-style dating is not considered proper. The groom may not even see his bride until the *coi mat* (koy maht), the meeting of the two involved families. A third person, or intermediary, is used to approach the girl's family on behalf of the boy's parents. Then an astrologer is consulted to see if the stars indicate that the marriage is meant to be (Muzny, 1989).

After the preliminary steps, the parents get together at the residence of the girl and thereafter meet frequently to clear up any questions about the marriage. Finally, the formal engagement party is scheduled at the girl's home, again with the blessing of the astrologer. Leading a procession, the groom walks (or more likely drives, today) to the bride's house bearing gifts for her. The first thing the groom does upon entering the bride's house is to bow or pray at the household shrine to the family's ancestors to show his respect. On the wedding day, another procession of the groom's family and friends goes to the bride's home. Wearing a ceremonial blue robe, the groom presents the red wedding dress to the bride, which she wears during the rest of the ceremony (Muzny, 1989).

Arab Courtship and Marriage

For Muslims in the Arab world, families are actively involved in courtship and marriage. Both families work to choose a spouse who most closely matches the personality and status of the bride and groom. In Egypt, there are even TV shows in which people dramatize the advantages and disadvantages of marrying someone richer, poorer, older, younger, and so on. After the family selects the potential bride and groom, an elaborate engagement reception, *i'lan al-khitbah* (i-lahn ahl-hit-bah), which means "publicizing the proposal," is held in the bride's home (Rugh, 1984).

Then the bride and groom write and sign a wedding contract, which is more strict and binding than an engagement in Western cultures; there must be official witnesses from the Muslim religious court who give their approval. The contract explains what the *mahr* (mah), or dowry, will be. Under Muslim law, a marriage without a dowry is illegal. The financial security of the woman is paramount in these arrangements. Usually, the dowry is paid in money, even though the bride's family may spend it on a trousseau (clothes and accessories for the wedding), jewelry, furniture, or land. One type of dowry is given to the bride and her father when the contract is signed. Another kind of dowry is an amount of money, land, or other material items that would be paid to the bride and her family only if the husband divorces the wife or dies and leaves her a widow. If the dowry promised is small, this usually means that the bride's family can take for granted that the groom will behave honorably and generously towards his wife (Prothro, 1974).

The wedding ceremony is an occasion for much celebration. The rite itself is simple and straightforward and takes place in the home of the bride. The bride and groom clasp right hands and express their consent to marry in front of an authorized *sheikh* (shake) and at least two witnesses. Selections from the Quran, the Muslim holy book, are recited. The bride then formally leaves her father's house accompanied by her groom and a group of relatives from both families.

Families often go into debt in order to pay for a wedding reception that reflects their status in society. One of the authors had the opportunity to attend a reception while living in Cairo:

> A great commotion in the usually peaceful lobby of the Cairo Hilton hotel in Egypt attracted my attention. Trumpets blared, cymbals clanged, and a belly dancer displayed her artistry at the head of a long procession winding among the lobby furniture and up the stairs to the immense main ballroom. Curious about the reason for the parade through the lobby, I spoke to one of the members of the procession. I was astounded to learn that the column of musicians and guests, with the women dressed up in high-fashion gowns and jewels and the men in fancy tuxedos, were escorting a new bride and groom to their wedding reception. The person with whom I spoke was a member of the bride's family. Reflecting typical Arab hospitality, she invited me to join the festivi-

ties. I witnessed a spectacular display of pageantry from a front-row seat at the family's table. The married couple was radiant, even though they may have been married officially days or weeks earlier, as I learned later. The most popular hotels in which to hold receptions are booked far in advance, so couples often have to hold the event many days, even weeks, after the day of the wedding.

The couple sat on a raised platform, much like royalty, and the guests came one by one to extend best wishes. Two orchestras alternated between playing Western and Middle Eastern pieces, and a famous radio and TV personality performed, as did several more belly dancers. A gigantic buffet provided mounds of all varieties of delicious meats, seafood, fruits, and pastries highlighted by decorative ice sculptures. When the couple cut the first piece of the many-tiered wedding cake, sparklers flashed their glittering white lights in the darkened ballroom and clouds of white fog rolled across the ceiling.

While this was a function of an obviously wealthy, upper-class Egyptian family, the lavish attention given to the most minor detail shows how significant courtship and marriage are as great events in Egyptian and many Middle Eastern societies. The reception was the result of an all-out effort by both families. The stars of the show were not only the newly married couple, but also the many relatives who played their roles, beginning with the selection of the spouse and ending when the last guest left the ballroom.

Activities

1. Discuss: What do your students think about arranged marriages? What are the advantages and disadvantages? Are there any students in your class whose parents will arrange their marriages? If so, ask them to explain the reasons for this custom. *(interpretive)*

2. Discuss: What do Muslim marriage customs say about the roles of men and women in Muslim cultures? What purpose does a dowry serve? *(interpretive)*

3. Discuss: Compare weddings in Viet Nam, the Arab world, and the U.S. What kinds of weddings do we have in the U.S.? Have the students describe any weddings they have attended. What is the difference between a Catholic wedding, a Jewish wedding, a civil wedding, etc.? *(cross-cultural, interpretive)*

Divorce in the Arab World

It is ironic that in many of the cultures where courtship and marriage are complex affairs and the family is involved every step of the way, the process for divorce is much simpler and more personal, a matter between the husband and the wife only. For example, while the Muslim courtship and wedding, as described above, is a family observance that may cover months from beginning to end, the divorce can be accomplished in minutes by a simple statement of the husband.

Before much of the Arab world adopted the Islamic religion, divorce was common. The husband simply pronounced a few words that dismissed his wife and then paid a fee to the wife's father or guardian. The Quran allowed for the concept of divorce, but it placed some guidelines and restrictions designed to make the procedure more fair, especially for women. A Muslim marriage can be ended in

SIDEBAR

**Proverbs:
Wives and Husbands**

Choose a wife to please yourself, not others.
—**Rumanian**

He who does not honor his wife does not honor himself. —**Spanish**

If the husband is the head, the wife is the crown upon it. —**Slovakian**

Husband and wife are like one flesh. —**Yiddish**

A good husband makes a good wife. —**English**

A good wife makes a good husband. —**English**

The husband is the head, the wife is the neck; she can turn him whichever way she wants. —**Russian**

A man without a wife is a man without thoughts.
—**Finnish**

A wife is a household treasure. —**Japanese**

When you have five wives, you have five tongues.
—**African (Ashanti)**

three ways. In the first form of divorce, called the *talaq* (tahl-ack), the husband may pronounce the divorce formula—equivalent to "I divorce you"—to his wife and have his action recorded by the religious court. The divorce terms of the marriage contract then go into effect and, if the husband hasn't done so already, he must pay the dowry. In the second form of divorce, called *mukhala'at* (mook-hah-aht), the husband and wife agree equally to the divorce, and she gives up all or part of her dowry payment—presumably to encourage the husband to divorce her—and the agreement is also recorded in the court. The third way, *tafreeq* (tah-freek), is a kind of separation equivalent to divorce; under this agreement, the husband and wife can remarry someone else.

If a husband pronounces divorce in the traditional fashion, the *talaq,* he has three months to reverse his decision. Within those three months, if the husband changes his mind and/or if his wife is pregnant, the husband can take her back—with or without her agreement—but they must sign a new marriage contract. During this three-month period, he is responsible for taking care of her. If he chooses not to take her back, the divorce becomes final. He can do this two times; the third time is truly final. To make the divorce final from the beginning, the husband pronounces the statement of divorce three times before witnesses. A man can marry immediately after divorce, but a woman must wait approximately three months. It is quite common for divorced Muslims to marry someone else sooner or later. If a woman does not marry, she most likely will be taken care of by her family.

Activities

1. Discuss: What do the Muslim divorce customs tell you about the status of men and women in Muslim cultures? *(interpretive)*

2. Discuss: Why do people in the U.S. get divorced? (List the reasons on the board.) Why should a married couple get divorced? When should a married couple not divorce? What can they do to avoid divorce and make their marriages work? *(constructive)*

Intercultural Marriage

The ways people date, get engaged, marry, and divorce vary all over the world. The differences can present a stumbling block for those trying to understand another culture, and especially for those who date or marry people from other cultures. Imagine the frustrations that might result between members of two very different cultures who want to marry—or to divorce. Intercultural marriage

is quite common in the U.S. Indeed many people in the United States are products of intercultural marriages, even though their parents may not have followed the marriage customs of their cultural heritage. The following activity concludes this lesson with an exploration of the marriage patterns of your students' own families or acquaintances.

Activity

Have each student (or pairs of students) find a married couple who does not share the same cultural background and interview them. Did the couple experience any problems because of their cultural differences? How did they solve some of these problems?

Ask the students to share and discuss their findings with the class.

Other students may prepare a report on their intercultural parents or family members.

Discuss: What are the problems and blessings of an intercultural marriage? *(constructive)*

Lesson 3

Family I

There are many different kinds of families in the U.S. It is quite difficult to point to one or another and call it "typical," and the same goes for cultures around the world. Moreover, people express their family ties in different ways, here and in other cultures. What some of us may consider a "normal" expression of affection for one's family members—a hug, a kiss on the cheek—can appear overly mushy and sentimental to others. In turn, what some cultures would call a "normal" family relationship might appear cold and stiff to us.

For example, a woman from the U.S. married a Japanese man and traveled with her new husband to his homeland to meet his mother and father. The husband had not been home for several years and was looking forward to seeing his parents. But much to the wife's amazement, he did not give them a kiss or even a hug when he greeted them; he instead simply bowed, as did they. The U.S. woman's first impression was that Japanese family members were cold and unloving toward each other.

Yet as she got to know his family and the Japanese culture better, she realized that her husband was showing deep respect and affection by bowing to his parents. It is when the Japanese are much younger that parents and children show their affection for each other in more physical ways. Japanese mothers are often physically closer to their children than are women in the West. Youngsters are not placed in playpens but are allowed to crawl and toddle at their mothers' feet. Babies are strapped to mothers' backs instead of placed in strollers for trips into the outside world, and at night the parents and young children sleep together on their floor mats, rather than in separate rooms. The U.S. woman had to take a much closer look at Japanese culture to understand and appreciate a different cultural way of expressing affection and respect for one's family.

Activity

Ask each student to write a paragraph or two describing the "typical" U.S. family. It might be fun to have them draw pictures of this family. Read some of the responses to the class and show the corresponding drawings. Compare and contrast them.

Discuss: How many students can say that theirs is a "typical" family? Is there really such a thing as a "typical" family? What other kinds of families are there in the U.S.? *(constructive, interpretive)*

The Family: The Arab World

Activity

The text on page 131 is excerpted from a tape made by a Syrian youth for his parents who were on a visit to the United States where two older brothers were studying. The message is typical of one a boy from that part of the world might send to his parents whom he misses.

Copy the letter for your students and read it with your class. Make three columns on the board: "Father," "Mother," and "Brothers." Discuss the letter, marking characteristics of the son's feelings for and behavior towards each family member under the appropriate column. See if your students can draw some conclusions about the character of these relationships in Arab families. *(interpretive, cross-cultural)*

Did You Know?

The only area of the world in which polygamy is actively practiced is found in sub-Saharan Africa. Having many wives is a sign of prestige for a man, and having numerous children means many helping hands. That area of the world also has the highest birth rate to be found anywhere, 6.3 children per woman (Bledsoe, 1990).

Hello father, hello mother . . . how is your health? How are my brothers, Samir and Walid? . . . I can imagine how they met you at the airport. I am sure they were over-whelmed with joy at seeing you.

I hope you will keep in contact and if you plan to stay longer I wish you would write often and send us your pictures. I miss you very, very much. I miss seeing my father. I miss seeing you coming home smiling. . . . I don't know what to tell you, my father. I want you to rest assured. I remain an ideal model for the whole village. Don't worry at all. . . . My time is totally devoted to the fields. I am taking good care of it. Don't worry. . . . I'm working more than if you were here. . . .

Now mother, it's your turn, my mother. I don't know what to say to you. First, your hands and feet I kiss . . . I always, always miss you. I miss the times when I say, "Mother, give me my allowance," when I embrace you, I kiss you, I cause you trouble and suffering. . . . My mother, I don't know my feelings toward you. When I say, "my mother," tears burn in my eyes. . . .

Now I come to my eldest brother, Walid. How are you my brother? How are you, my eyes, my soul, the one we are proud of wherever we go? We raise our head [notice he does not say "heads," because the family is one head] among people. You are a model for everybody. May God protect you from the eyes [evil eyes] of people. I'm sure you are very happy with my parents. . . .

Now you, the love of my heart, you, Samir. You, my brother. There is nothing more beautiful than the word "brother." May you finish your studies and come back, and I can call again to my brother. Samir, I don't know what to say. By God, by God, I miss you very, very, very, much, my brother. . . . Please, tell me your feelings when your parents arrived at the airport, please. I miss my parents very much.

My grandfather misses you very much. He cried a lot after you left and sobbed, "Would my son come back before I die?"

Hello, father. How are you, father? There is one thing I forgot to tell you. I have sprayed the apple trees. . . . Do not forget to bring back the camera and film. And you, mother, don't forget to get me what I asked for. Whether you bring it or not, I am always grateful to you. My mother, my mother. My God, I'm right now sitting in the room by myself and recording on the bed. I don't know, mother, my mother, how much I miss you. . . . I hope you return safely. I don't know how, when I pronounce the word "mother," my heart inside contracts. . . .

I conclude, my father, my mother, and my brothers, by kissing your hands, father, and asking for your blessing. The son realizes all his dreams if he has the blessings of his parents. My mother, my eyes, my soul, you are my heart, you my mother. My mother, when I say the word "mother" it rises from deep inside me. My mother, please don't cry when you hear this tape. Please don't cry; don't worry. My brothers, my father, my eyes, I will conclude by asking for your blessings and particularly the blessings of my father. Father, you can't imagine how happy I am for you. I'm happy for you, you cannot imagine how. . . . My mother, I asked you to bring me some underwear, to put it frankly. I like American underwear. My brother, don't forget the camera and the bottle of perfume. My brother, when I say the word "brother" I almost collapse. You are two, but I am alone. I'm alone in the world. I'm alone in the world. But God is generous, I hope to be with you. I conclude by kissing your hands and feet, my father, and you, my mother, I kiss your hands and feet. I ask for your blessing. With your blessings, my father, I can face anything. My brother Walid, I kiss you, I kiss your cheeks. You Samir, how I miss your smile and your eyes. With regards. . . .

Source: Halim Barakat, "The Arab Family and the Challenge of Social Transformation," in *Women and the Family in the Middle East,* edited by Elizabeth Warnock Fernea. (Austin: University of Texas Press, 1985.) Used by permission.

This letter illustrates "many aspects of Arab family life, including its interdependence, sentimentality, commitment, and self-denial" (Barakat, 1985). The family has been the center of existence throughout the Arab world for centuries, and it has always provided for the needs of its members. An Arab can count on his or her family for financial security, a place to be cared for when one is out of work, sick, and retired. Only in very recent years have retirement homes and orphanages come into being in the Arab world, and they are very, very rare even today. The family takes care of each and every member, however distant a relative.

With these things in mind, it is interesting to consider how an Arab might view family relationships in the U.S. Would he or she think that many in the U.S. are cold and unfeeling toward each other? The following could be a typical letter from an eight-year-old, middle-class U.S. girl, writing from summer camp to her parents back home. It provides a stark contrast to the letter from the Arab boy to his parents.

Hi Mom and Dad,

Our team won the baseball playoffs, so we are going to get a trophy. We really have a good pitcher. I'm learning to swim and made it all the way to the end of the pool yesterday. The food stinks! Could you send me some cookies? Visitors' day is next week. See you then.

Love,
Janie

P.S. I sure could use some extra money. There are all kinds of things I'd like to buy in the camp store.

Activity

Ask the students to pretend they are visiting a relative or attending camp for a month during the summer, and have them write a letter home to their family.

Then have them write the letter as an Arab kid might write it. (If you have Arab or Arab American students in your class, turn the exercise around so that they imitate a letter-writing style of what they consider a typical U.S. kid. Perhaps there may not be a huge difference. Explore this.)

Choose a sample of these pairs of letters to discuss with the class. Have them make comparisons and contrasts. What can they conclude about the various ways children express their ties to their families in the U.S.?

Did You Know?

When women take more than one husband, it is known as *polyandry*. This type of relationship can be found within two different groups in two pocket areas of India. The first group, known as the Todas, live in the Nilgiri Hills in the south of the subcontinent, and the second, called the Jaunsar-Bawar, can be found in the Himalayas to the north. Sometimes several brothers will share one wife. A primary reason for this arrangement is economic. One man does not have the means to support a wife, and so the financial responsibilities are divided among the different husbands. This practice, however, is dying out in India (Chatterjee, 1983).

What do they think an Arab kid would say about this? (If you have Arab students, what *do* they say?) (*cross-cultural, constructive*)

The Extended Family: The Arab World and Africa

Many Arabs live in extended families. An extended family includes the father, mother, children, grandparents, husbands, and wives of the family members and often aunts, uncles, and cousins. These extended families usually live together in the same home or a group of nearby homes. In the traditional Arab family, father is considered the head of the family, the "patriarch." He is distant from the children, particularly during their younger years, while mother is the one to whom the children come with their problems. Prior to Islam's emergence on the Arabian peninsula in the seventh century, men in the Arab world could have many wives. Now a husband, by Islamic traditions, is allowed to have four wives, but each must be treated equally. By limiting the number to four and making sure each one is as important to the family as the others, the status of women improved in Arab society. However, polygamy—the system that allows a husband to have more than one wife—is very rarely practiced today in the Arab world.

In the extended family arrangement, married sons, their wives, and their children, as well as unwed daughters, live together or at least close by. What is one family member's success or failure is everyone's success or failure. The family shares in each other's glory and shame. If a son or daughter loses temporary favor with the family,

SIDEBAR

PROVERBS:
FAMILY

A family divided against itself will perish. —Indian (Tamil)

Family quarrels sow the seeds of poverty. —Japanese

As the family is, so is the offspring. —Russian

Whoever is ashamed of his family will have no luck.
—Yiddish

Large families bring poverty. —Greek

If the family lives in harmony, all affairs will prosper.
—Chinese

---

e or she still cannot be disinherited because the head of e household may not leave more than one-third of his tate to anyone outside the family circle. However, the mily's honor rests on each and every member. A girl, pecially, must maintain her honor, and even a hint of andal, which could be brought about by being seen holdg hands with a boyfriend, could bring dishonor to the tire family.

The sense of family penetrates Arab society, includg the workplace. While the U.S. discourages nepotism e practice of hiring one's relatives to work at one's mpany), an Arab will consider it perfectly logical and tural to look after members of his family by giving them bs. Moreover, teachers, political leaders, and employers e thought of as "fathers" while their students, citizens, d workers are held in a parent-child relationship. Even college, professors talk of their students as "my chilen." "Arab society, then, is the family generalized or larged, and the family is society in miniature," says arakat (1985).

The ways families live and fit together in the many untries of the Middle East, as well as the amount of eedom certain members, especially women, have, pends on many different things: how the local commuty practices the Islamic religion; how much wealth and lucation the family members have; how much the couny has modernized; and whether or not the country has er been occupied by a Western power. The above scriptions of family life pertain to very traditional Arab

societies. Saudi Arabia, for example, is one of the most traditional cultures in the Middle East, and this is due in large part to a very conservative branch of the Islamic faith known as Wahabism. Saudi Arabia also has the distinction of being the only Arab country never to have been occupied by a Western power; it therefore escaped being influenced by many of the laws, regulations, and cultural customs of Western society.

The extended family is also found among African tribes. In many traditional African societies, children do not really "belong" to their parents, as they do in Western societies. Instead, they are members of either their mother's or their father's family. If they are considered part of the mother's kin, the society is known as *matrilineal.* But if the relationship is on the father's side, it is known as *patrilineal.* Children may call all their mom's sisters and friends, "mother," or all their dad's brothers and friends, "father." People are not so concerned about the actual biological parents but instead about the roles people actually play, and many people in the community may act as parents toward the youngsters.

These extended family members are always around to lend a hand when needed. An African living temporarily in the U.S. expressed her sadness at not having her family close by: "Every day my nieces, nephews, and other family members filled my home. I was never alone. I find it very lonely here in the U.S. where large groups of family members are only present for special occasions." In Africa people do not worry about who will take care of them when they are ill, or what will happen when they are too old to live alone. The family is always there to provide any assistance that might be needed.

Family and friends are not "invited" to each other's home. They simply go. No one is surprised to find one or two "guests" on the doorstep at dinner time. But there is always an abundance of food, for contrary to the U.S. practice of preparing enough food for those who will be present for the meal, Africans cook in large quantities for unexpected guests. A certain portion of the prepared foods are always held back, just in case someone were to appear during the meal. If no one shows up, the children are probably allowed to eat the left-over food a little later.

Many changes are coming to the traditional African family. Schooling, industrialization, conversion to Christianity, and new laws are encouraging a sense of individualism. This does not result in nuclear families like those found in Western cultures. Instead, single-parent families are emerging that have close ties to either a mother or a father (Priso, 1989).

Activities

1. Discuss: Why do we form and live in families? What purpose does a family serve? Why do parents have children? *(interpretive)*

2. Make three columns on the board: "Mother," "Father," and "Kids." Under each column, list characteristics that your students suggest that describe the role each member plays in the family unit. In other words, what is a mother's responsibility in the family? What do kids contribute to a family? And so on. If you receive a large variety of responses, that only underscores the fact that there is no such thing as a "typical" family. Those characteristics upon which many students agree reflect some common cultural attitudes about family in the U.S., or at least in your community. *(constructive)*

3. Discuss: What is an extended family? Do any of your students live in extended families? What are the benefits to living in an extended family? Discuss the roles of friends and relations in an African family. Do the students have a close family member or family friend who assumes the role of "mother" or "father"? How do they feel about this? Is it resented, or do they find it helpful? Would they like to have such a relationship with another adult? *(interpretive)*

4. Is the sense of family as important in the U.S. as it is in the Arab world and Africa? Can your students think of examples in which family is more important than, or not as important as, say, nation, city, church, etc.? For instance, what if your sister were dealing drugs or planning to assassinate the president? Would you turn her in to the police? Can the students invent other ethical dilemmas that would force them to choose between family ties and other loyalties?
(interpretive, constructive)

The Rural, Lower-Class Family in Egypt

In many societies, a family's economic level has a large influence on how it fits together, how it lives, and how much freedom of movement its members have. In Egypt (as in many other countries, including the U.S.) more wealth often means more education, which in turn often means more opportunities for international travel and highly skilled careers, especially for women. Let's take a quick look at the way a rural, lower-class family might live in Egypt.

Did You Know?

In a recent survey of twelve European countries, it was discovered that nearly half the married women are employed. Yet even when women are working outside the home, they do far more of the household chores and child-rearing than the men do. In France and England, for example, a working woman does three times more housework than the husband does.

One of the biggest changes that has come to family life in Europe since the mid-1900s has been the increase in single-parent families. The children usually live with the mother. This is true of 90 percent of single-parent families in France and 93 percent in Denmark (Michel, 1989).

For many lower-class, rural Egyptian families, the fathers have been forced to seek a source of income away from the land that they had always farmed. Egypt provides very little land for farming; what is available lies in narrow strips along the Nile River and through the delta that fans out near that river's mouth along the Mediterranean Sea. Yet with the country's population explosion, there simply is not enough land to go around. Cairo, Egypt's large capital city, has become one of the most popular destinations for these uprooted people, and here they settle into those sections of the city where many, many people live close together. These families often bring with them chickens and goats and a way of life common to the rural village where nearly everyone knew each other or was related. They may leave some relatives behind in the village, but they try to keep close contact with them by visiting often and sometimes arranging marriages between their own children and cousins or close friends back in the village.

Not all rural families look for new opportunities in the big cities. Some of the men head to the oil fields of neighboring Arab countries to seek their fortunes. They send their money back to wives who stay behind with the children. With their husbands gone, the wives assume new roles as the heads of their families.

For those who move to the city, the neighborhood is very important to the family's life. Men will gather in the local coffeehouses to play dominoes and gossip with their friends while the women gather on the apartment rooftops

or sit on buildings' stoops to talk with their neighbors. "Who is your family?" people will ask of those who have just arrived from the village, because knowing the family name usually establishes the newcomer's reputation, which is far more important than his wealth. The neighborhood streets are busy with stalls and shops on the lower floors of the apartment buildings. Young girls scurry along on family errands, and boys gather for street games (Rugh, 1984). It is a busy, loud, and colorful scene.

In the early morning hours as the neighborhood comes to life, men shout greetings from their windows to passersby: *"Sabah el khair"* (sah-bah el ka-heer, "Morning of brightness") or perhaps *"Sabah in nur"* (sah-bah in nur, "Morning of the thick cream that rises to the top of the milk") (Rugh, 1984). There is a sense of sharing in the neighborhood, much as there was back in the village. Women rush to help neighbors in crisis or use the apartment building's common oven. If the family is lucky, they will have a water faucet, but sometimes they must run down the street to a common tap. Throughout all class levels there is an overall concern for the females of the family, but in these neighborhoods it often means that young women, heading to their jobs, are accompanied to the bus stop by a male member of the family (Rugh, 1984).

While emphasis traditionally is on the male side of the family, once people move to the city this, out of necessity, changes. The father's side of the family may not be around, but mother's side is. With a longing to be close to relatives, mother's family is substituted for father's. Even when jobs provide an income that allows individuals to move to better housing and neighborhoods, many choose to stay where they are in order to be close to family.

Arab Women in the Workplace

In many countries throughout the Middle East and the Arab world, family life is changing, and one of the basic changes comes as women leave their protected lives at home for jobs in the outside world. Sometimes the women find more equality with men in the workplace than women in the U.S. do. In the Arabian peninsula country of Oman, for example, women receive the same pay and job opportunities as men. They are permitted to join the military, the police force, and government services. These women also have a special perk rarely found in the U.S. For six months following the birth of a baby, a woman in Oman is allowed an hour off each morning to go home to feed the infant. These conditions are especially surprising in light of the fact that before 1970 no girls and very few boys attended school and that a university did not even exist in the nation until the late 1980s. In Oman changes have been dramatic.

The upper-middle-class women in Egypt have more opportunities to attend college, pursue professional careers, and travel to other cultures than women in the lower classes. Although highly educated, successful in their careers, and well traveled, many of these women lead independent lives outside their homes but still submit to their husbands' wishes inside. Many Egyptian women who are educated in other languages accept jobs with international corporations based in Cairo. Sometimes these well-educated women go into businesses with their husbands or open small shops of their own. The fields of journalism and aviation, as well as other professions are also open to qualified women.

Activities

1. Discuss: Why would a family's economic level, or amount of money they have, influence how they live and fit together? (For example, if both father and mother work to earn money, kids have less time with their parents, etc.) What else influences how a family lives? (For example, level of education of parents, the kinds of jobs parents have, single-parent families, etc.) List students' suggestions on the board. (*interpretive*)

2. Have the students write a paragraph or two on this question: If your family won millions of dollars in the lottery, how would your family live? *(constructive)*

3. Discuss: What careers are open to women in the U.S.? Are there any limits to what women can do or achieve? What are they? What does a woman need to be successful? *(interpretive)*

SIDEBAR

Under Confucian principles, a patriarchal society (one in which men were the heads of the family and women were obedient to all males) existed in East Asia. It was said that a woman had three masters in her lifetime: first her father, then her husband, and in old age her son. But before Confucianism fanned across the area, women played important roles in East Asian societies. In Korea, for example, newlyweds often went home to live with the wife's family, and both sons and daughters were allowed to share equally in inheritances. Many of the same attitudes prevailed in Japan where a woman warrior once led her troops into battle, and the people traced the ancestry of their emperor back to a sun goddess, Amaterasu, rather than to a male god. Women were thought to have supernatural powers in the early days of Japanese history, and until the fourteenth century the country lived as a matriarchal society—one in which women had power in families and society (Iwao, 1993).

Lesson 4

Family II

The Family: East Asia

Great emphasis is placed on the family in East Asia, just as it is half way around the world in the Middle East—but with a difference. While the Islamic religion has a strong influence on family life in many Arab countries, in East Asia the roots are firmly planted not in a religion, but in a philosophy—Confucianism. This philosophy was developed about five hundred years before Christ through the teachings of an educator named K'ung-fu-tzu, whose name was Latinized to "Confucius." He, along with many of his disciples, some of whom were not around until nearly two hundred years later, left an indelible mark on family relationships throughout East Asia, a mark that is still visible today.

Long before Confucius, the Chinese grounded their social and economic values within the family, and that ancient philosopher reinforced these values. Confucianism began in China and spread over the centuries to other East Asian countries. Confucius said there were five basic relationships in life on which society was to build: those between father/teacher and son, ruler and subject, husband and wife, older brother and younger brother, and friend and friend. Three of the five relationships focused on the family, and devotion and dedication of children to parents was the key to a good and serene life. The concept of family was so important to East Asian societies—and still is—that many East Asians place more emphasis on family than on God or their country.

Moreover, the relationships that Confucius said were basic to life were also meant to indicate how those relationships should be lived. In each pair, the second person had to give respect to the first person. In other words, the son must honor the father/teacher, the subject must bow to the ruler, the wife must submit to the husband, and the younger brother must pay respect to the older brother. This system of honor contributed to the great sense of hierarchy in many East Asian societies today.

It is important to keep in mind that while Confucianism has had a strong influence on family life and the roles of women and men in East Asian cultures, other forces helped to shape family life differently in each country.

Did You Know?

Traditionally, the ideals of family life in East Asia included the following: separating boys and girls at an early age; holding back one's emotions; worshipping or at least great respect for one's ancestors; and living with one's extended family. But the ideal plan was not always the actual plan. Just as in the U.S., where there is a tendency to believe that the past was simpler and more ideal than the present, so it is with traditionalists of East Asia. Having several generations of one's family live under one roof was not always the case in China, and never the common practice in Korea and Japan (Martin, 1990).

Did You Know?

Beauty, not intelligence or education, was previously considered the most important attribute a Chinese woman could have. Only the man was expected to be educated, and it was said that "a lack of culture is a virtue in women." Even into the early part of the twentieth century, tiny feet were considered a form of feminine beauty. In order to keep the feet small, they were bound with string to prevent them from growing and to shape them into "crescent moons."

In China the language itself helped to reinforce the concept of family relationships. Because of the importance placed on precise positions within society and the family, the Chinese language developed with exact terms for family titles. Relatives even today are not simply "aunt" or "uncle," "brother," or "sister" but *Jiu Jiu* (joh joh, maternal uncle), *Shu Shu* (soo soo, father's younger brother), *"Sheng Sheng"* (sheng sheng, wife of a father's younger brother), *Jie Jie* (jay jay, elder sister), and *Di Di* (dee dee, younger brother) (Qi, 1989). Respect and obedience are given to those above oneself. With large families and great age spans, uncles might be younger than nephews, and nieces older than aunts, but it makes no difference. Everyone always submits to those of a higher rank within the family, regardless of age.

Confucianism still has an influence on family relationships in East Asia, but East Asians rarely think about it. Changes have been dramatic throughout that part of the world, not the least of which was the end of the practice of feet-binding at the beginning of the twentieth century. A completely different way of thinking about women and family life began to creep into East Asian societies before World War II, but really took root following that war, only to blossom in full strength at the end of the twentieth century. While some might say East Asian societies have "Westernized," becoming more like U.S. and European cultures, it would be more accurate to say they have *modernized,* for the influence of ancient East Asian culture and tradition persists to this day.

Activities

1. Discuss: By what names or titles do you call members of your family? Are they different from the ones used by your parents or grandparents when they were children? Have we become more formal or informal, creative or traditional, in our ways of addressing family members from a generation ago? How do you think someone from East Asia might think about your way of addressing family members? *(interpretive, cross-cultural)*

2. Discuss: Confucianism plays a subtle but important role in family relationships in East Asia, and the Islamic religion serves the same role in the Middle East. What force, if any, do you think greatly influences family life in the United States? How? *(interpretive)*

3. Discuss: Not too long ago in China, women's feet were bound because having tiny feet was a sign of great beauty. What do we in the U.S. think is beautiful about a woman or man today? Have our definitions of beauty changed since a generation or two ago? Think of old movies shown on television and what was considered a beautiful woman or a handsome man in them. Consider the hair, clothes, makeup. What do you think your children will say is strange about what we think is beautiful today? What do you think someone newly arrived in this country might think is strange about our definition of beauty? *(interpretive, cross-cultural)*

Women's Roles in East Asia

There are many similarities among family lifestyles in today's East Asian cultures, and one is the woman's role as head of the household finances. In Korea, nine out of ten men give their paychecks completely and directly to their wives. The wife is even responsible for buying the house (Kim, 1990). The Japanese wife also controls how the money is spent in the family; she is the one who gives her husband an allowance, and it is she who will decide on such major purchases as a new refrigerator. Chinese women share in their family's financial responsibilities. Allowing the women to handle the money, some scholars have suggested, is due to the fact that traditional Chinese society looked down on anything having to do with money. Financial matters were left to the lower classes, the merchants, while the upper classes, scholars, and government workers, did not concern themselves with financial matters. Therefore, leaving the money matters to the women does not mean that it is a high honor for them (Morse, 1987). Women's roles in East Asia are changing quickly and greatly with more and more women joining the work force, receiving college and graduate degrees, and selecting their own mates.

The Japanese Woman

Traditionally, the young Japanese bride went home to live with her husband's family. Her position in the family was almost one of a servant. She had to please her husband's mother, which meant getting up first in the morning and going to bed last at night. She also was to have her bath last. These attitudes have changed today. The newlyweds rarely go home to live with the husband's parents, and the young woman is no longer thought of as a servant for her mother-in-law. If parents and adult children are to live together today, it is more likely that the elderly will move in with a grown son or even perhaps a daughter.

Once a woman settles into her own home with her new husband, she experiences a great deal of independence. Not only does she manage the family finances, but she also has an enormous amount of free time in which to do as she pleases. Gone are the days when Japanese wives had to serve their husbands (which was quite common until just after World War II). In those days a wife helped her husband dress and undress, quickly placed a cup of tea in his hand if he started to reach for one, and generally lived to serve her spouse and run the home (Iwao, 1993).

Japanese homes are usually on the small side by U.S. standards (see Space chapter). This, in addition to having modern appliances, has drastically cut the hours needed to keep the home running efficiently. With her husband usually leaving home early in the morning for a long commute to the office, returning late at night after a round of business parties, and the children in school, the average wife has many choices. She might decide to join a culture club, meet with friends, watch a soap opera on television, or take a job. Her attitude about having a career is very different from that of many women in the U.S. Therefore it would be unfair to judge her with U.S. cultural eyes. Betty Friedan, the famous U.S. feminist, once made that mistake during a speech to Japanese women. She told them how sorry she felt for them because they were left at home to take care of the children while their husbands went out to parties every night. This was a mistake because Japanese women do not expect and do not necessarily want to be invited to their husbands' business parties (Iwao, 1993). A Japanese woman told us the same thing: "I would not want to act as hostess for one of my husband's parties," she said. Japanese women in the workplace do not seek the same goals as women in the U.S. They may want equal pay for equal jobs, but they do not particularly want the equal job.

Japanese men work long and hard, and many Japanese women simply do not want to have the men's long

Did You Know?

For various reasons, people live longer in Japan than in any other country in the world. A Japanese woman can expect to live to the age of 81.7, and a Japanese man to 75.9. (According to the 1994 *World Book Encyclopedia,* life expectancy for U.S. women is 78.3; for U.S. men, it is 71.5.)

Did You Know?

Rather than having their married children come home to live with them, many Japanese parents in their old age will go to live with their children—either their sons or their daughters. Yet things are changing in Japan, and parents are going to live with their children less and less. The elderly are beginning to live alone, and in Japan retirement homes are becoming more common, as they are in the U.S. (Reischauer, 1988).

hours and heavy work loads. Instead, they look for jobs that may be fulfilling but not as demanding. Often, they will hide the extra money in a secret fund known as *hes-okuri* (heh-soh-koo-ree), or "belly button savings," so called because this secret money hideaway once was held in the sash that encircled the kimono (Iwao, 1993).

Activities

1. Discuss: Who does the finances in your students' families or homes? Why? *(interpretive)*

2. Have the students pretend they are responsible for keeping track of their families' money and paying the bills. Ask them to write a family budget. What are the family's expenses (food, rent, etc.)? What can kids do to help their family stick to their budget? What does a family need to get by? *(constructive)*

3. Discuss: In what way is a Japanese woman's sense of independence different from a woman's in the United States? *(interpretive, cross-cultural)*

4. Discuss: Are women treated equally to men in the U.S.? If not, give some examples. Should we judge the goals of men and women in other cultures by our own standards? Why or why not? *(interpretive)*

Family in Japan

Let's look now at one specific East Asian culture, the Japanese, and examine in more detail one very special family relationship—that between a mother and a child.

Family is still very important in Japan, but today it usually refers, just as it does in the United States, to a *nuclear* family. Unlike an *extended* family, a nuclear family is made up simply of parents and their children. Yet in the Japanese family, ties between parents and children are

closer and the parents' authority is stronger than it is in the U.S. (Reischauer, 1988).

In the U.S., most children are reared to be independent and self-reliant. In Japan, on the other hand, one of the most important values is the sense of dependence people have on one another (this will be explored in more detail in the next chapter). That sense of dependence begins at home, where the bond between a parent and a child is formed. Actually, that bond is greater between the Japanese mother and her children than between the Japanese father and the children. One of the reasons for this simply is that the Japanese father is at work most of the day, even weekends, and must attend business parties at night. The bond between a mother and a child is the highest form of dependence; it is the yardstick by which all other dependent relationships in Japan (such as that between a teacher and a student or a boss and his employee) are measured. While the father-figure seems to be quite important in many Western cultures, in Japan it is the mother-figure, a representative of caring, non-judgmental, all-accepting love (Doi, 1973). When her children are very young, the Japanese mother will shop, cook, and clean with her children strapped to her back. One hardly ever sees babies in playpens or strollers, and babysitters are very rare. The children usually sleep with their mothers, too.

Much love and acceptance, not strict authority, goes into rearing children in Japan. While many U.S. mothers attempt to prepare their kids for school by teaching them discipline, Japanese mothers tend to be very indulgent with their young children and leave it to the school to teach the children how to behave well. They rarely criticize or discipline them. The don't make their children pick up after

PROVERBS: PARENTS AND CHILDREN

Parents are the first teachers of the children.

—Burmese

The parents can see best the character of the child.

—Japanese

When the question was put to the prophet Muhammad, "Whom should you respect?" he answered, "First your mother and then your mother and then your mother." —Arab

Like father, like son. —English

Like mother, like daughter. —English

If the father is a good man, the son will behave well.

—Vietnamese

A child should not speak while an adult is talking.

—African (Jabo)

A wise man was asked, "Which of your children is your favorite?" The wise man replied, "The young one until he grows up, the sick one until he recovers, and the absent one until he returns." —Arab

A child that is given everything that he asks for will rarely succeed in life. —Philippine

A good child is a crown of honor for his parents.

—African (Swahili)

mothers, will reinforce these teachings. Instead of saying "You are a good boy" or "You are a bad boy," and instead of punishing a child or getting angry for something the child has done wrong, a Japanese mother will tell the child that he or she has brought great shame or embarrassment to the family.

The Japanese have a word, *ninjo* (nin-joh), which means a sense of spontaneous good feeling or affection for someone; ninjo is entirely natural in the mother-child relationship. In return for the mother's devotion, Japanese children grow up giving their mothers the deepest "filial piety"—a term that means respect for one's family members. They learn to be thankful for their mother's devotion by honoring them and being obedient to their wishes for the rest of their lives. What is more, Japanese children carry this sense of devotion with them to school and later to their jobs. The close bond they have with their mothers helps them when they enter school to form close relationships with their teachers and classmates. In school, they express their devotion and obedience to their teachers and classmates, and later, on their jobs, they express the same sense of dependence on their co-workers, bosses, and employers. In return, teachers and classmates offer the kind of devotion the young child experienced from his mother, and bosses and employers will take good care of their workers, usually for life. Every step of the way through life—from home, to school, to work—the Japanese person experiences a sense of family.

Activities

1. Discuss how Japanese children are reared at home. Ask your students how their parents disciplined them at home when they were younger. If they did something wrong, what did their parents say? Compare this to how Japanese mothers treat their young children. How did your students learn to obey parents and teachers? *(interpretive)*

2. Discuss: Are kids in the U.S. taught to be independent or dependent on others (parents, teachers, peers, employers)? Why do you think we are taught to be independent in the U.S.? What does it mean to be independent? Is it necessarily better than being dependent? What are the advantages to being taught to be dependent, as the Japanese are? *(interpretive, cross-cultural)* (This discussion leads into the theme of the following chapter: "The Individual and the Group.")

themselves (Peak, 1991). Instead of yelling at them to behave or stop crying, the mother might give her child a piece of candy to make him happy. Children are taught at home to understand *why* their mothers want them to do something, rather than to do it because "I told you so." Mothers might say how hurt they feel by a child's behavior.

During the early years in school, children learn that they must avoid hurting others' feelings and that it is extremely important to maintain harmony within one's group, whether that group is one's family, one's class, one's study group, or one's company. They learn that they should never cause others to "lose face" or make others feel embarrassed or ashamed; they should always be sensitive to others' feelings and needs. Parents, especially

3. Have the students interview family members for stories handed down through their families. These stories should feature an event in the family's history, an esteemed ancestor, some special hardship overcome by family members, or whatever else the student and his or her family feel is important. Ask the students to write these stories in their own words and even illustrate them. Compile these stories in a classroom book with a cover and contents page. Have the students give it a title. The finished product may be a fascinating and inspiring book worth displaying to the school and sharing with students' families. *(constructive)*

Resources

Banks, James A. and Cherry A. McGee Banks. *Multicultural Education: Issues and Perspectives.* Boston: Allyn and Bacon, 1993.

Barakat, Halim. "The Arab Family and the Challenge of Social Transformation." In *Women and the Family in the Middle East: New Voices of Change;* edited by Elizabeth Warnock Fernea. Austin: University of Texas Press, 1985.

Bledsoe, Caroline. "Transformations in Sub-Saharan African Marriage and Fertility." *Annals of the American Academy of Political and Social Science.* July 1990: 115–25.

Carroll, Raymonde. *Cultural Misunderstandings.* Translated by Carol Volk. Chicago: University of Chicago Press, 1987.

Chatterjee, Bishwa B. "Training and Preparation for Research in Intercultural Relations in the Indian Subcontinent." *Handbook of Intercultural Training.* Edited by Dan Landis and Richard Brislin. New York: Pergamon Press, 1983.

Condon, John C. *Interact: Guidelines for Mexicans and North Americans.* Edited by George W. Renwick. Chicago: Intercultural Press, 1980.

Crane, Paul S. *Korean Patterns.* Seoul, Korea: Hollym Corporation, 1968.

Doi, Takeo. *The Anatomy of Dependence.* Translated by John Bester. Tokyo: Kodansha International, 1973.

Heusinkveld, Paula Rae. *The Mexicans: An Inside View of a Changing Society.* Worthington, OH: Renaissance Publications, 1993.

Howe, Russell Warren. *The Koreans: Passion and Grace.* San Diego: Harcourt Brace Jovanovich, 1988.

Iwao, Sumiko. *The Japanese Woman: Traditional Image and Changing Reality.* New York: Free Press, 1993.

Kim, Suk-hoyn. Article in *Korea Daily.* October 28, 1990.

Martin, Linda G. "Changing Intergenerational Family Relations in East Asia." *Annals of the American Academy of Political and Social Science.* July 1990: 182–213.

Michel, Andree. "Marina, Sarah, Michel and Jean: The Family Past and Present, Europe." *UNESCO Courier.* July 1989.

Mieder, Wolfgang. *The Prentice Hall Encyclopedia of World Proverbs.* Englewood Cliffs: Prentice-Hall, 1986.

Morse, Ronald A. *Wild Asters: Explorations in Korean Thought, Culture and Society.* Washington, DC: Lanham University Press of America, 1987.

Muzny, Charles C. *The Vietnamese in Oklahoma City: A Study in Ethnic Change.* New York: AMS Press, 1989.

Peak, Lois. *Learning to Go to School in Japan: The Transition from Home to Preschool Life.* Berkeley: University of California Press, 1991.

Priso, Manga Bekombo. "Lines of Descent: The Family Past and Present, Africa." *UNESCO Courier.* July 1989: 23–27.

Prothro, Edwin Terry and Najib Diab Lutfy. *Changing Family Patterns in the Arab East.* Beirut: American University, 1974.

Qi, Yanfen. "The Empire of the Ancestors: The Family Past and Present, Ancient China." *UNESCO Courier.* July 1989: 17–21.

Reischauer, Edwin O. *The Japanese Today: Change and Continuity.* Cambridge, MA: Belknap Press, 1988.

Rugh, Andrea B. *Family in Contemporary Egypt.* Syracuse: Syracuse University Press, 1984.

Selected Readings for Fulbright Scholars to Korea. Compiled by Korean-American Educational Commission, 1992.

Topolnicki, Denise M. "A Look into Family Life: Japan." *Money Magazine.* October 1991: 94–107.

Whyte, Martin King and William L. Parish.
Urban Life in Contemporary China.
Chicago: The University of Chicago Press, 1984.

Welcome to Cairo. American Embassy Publications.

The Individual and the Group

Goals

This chapter explores several basic aspects of individualism and group orientation and their implications for cross-cultural understanding. The information, stories, examples from various cultures, and student activities are designed to help your students achieve the following goals:

1. To understand that some cultures tend to value the individual over the group and that other cultures tend to value the group over the individual.

2. To explore the concept of individualism, especially as it is experienced and promoted in the United States.

3. To think critically about the concept of U.S. individualism, particularly in light of the group orientations found in other cultures.

4. To think about a class system while learning about the class systems in the U.S. and England, and to speculate about the limitations and benefits of class systems.

5. To understand the various ways people express their loyalties to groups (whether those groups are nations, countries, families, or study groups), how cultures with group orientations live and interact, and the advantages of such group orientations.

6. To grasp the concept of hierarchy and to learn about the forms of hierarchy found in the Japanese and Indian cultures.

7. To learn about the Indian caste system and to be able to compare a caste system to a class system.

Cross-Cultural Attitudes and Skills

As students work toward these goals, they will develop the following cross-cultural attitudes and skills:

1. They will continue to become more conscious of the cultural values that shape their attitudes and behaviors as well as to think more critically about these values.

2. In their collaborative activities, they will experience the value of a cooperative group orientation.

3. They will think more deeply about their own identities and the process by which their identities are formed.

4. They will practice their interpretive and empathic skills as they engage in self-exploration as well as role-playing aspects of other cultural perspectives. In this way, they will continue to explore how the world looks to them and how it looks to others—a vital cross-cultural experience.

GENERAL INTRODUCTION

Almost from the time we are born, we begin to learn how our culture expects us to fit into society. In the United States, it often starts with the compliments showered on us at birth, compliments that intend to make us stand out from others: "That is the most beautiful baby I've ever seen!" "Those eyes are gorgeous!" U.S. mothers graciously accept the remarks on our behalf; they hope their babies will grow into distinct, unique, and special *individuals*. In many other cultures, however, a mother denies such compliments as the first step in teaching the infant humility and the need to blend in with the *group*. A young Korean woman who had recently arrived in the United States from her homeland gave birth to a baby girl in a large Midwestern hospital. She soon startled staff and visitors alike by announcing to everyone that her newborn infant was ugly. "Oh no," everyone tried to reassure her, "the baby is very pretty." No one realized that the young mother was simply following the unwritten rules of her home culture. To accept such a compliment indicates that you agree with it, and it is not appropriate in many East Asian cultures to think of yourself or your child as standing out from the group.

Around the world, as babies grow into toddlers and toddlers into children, parents pamper and punish according to the customs of their cultures. In some cultures, parents place more emphasis on coddling and appeasing their very young children than on reprimanding and disciplining them. For example, a mother in one culture may traditionally quiet her child's stubborn whimpering with a piece of candy, but in other cultures, a mother will be more apt to give a stern reprimand and advise her child not to be a "crybaby." When children enter school, teachers also play important roles in shaping the youngsters' personalities and preparing them for life beyond the classroom. While children may be taught how to get along with others and to give and share with their classmates, they also may be strongly encouraged in some societies to be independent, to stand on their own two feet, and to prepare to face the world as strong, self-reliant individuals. Yet in other cultures, the lessons center on blending into the group, conforming, and learning not to be different. These lessons are not labeled as cultural training sessions. Indeed, children rarely know that they are being taught how best to fit into their cultures. Sometimes the cultural instructions come in the form of scoldings from parents: "Don't tell me you want to do that simply because everyone else is doing it! That's the poorest excuse of all," a U.S. parent often says. At other times the lesson weaves its way into a proverb, as it does with the very popular Japanese saying: "The head of the nail that sticks out is pounded down." Youngsters in Japan understand that to "stick out," or to be different, is not acceptable. Early on, children everywhere learn to respond to situations according to the value a culture places on the group or the individual.

Most cultures care about both the individual and the group, but they usually value one more than the other. The U.S. is known around the world for its sense of rugged individualism. Japan is known for its exemplary teamwork and cooperation. Cultures also have different social structures into which individuals and groups are organized. Some cultures have a class system and others have a hierarchy. A hierarchy can be compared to a stairway on the steps of which individuals or groups are located with someone or some group either above or below them in social status. Class systems and hierarchies vary from culture to culture, as we shall see in the lessons that follow.

We often are completely unaware of the cultural values that shape our attitudes and behavior. In fact, we sometimes are unable even to identify the values themselves. In the U.S., a child grows up wanting to be accepted by his or her peers but at the same time repeatedly hearing from his elders that it is important to "be himself" and not to be concerned with others' opinions, as long as he is "doing the right thing." Yet he would have difficulty identifying this as a cultural value that emphasizes the individual over the group. The following situation illustrates this particular cultural value:

The school class is having a game of dodge-ball on the playground while the teacher stands quite a distance away near the school building. Suddenly, Johnny, one of the members of the group, decides he no longer wants to play the game, and he grabs the ball and runs to the other end of the school's lot. There he begins to bounce the ball against the building while the other children complain that they want to continue with the game.

How would a child in the U.S. typically respond to such a situation?

Would he or she run to the teacher and say, "Our group is having a problem out here, and we are unable to continue with the game"?

or

Would the child run to the teacher and say, "Johnny took our ball, and we can't go on with our game. Please make him give it back"?

Most U.S. children would respond in a way that identifies an *individual* as being the cause of the problem. In our culture, we are quick to point the finger of blame at an individual, but we also are anxious to accept personal praise for a "job well done."

As students are introduced to the concepts of individualism and group orientation in this chapter, they will gain new insights into how their own culture and other cultures value one over the other, as well as how these concepts influence the attitudes and behavior of the members of their own and various other cultures.

What Went Wrong?

These introductory activities are designed to introduce your students to the value a culture places on the individual or the group, and how a contrast in cultural values can cause cross-cultural misunderstanding. Most students will not know the correct answer to each, but that is not the point. The point is to initiate curiosity and discussion and to stir their interest in pursuing this topic.

Teacher's Instructions: Divide your class into groups of four or five students. Hand each group a copy of each of the following worksheets. Have each group work together to decide which answer best explains the behavior described in "What Went Wrong?" Then, as a class, each group will explain its reason for choosing the answer. After each group has spoken, reveal the correct answer and discuss it. An explanation to each one has been given below. Do the same with each "What Went Wrong?"

Some discussion questions include:

1. Why did your group choose this answer over the other answers? Were there clues given, did you simply eliminate the other answers, did you choose by instinct, or did you apply some assumptions you already had about the cultures mentioned? If you applied some assumptions, what did you already assume about the people from that culture?

2. How would you have felt in this situation?

3. What would you have done next?

4. What does this exercise show you about the different ways people from different cultures respond to the same situation?

Answers and Explanations

WHAT WENT WRONG? #1 = Answer #2

Mark and his father thought the British did not like people from the U.S. because they did not appear to be pleased with the invitation to a soccer game. The real reason was that in England soccer is associated with the working class, and members of the upper-middle class usually do not attend soccer matches. There have been violent demonstrations at these games. Experts who have made studies of these riots chalk them up to dissatisfaction with economic conditions rather than emotional outbursts strictly associated with the outcome of the game. On game days in London, police are posted at the subway stops—there known as *tube* or *underground* stations—that are along the line taking spectators to the stadium where the match will be played. The officers have been posted to curb any signs of violence that might erupt. The parents of Mark's friend reacted in a manner typical of many members of their class. They do not have a deep interest in the sport, and they also are fearful of any demonstrations that might take place.

WHAT WENT WRONG? #2 = Answer #3

Baseball is one of the most popular sports in Japan for young and old alike. While the rules of the game may be the same as in the United States, attitudes toward the sport are different. Shigeo could not understand why he was not allowed to play just because his arm was sore. In Japan one perseveres in spite of problems. One professional team member in the Japan Series, the equivalent of the U.S. World Series, continued to play with a broken foot. Team members are ever loyal to the group and do not criticize their coach or discuss their personal problems with team members. Shigeo was also surprised by the choice of team captain. In his country the member of the team who is oldest and has been a member the longest is chosen over someone who has outstanding sports' skills and leadership ability. This means that a junior would never be selected over a senior as captain. One of the biggest surprises for Shigeo came with the last game. In Japan the baseball season does not end with regional playoffs but with a national tournament. It is the most important high school sporting event of the year, and nearly half a million spectators cram the stadium to see the playoffs. Others are glued to radios and television sets to hear every detail, which includes not only a description of the plays but a complete rundown on *seishim* (say-shim), or the spirit displayed by team members.

WHAT WENT WRONG? #3 = Answer #4

The Bradleys were very surprised when their Indian hosts did not join them for dinner. But the Indians whom they were visiting were following the strict customs of their culture, customs that may have faded in the big cities of India but still exist in the smaller villages. Indians regard themselves as belonging to certain groups, each of which is above or below another group in status. They are born into this group, known as a *caste,* and are associated with it for life. Many strict rules of behavior are associated with the caste system, and food preparation is one of them. These strict rules are followed more in the villages than in the cities. Eating is not thought of as a time to get together for fun, conversation, and relaxation, as it is in the U.S. Sometimes people bring their own prepared food to another's home, so there is no danger of mistakes being made in its preparation. Members of the Brahmin caste are on the very top step of this country's hierarchy. They perform many purification rites before they eat their food, and then they often eat this food alone. In order to keep themselves and their food pure and to protect themselves from what is called "pollution," these Brahmins sometimes simply offer food to their guests but do not eat with them. Indians are very hospitable but, like people in other parts of the world, they follow the customs of their country. They really had wanted to entertain the Bradleys, but they also wanted to do it within the framework of their culture's customs.

S t u d e n t

Worksheet

NAME _____

DATE _____

WHAT WENT WRONG? #1

Twelve-year-old Mark Pela and his family moved temporarily to London, England, from Atlanta, Georgia. Mr. and Mrs. Pela were searching for antiques and unusual gift items in order to open a shop back home. The Pela family settled into an upper-middle-class neighborhood, where Mark became friends with his immediate next-door neighbor through a scouting program. Mark had been an avid soccer player back in the States, and he could not wait to see his first professional game in England. He knew he would be watching some of the best soccer action in the world. His father purchased three tickets to a professional game and told Mark to ask his new friend to go along. The boy accepted, but he and his parents did not appear to be very pleased with the invitation. The Pelas were both surprised and hurt by this reaction. "I guess they just don't like Americans," Mark and his father reasoned.

Why was the British friend displeased with Mark's invitation to the soccer game? (Circle the answer that best explains their behavior.)

1. British parents do not like their kids to play with kids the parents have never met. Since the parents had never met Mark, they would not let their children go to the soccer game with him.

2. In England, people who are members of the upper-middle class, as Mark's friend was, do not tend to like the sport of soccer or to go to soccer games. Usually it is the working class who prefers soccer games, and sometimes riots break out at these games as the fans get too rowdy. The upper-middle-class parents of Mark's friend probably did not want their son going to a soccer game because the crowd might get violent and also because they were not interested in soccer in the first place.

3. It would have been more appropriate and polite if Mark's father had bought two extra tickets so that Mark could have invited another neighbor and his father. Politeness is very important in England. When Mark invited only one, it was probably considered rude.

4. Mark's friend was a member of the upper-middle class, people who are very, very wealthy. They have their own set of high-society friends and many things to do on the weekend. They probably did not have the time to go to the soccer game with Mark, and perhaps they were not thrilled about doing something with him, since people from the U.S. are considered beneath their class level.

Student
Worksheet

NAME _____

DATE _____

WHAT WENT WRONG #2

Shigeo Murakami moved from Osaka, Japan, to Seattle, Washington. Back home he had been pitcher on his high school baseball team, and he managed to win the same position on his U.S. school's team. However, he had problems adjusting to the U.S. way of playing baseball. The team's trainer would not allow him to play in one game because his arm was sore. Shigeo also was very surprised when his teammates elected a junior as captain of the squad, and he was amazed still another time when classmates complained that they were not being played enough. But the biggest surprise of all came when the season stopped after his school won the state title. "Baseball is very strange in the United States," he thought to himself.

Why did Shigeo think U.S. baseball was so strange? (Circle the answer that best explains Shigeo's reaction.)

1. Shigeo expected to be elected the captain of the team because in Japan the pitcher is always the captain. He felt he was not being given enough respect on the team.

2. People from all cultures judge what they see with their own cultural eyes. Shigeo simply thought that the Japanese way of playing baseball was better than the U.S. way of playing baseball and could not understand why baseball is not played in the United States as it is in Japan.

3. Baseball in Japan may have many of the same rules as baseball in the U.S., but the people who play it have different values. For example, back home, he would have been able to play with a sore arm, a senior would have been elected over a junior as captain, and team members would never complain or criticize their coach. Shigeo was surprised at this difference in values.

4. Shigeo was probably uncomfortable in this new culture, especially because Japan and the U.S. are so very different. He loved baseball, and it was the one thing Shigeo thought would remind him of home. When he discovered a few differences in how the game is played, Shigeo was very disappointed and felt homesick. This game did not seem like baseball at all.

S t u d e n t

Worksheet

NAME _____

DATE _____

WHAT WENT WRONG? #3

Tracy Bradley accompanied her U.S. parents on a trip to New Delhi, India, where Tracy's mother was to take part in a conference at a local university. In one of her discussion groups, Dr. Bradley met an Indian woman from a village outside of the city and was extremely pleased when the Indian woman invited the entire Bradley family to her home for dinner. "I understand the family belongs to the Brahmin caste," Dr. Bradley explained to her husband and daughter. "This is the most elite caste in the country." The Bradleys looked forward to their visit and were truly pleased when they were offered a meal shortly after arriving in the Indian home. But their pleasure turned into bewilderment when they discovered that the Indian family did not eat with them but simply served them the food. "What went wrong?" wondered the Bradleys. "Didn't they want to eat with us?" The Bradleys decided that maybe they should have refused the food or insisted that the Indians eat with them. They really were very embarrassed about the situation.

Why did the Indian family not eat with the Bradleys? (Circle the answer that best explains their behavior.)

1. Because the Indian family belonged to the most elite group in the country, they were not allowed to eat with inferior people, and people from the U.S. are considered inferior. Yet they wanted to be polite, so they asked the Bradley family over to dinner even though they could not sit down to eat with them.

2. When the Bradleys arrived, the Indian family discovered that they were rude and loud. They wanted them to leave their house as soon as possible, so they gave them the food but did not eat with them, since that might have kept them there longer.

3. The Indian family was simply following an Indian custom: you do not eat with your guests. They feel that to be polite, they must act as servants and serve the food while the guests eat.

4. The Indian family belonged to the most elite caste in India, and this caste has strict rules for preparing and eating food. Members of the Brahmin caste perform purification rites before they eat their food, and then they often eat it alone. They are supposed to keep their food pure, so to eat with the Bradleys, who are outsiders, would be to pollute the food. These customs have faded in India's big cities, but they still exist in some of the smaller villages. Like many Indians, this family was very hospitable and they really wanted to entertain the Bradleys; but they also wanted to do it within the framework of their culture's customs.

Lesson I

Individualism

Off and on since early history, humans in cultures all over the world have attempted to achieve some form of individualism. The idea of individualism has been rejected by different civilizations for various reasons. The group remained more dominant, and it really was not until rather recent times, historically speaking, that the individual became more important than the group in many cultures, especially Western cultures.

The idea sprang to life again in England during the 1600s. This time it really took hold. Many of the early American colonists who came from England brought with them the concept of the individual being more important than the group. They had no name for this idea, but they talked about it in many different ways. And it gradually took root as one of the guiding values of the young republic. Benjamin Franklin, one of the founders of our country, reflected this emphasis on the individual when he made popular a seventeenth-century English proverb:

> God helps those who help themselves.

This proverb reflects one of the basic principles of individualism: self-reliance, or not depending on others for help, is an important factor in getting ahead.

"Everyone has a right to a dream and to pursue it," said a Chicago Bulls player during his speech at a high-school assembly program. But is it a right? Those who believe in individualism say "absolutely." But those who put the group first have a different view. A foreigner once commented that people in the United States make business decisions based on their desire to promote their own personal goals (Stewart, 1991). Many observers from other cultures think that our belief in our individual "rights" often makes us selfish, that we will step on others to get what we want for ourselves. Is this true? Are we in the U.S. encouraged by our culture to pursue our personal dreams at the expense of others? It is a question to consider.

Did You Know?

No one had a name for the idea that a person was more important than the group until about a half-century after the birth of the U.S. It was then given a name by a French writer named Alexis de Tocqueville who came to the United States to observe and reflect upon democracy in U.S. society. After observing people's independent attitudes in the U.S., Tocqueville coined the word "individualism," but "individualism" was not necessarily a word of praise. He thought it was a bit selfish of people to put themselves, their immediate families, or their close friends first. The good and bad of individualism have been debated ever since those days of Tocqueville's visit. How one regards individualism depends upon one's politics and the views of the culture in which one lives.

Activities

1. Ralph Waldo Emerson was one of the fathers of American individualism. His famous essay "Self-Reliance" (1841) is a major text in the history of American individualism. It is too difficult and too long to assign to your students but the following representative excerpts may provide a fruitful source of interpretation, discussion, and self-reflection.

   Give the students some biographical background on Emerson. Then divide the class into groups of four or five and assign each group two or three of the quotes to read, grapple with, interpret, and discuss. They will need to look up difficult words in the dictionary and may require your assistance in getting the main point. But let them try to reconstruct the meaning for themselves first. After discussion, have them complete the Agree/Disagree chart on page 155 individually. *(interpretive, collaborative)*

From Ralph Waldo Emerson's "Self-Reliance" (1841):

#1   To believe your own thought, to believe that what is true for you in your private heart is true for all men—that is genius.

#2   Trust thyself: every heart vibrates to that iron string.

#3   Whoso would be a man, must be a nonconformist.

#4   What I must do is all that concerns me, not what people think. . . . [Y]ou will always find those who think they know what is your duty better than you know it. It is easy in the world to live after the world's opinion; it is easy in solitude to live after our own; but the great man is he who in the midst of the crowd keeps with perfect sweetness the independence of solitude.

#5   We must go alone. I like the silent church before the service begins, better than any preaching. . . . So let us always sit. Why should we assume the faults of our friends, or wife, or father, or child, because they sit around our hearth, or are said to have the same blood? . . . Friend, client, child, sickness, fear, want, charity, all knock at once at thy closet door, and say,—"Come out unto us." But keep thy state; come not into their confusion. . . . No man can come near me but through my act.

#6   Say to them, "O father, O mother, O wife, O brother, O friend, . . . I must be myself. I cannot break myself any longer for you, or you. If you can love me for what I am, we shall be the happier. If you cannot, I will still seek to deserve that you should. I will not hide my tastes or aversions. . . . If you are noble, I will love you; if you are not, I will not hurt you and myself by hypocritical attentions. If you are true, but not in the same truth with me, cleave to your companions; I will seek my own. I do this not selfishly but humbly and truly.

#7   And truly it demands something godlike in him who has cast off the common motives of humanity, and has ventured to trust himself for a taskmaster. High be his heart, faithful his will, clear his sight, that he may in good earnest be doctrine, society, law, to himself, that a simple purpose may be to him as strong as iron necessity is to others!

#8   Insist on yourself; never imitate . . . . That which each can do best, none but his Maker can teach him. No man yet knows what it is, nor can, till that person has exhibited it. Where is the master who could have taught Shakespeare? Where is the master who could have instructed [Benjamin] Franklin, or [George] Washington, or [Sir Francis] Bacon, or [Sir Isaac] Newton? Every great man is. . . .unique.

#9   Do that which is assigned you, and you cannot hope too much or dare too much. . . . Abide in the simple and noble regions of thy life, obey thy heart. . . .

#10   A political victory. . . the recovery of your sick, or the return of your absent friend, or some other favorable event, raises your spirits, and you think good days are preparing for you. Do not believe it. Nothing can bring you peace but yourself.

2. Copy the list of proverbs on page 156 for your students. Ask them to mark with an "I" all those proverbs that emphasize the value of the individual. Mark with a "G" all those proverbs that emphasize the value of the group. Choose a few to interpret, paraphrase, and discuss with the class. Ask the students to write their own proverbs about the value of the individual or the group. Have them share the proverbs with the class and/or print them on classroom signs. *(interpretive, cross-cultural)*

3. Pose the question found right before these activities to your students. What do they think? Do they feel it is acceptable to step on others to pursue their individual dreams? Can they think of examples? Are there any people who are famous because they have or have not done just that? *(interpretive)*

What Individualism Means in the United States

Activity
Just for fun, copy the True/False worksheet on page 157 for your students and ask them to complete it. Discuss the reasons for their answers to each T/F statement. *(interpretive)*

Worksheet

NAME _____

DATE _____

Instructions: After you have read and understood the ten quotes from Ralph Waldo Emerson's essay "Self-Reliance," fill in the chart below by putting a check in the "Agree" or "Disagree" column if you agree or disagree with the meaning of each quote. Then choose one quote and explain WHY you agree or disagree with Emerson's point.

AGREE/DISAGREE CHART

Emerson Quote	Agree	Disagree
Quote #1		
Quote #2		
Quote #3		
Quote #4		
Quote #5		
Quote #6		
Quote #7		
Quote #8		
Quote #9		
Quote #10		

WHY I AGREE OR DISAGREE:

Quote # ___ :

_____

_____

_____

_____

_____

_____

_____

_____

_____

_____

_____

Proverbs: The Individual and the Group

A boat does not go forward if each one is rowing his own way. —African (Swahili)

Help yourself and God will help you. —Dutch

Let every bird sing its own tune. —Danish

Different strokes for different folks. —United States

If one link snaps, the whole chain falls apart. —Yiddish

To each his own. —English

Every head must do its own thinking. —African (Jabo)

People are not alike like guinea fowl, nor identical like quail. —African (Ovambo)

He who does not mix with the crowd knows nothing.
                                        —Spanish

The unselfish person will draw the prize. —Japanese

Student
Worksheet

NAME _____

DATE _____

Are You an Individualist?

Instructions: Circle the answer you personally believe to be correct.

1. If your school announces that baseball caps may no longer be worn in the classroom, a reason for the new rule should be given.

   T F

2. Cindy and Shannon had been best friends for several months. One night they planned to rent a video and order a pizza. Cindy thought horror movies were cool while Shannon hated watching them. Cindy wanted only cheese on the pizza, but Shannon wanted pepperoni on it. These were not reasons to break up the friendship.

   T F

3. Ryan's mother always complained about his dirty room. One day he surprised her by picking everything up and putting the room in order. His scout master was coming to dinner that night. He probably cleaned his room because he did not want this man to think he was a slob.

   T F

4. Jamal Thompson's father announced one evening that a former co-worker, who had left the company for another job in a city several hundred miles away, was coming back into town with his family for a visit. Mr. Thompson wanted to invite them to his family's home for dinner. The two families, including the children, had been friends. The Thompson family probably thought this invitation was a good idea.

   T F

5. Jennifer poured through her junior dictionary every evening in preparation for a district spelling bee that was taking place in her town in a few weeks. She had decided to compete and compete hard. She probably wanted to win the match.

   T F

6. Bobby's younger brother kept coming into Bobby's room to check out what was new or going on. Bobby finally put a sign on his door that said "Keep Out." Bobby had a right to do this.

   T F

7. Vanessa was a new girl in the sixth-grade classroom. Every day she came to school in a very expensive and different outfit. She appeared to have no interest in making friends with anyone in the class. In fact, when she did speak with anyone, she told them about all the important activities that were taking place in her home and the very expensive trips her family was planning to make. The class was justified in thinking she was a "snob."

   T F

8. Mr. Rodriguez received his property tax bill and was very angry. His taxes had increased $300 from the year before. He decided to challenge his local government by filling out a petition. He had every right to take this action against the tax assessors who had sent him the new bill.

   T F

HOW YOU RATE ON THE INDIVIDUALISM SCALE

Number of answers given as "True"	2–3	4–5	6–7	8
How important individualism is to you	Not at all	Somewhat	Very	Completely

Below, students will discover how each of the statements on page 157 points to a specific element of U.S. individualism. Let's take a look at these elements in more detail.

Think for Yourself

People in the U.S. tend to dislike being ordered to do something. They usually believe that they can judge for themselves what is best. If a new order is given or a law is made, they want to know the reason behind it. They respond better to persuasion and reasoning than they do to commands and rulings that contain no explanations. U.S. students would expect to be given some explanation as to why they no longer could wear their baseball caps. One reason recently given for such a rule in an urban high school was that the administration felt such head gear might be associated with gang identification. Traditionally, members of the military in any society have been expected to respond to orders without questioning them. But people in the U.S. believe that under certain circumstances, individuals must defy orders when they personally believe the orders are immoral or illegal. After World War II, the U.S. and its allies arrested many German officers whom they believed had committed war crimes and atrocities. The German officers argued that they had only been following orders. But the U.S. and its allies said that excuse was not good enough, that individuals must be responsible for their own actions.

To Each His or Her Own

We do not have to agree with every belief, attitude, and taste a person has in order to be his or her friend. In the U.S., everyone supposedly is allowed to be his or her own person, and it is not necessary for us to accept the whole individual. We can pick and choose what we like about someone and can work and play with people who have different religious beliefs or politics. In some cultures, such as that found on mainland China, one's different political beliefs can lead to his or her being an outcast.

Do It Yourself

It is a firm belief in the U.S. that people perform best when they are self-motivated. All the arguments as to why one should do one's homework or the advantages of getting a good education are usually not very effective unless the individual really understands and wants to do it herself or himself. Ryan finally decided to clean his room when he believed he had a good reason for doing so. Self-motivation is one of the basic principles of individualism.

Change Is Good

In the U.S., change and variety are qualities usually admired. This is not always true in other cultures such as Japan, where leaving a company for another job is considered disloyal. Anyone in that Asian country who would do so would be considered outside the group, and the group would no longer be expected to show him friendship and respect. But in the U.S., respect for other individuals, whether or not they are inside or outside our close circle of friends and co-workers, is considered admirable. The Thompson family thought it perfectly normal to invite an old business associate and his family to their home. They respected anyone's right to change jobs, and they did not consider this former employee an outsider simply because he did not work with Mr. Thompson anymore.

Look Out for #1

Jennifer no doubt wanted to win the spelling bee. Many people in the U.S. are fierce competitors on an individual basis. Many of us believe it is our right to compete and to try to get ahead. Competition is greatly admired in the U.S., and it often is valued more highly than cooperation. Yet in recent years, some of us have begun to see that the cooperative spirit shared in some cultures has its advantages. Children in Japanese classrooms, for example, place their desks together in small groups called *hans* (hahns). In the han, each person helps the other; slow learners and advanced students are not separated from the mainstream but work together in order to help each other. The new emphasis on cooperative learning in the U.S. classroom takes advantage of the spirit of cooperation that can enable students to teach each other and learn from each other in fascinating and effective ways. While we may always compete with one another in the U.S., we are learning that sometimes we can achieve more if we cooperate with others.

Did You Know?

Having had little experience of being able to be alone behind a closed door, Russians tend to find privacy within themselves, whether or not they are surrounded by people. Daydreaming is a form of privacy into which no one can intrude. This way, the need to be alone is fulfilled, even though the person may have no privacy in the U.S. sense of the word.

"Private! Keep Out!"

The right to privacy has always been considered important in the U.S. We do not share certain information even with our friends. It is not unusual for a child who has her own room to put a sign on the door that says, "Private! Keep Out!" It is considered perfectly normal in U.S. culture for each person to have a space of his or her own—a special drawer that no one is to invade, a hideaway where one can be alone with one's own thoughts, or an office that is walled off from other workers. But this is not always the case around the world. While the English are firm believers in individualism and its principle of privacy, they often express it in a different way than we do. The English do not always need "walls" or a special area to mark off their own personal territory. Many of them, particularly in the upper-middle or upper classes, shared a nursery room with their brothers and sisters when they were very young and did not have rooms of their own. In other words, walls did not provide privacy. Instead, these youngsters learned to shut out others mentally rather than physically. In some cultures, such as the Russian, Japanese, and Arab, there is no word for privacy. Being alone is either not possible because of lack of space or it is not considered important.

The Embarrassment of Riches

In the U.S., individualism walks hand in hand with egalitarianism, a sense that everyone should be equal no matter how much money, power, or fame he or she has. Many in the U.S. are quick to resent others who try to impress them with their position and wealth. While individuals in the U.S. often strive to attain more money and material goods, they do not like to hear other people brag about how rich and successful they are. They may be obsessed with how to achieve success, but they tend to dislike those who act as if their success makes them superior. They are quick to label those kinds of people "snobs."

Did You Know?

Most Norwegians are fiercely egalitarian, so much so that they tend to resent or mistrust someone who claims to be better than others, and they are embarrassed if they receive too much individual attention. It was typical at the 1994 Winter Olympics in Lillehammer, Norway, that the mayor of Lillehammer apologized when the Norwegians won so many medals.

Nothing expresses these Norwegian values better than a famous set of laws found in a story with which almost all Norwegians are familiar. It is called the *Janteloven* (**Yahn**-te **lov**-en, "Jante's Law"), and it is supposed to be the voice of society:

1. You shall not believe you *are* something.
2. You shall not believe you are as good as us.
3. You shall not believe you are wiser than us.
4. You shall not fancy yourself better than us.
5. You shall not believe you know more than we do.
6. You shall not believe you are greater than us.
7. You shall not believe you amount to anything.
8. You shall not laugh at us.
9. You shall not believe that anyone is concerned with you.
10. You shall not believe you can teach us anything.

"Question Authority"

People in the U.S. believe that as individuals they have the right to question and challenge their government. They demonstrate, vote in or cast a ballot against issues, petition those in authority, and generally make their voices heard through any number of actions, all of which are considered legal. These rights are guaranteed to them in the first ten amendments of our Constitution, which have become known as the Bill of Rights. Mr. Rodriguez responded in a manner typical of our culture and within the boundaries of the law when he filled out a form to ask for a review of his property taxes. Many individuals in our country also share a belief stated by the famous U.S. author and naturalist Henry David Thoreau: "The government that governs least, governs best."

All of the above examples point out the importance of the individual self in U.S. culture. This does not mean, however, that people in the U.S. do not value community and group affiliation or that they are opposed to joining groups. Each person is associated with a group in some way: family, neighborhood, economic class, ethnic identification. These all help to shape values and identities. The U.S. also is a nation of joiners. Many children belong to boy or girl scout troops, sports teams, and clubs. They proudly identify themselves as belonging to a certain school by wearing a sweatshirt with the school's name emblazoned across the front. Adults join service and social clubs as well as sports groups. There probably is not a cause or an idea that is not represented by some kind of organization in the U.S. Yet each of these groups is considered a collection of individuals. According to deeply entrenched U.S. ideology, no one is supposed to lose his or her identity within any of these groups. He or she is supposed to remain his or her "own person."

While it is possible to identify some of the significant aspects of U.S. individualism, it remains a complex matter. The following activities are designed to help students become more aware of U.S. culture's emphasis on the individual while enabling them to think more critically and deeply about the complex relationship between individuality and group affiliation. They should begin to understand that their self-images are formed somewhere in the intersection between their sense of individuality and their need for their group's perspective. Some important cross-cultural sensitivities can be developed with that understanding—sensitivities such as empathy, self-knowledge, a sense of dependence on others, an appreciation for one's group affiliation, and an ability to think critically about cultural stereotypes passed on through the media (as in Activities 5 and 6).

Activities

1. Go over each statement in the T/F quiz and share the information that follows the quiz, going point by point and discussing each as you go.

   Then have the students construct a "Mind Map" of these points. Copy the Mind Map on page 161 and ask the students to fill in the major points that are associated with the central idea. Then ask them to expand the map with any ideas they feel relate to the ideas in the circles. Their ideas should be written in new circles that radiate off the other circles. This exercise helps students to stimulate and organize their thoughts and to construct a visual representation that is easily remembered. *(constructive)*

2. Have the class—in small groups, as a whole, or individually—write a "List of the Individual's Rights." Come up with twenty of them, but have the class vote on the top ten. Post the list in the classroom. *(constructive)*

3. Pose the following questions for debate or a writing assignment. Some research may be needed. *(interpretive, constructive)*

   In recent years, many people have said that affirmative action programs in the U.S. have infringed on the rights of the individual. These are programs that enable members of minority groups to get jobs or attend schools they otherwise might not have the opportunity to enjoy because of discrimination in hiring and school admissions. Affirmative action programs say that a number of spaces must be offered to minorities. Sometimes people have gone to court over this issue. For example, a white medical school applicant sued when he was rejected admission and a minority student with lower grades was selected instead. Some argue that this discriminates against white people, especially men. Others say that an individual's right must be put aside for the good of society, and society cannot improve unless minorities are offered opportunities to enter professions that have been closed to them.

   Do you believe that the individual is less important than the social goals that are being attempted with such a program? Or do you think the individual's rights should always come first, before that of society?

4. Discuss: When is the group more important than the individual? Give examples. Another route to pursue might begin with this question: Does society make the individual evil or does the individual make society evil? *(interpretive)*

5. Ask the students to look through magazines for advertisements that promote the value of the individual or the group (ads that promote the latter, for example, will appeal to peer pressure—"everybody's doing it"). Have them share and discuss the ads with the class. *(interpretive)*

A Mind Map

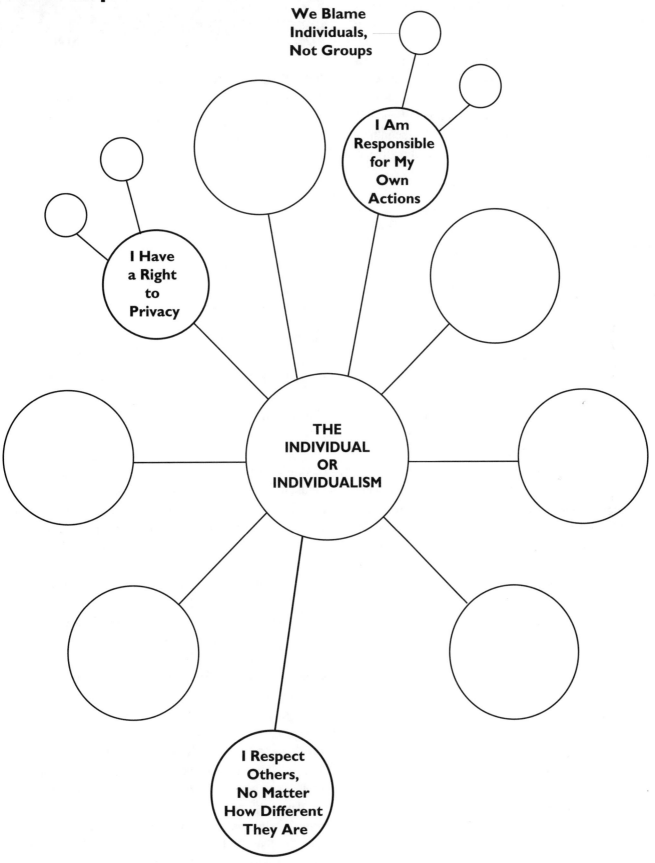

The circles may contain phrases ("I have a right to privacy") or key words ("Privacy").

6. Divide the class into groups and give each group a newspaper from a different day of the current week. Have each group look for articles that in some way are about blaming an individual for some problem and other articles that are about the fault of a group, such as a school, a political party, the welfare system, etc. Ask the groups to count up the number of each kind of article. Why do they think there is a larger number of one or the other? Do people in the U.S. usually blame individuals over groups? Why? Is it easier? Does it really solve social problems? *(interpretive, collaborative)*

7. Ask the students to complete the line, "I am a(n)_____" by listing their identities from the most important to the least important.

   Example:
   Valerie: I am a
   1. girl
   2. student
   3. hard worker
   4. daughter
   5. future lawyer
   6. sister
   7. African American
   8. New Yorker
   9. U.S. citizen

Which of the identities come from being associated with a group (such as any reference to one's gender, ethnicity, nationality, etc.) and which come from one's individuality (such as any quality of character)? *(constructive, interpretive)*

Lesson 2

The Class System

A class is a group of individuals in society who share several characteristics in common. Generally speaking, the following characteristics help to describe one's class in society:

One's level of income

One's occupation

One's level of education

One's residence and lifestyle

One's kinship or family

One's level of power in society

One's membership in organizations

These characteristics will not be the same in every culture with a class system. In a class system, it is the individual members who give the class its character or definition. This is quite different from a caste system, which we will explore in Lesson 4. In a caste system, the caste stamps its characteristics on the individuals within it (Beteille, 1992).

The importance society puts on class greatly influences its structure. If little emphasis is placed on one's position, the class system is usually more flexible, making it easier for an individual to move up or down on the social scale. Status is acknowledged in a variety of ways in different cultures. Frequently, this is done by the way a person is addressed or spoken to, as we saw in Chapter 1 on language.

The Class System in the United States

An Englishwoman who had come to the United States wrote about her bewilderment upon answering the door one day in this new land. There stood a stranger who immediately inquired, "If the woman of the house be at home for I am the lady that have come to help her cook" (Harris, 1992).

Can you tell what baffled the Englishwoman? Overlook the grammar and instead concentrate on the use of two words: *lady* and *woman*. According to the Englishwoman, the inquiry should have been, "If the *lady* of the house be at home, for I am the *woman* that have come to help her cook." The employer, she thought, was entitled to the more prestigious title of *lady*, but the hired help could only claim the title of *woman*. Such class distinctions are not often made in the U.S., where people pride themselves on ignoring where people stand on the social scale. Foreigners often are amazed at how quick we are to call our bosses by their first names, and to address anyone, short of the President, by his or her given name rather than the family or surname. In a guidebook prepared for Britons planning a trip to the U.S., one British author warned that people in the U.S.

> . . . will simply start talking to you—whether you want them to or not. You will notice that Americans get uncomfortable about talking to people unless they know their names. Almost every American will therefore rapidly tell you his or her name—and you are supposed to reciprocate. . . . They will also want to know where you are from and what you do (Trudgill, 1982).

Woodrow Wilson, who was President of the U.S. during World War I, had a word to say about the "classless" attitudes found in the U.S.; he said that people in the U.S. like to think that "this is the country where there is no distinction of class, no distinction of social status" (Pessen, 1992). In other words, we may have a class system, but we do not like to believe that class in any way limits us or makes us superior or inferior to others. Whether that is true is something to question.

Activities

1. Discuss: Is a class system fair? Does it limit you? Does one's class matter very much in life? Can you ever move into another class? How? How do you treat members of another class? Do you ever think about class? *(interpretive)*

2. Look through magazines to find and clip advertisements that represent class in some way (pictures of families from various classes; ads that depict material wealth, etc.). Discuss these images. What class do the majority of ads seem to represent? What are they appealing to? Do some magazines appeal to certain classes? Do their ads reflect that? *(interpretive)*

Did You Know?

Colonists of early America were very class-conscious. In New England a judge was addressed in passing as "Master So-and-So," and his wife as "Madam." But a blacksmith or tradesman had his name preceded with "Goodman," and his wife was called "Goodwife" or "Goody." People also received punishment for their crimes according to their station in life. A gentleman caught stealing would lose the privilege of being addressed as "Master," but a servant would receive a thrashing (Furnas, 1969).

The Class System in England

We can gain an interesting and informative insight into the dynamics of a class structure by looking at that system existing in England. It is one of the world's most democratic countries. At the same time, a structured class system, from royalty to "working class," has its subtle influence on many aspects of everyday life. A comparison of the rather class-conscious society in England and the relatively flexible social structure in the U.S. will illustrate how so-called sister countries can differ from each other.

A U.S. woman living in London tells the following story:

> We had been in our new home only a few days when I heard the milkman arriving at the door. I called out the upstairs window to him and said, "Sir, will you please leave two bottles of milk? I shall be right down." When I reached the door, the milkman was rather disturbed. "Please do not call me 'sir'," he said. "I am John." I then told him that he should also call me by my first name, Betty. He said that he couldn't do that. It was not his place to address me by my first name.

While the distinct lines among British classes have softened in recent years, there still exists a certain awareness of class differences that customarily is not found in the U.S. The importance of class lines is stronger in England than in the U.S. This, coupled with a sincere belief that you should not invade another person's privacy, restricts casual conversation with strangers in England. "Hi, I'm Joe. What's your name? What kind of work do you do?" These questions generally are not exchanged among British strangers. If you were to ask a British person about his job, he may think you are asking about his class level, because in England, more so than in the U.S., particular jobs usually are associated with specific classes. In recent years, these restrictions have relaxed, but many Britons still relate jobs to class level.

In the U.S., class distinctions are often blurred. In England, however, the most telling factor is the accent with which someone speaks. The British, like people in the U.S., have regional accents—accents that are used in a particular region of the country—but these are not nearly as important as the accent associated with their class. Not only do people pronounce words differently according to their class, but they also sometimes use a different vocabulary. For example, the upper class would never dream of addressing a stranger as "luv" or "governor," as does the working class.

An accent can help or hinder one in getting ahead in England since it identifies one's class status. Upper-class accents are usually expected in the more prestigious jobs. Why then wouldn't an individual in a lower class assume an upper-class way of speaking? Some do, but there is a degree of risk in undertaking this task. There are traditions, a sense of belonging, and pride associated with one's class, and attempting to speak above it can cut a person off from friends and family who may very well resent it.

The Upper Class in England

There are many subdivisions within each British class. At the very top is the *royal family,* and the ruling monarch is Queen Elizabeth. She is said to be one of the richest individuals in the world, but her riches, of course, did not make her queen; they are a result of her being born into the long line of British royalty. In London she lives in Buckingham Palace, which has more than six hundred rooms, but she also has many other homes scattered throughout England and Scotland, some of which she personally owns and others that are retained by the state.

The *titled aristocracy*—among them the dukes, duchesses, earls, and viscounts—rank just below royalty. They are treated with great respect and courtesy. These titles, along with large amounts of property, or landholdings, were given to the ancestors of these titled people many generations ago, and they have been handed down through the eldest son in the family. Many of these aristocrats are no longer as wealthy as their ancestors, thanks in part to high death taxes, but—money or no money—they still hold the highest positions in society. Each year the queen "knights" people in recognition of their outstanding accomplishments and service. A man who is knighted is

called "Sir," as in Sir Laurence Olivier, the actor, and a woman who is knighted is called "Dame," as in Dame Iris Murdoch, the novelist. This is only a lifetime title and cannot be inherited by family members.

Also in the very upper classes of England—right below the titled aristocracy—is the *landed gentry.* These people usually do not have titles but do own enormous estates, which include beautiful grounds and magnificent mansions. They usually live outside the London scene and away from the royal circuit. Sometimes, however, members of this group will marry into the titled class, even the royal family.

The titled aristocracy and the landed gentry have many characteristics in common. They often attend the same public (private) schools and, if academically eligible, go on either to Cambridge or Oxford University, the most prestigious universities in England and among the top institutions in the world. If they do not live strictly off inherited wealth, they often go into the military, banking, government, the church, or the diplomatic corps. They may sit on boards of large corporations, but they usually do not go to work as full-time employees of these organizations. Although they make up only a small percentage of the population, their power is felt throughout government, banking, and industry, and forms of what is called "the old-boy network." Through personal and powerful connections, much can be accomplished.

The upper classes often hold memberships in numerous clubs, located in old but prestigious buildings in London. Only recently have women been allowed to step foot inside these exclusive institutions. The upper classes usually choose sports that formerly were associated with survival, such as hunting, shooting, and fishing. Polo is also a favorite pastime. Horse racing transcends all classes to capture the hearts of nearly everyone in the country.

Activities

1. Go over the new terms associated with the upper classes in England. Clarify any confusion the students may have, or assign each term as a small group project to research and report. *(constructive)*

2. Discuss: What do the students know of the British royal family? Where do they get these images and ideas? Why do they think people in the U.S. are fascinated with the royal family? Do the students wish we had one? Why don't we have one? *(cross-cultural, interpretive)*

Did You Know?
The word *sportsmanship* originated with the British. "It is not whether you win or lose, but how you play the game," has been their motto.

Did You Know?
The pub often serves as the neighborhood social center in England. It is more than a place in which to stop for a drink. Here friends and neighbors gather for gossip, singing, and perhaps a game of darts. Pubs also supply some excellent, traditional English dishes.

3. Discuss: Do we have an aristocracy in the U.S.? How are the upper classes in England different from those in the U.S.? *(interpretive)*

4. Have members of the class help to draw a Mind Map of the class system in England on the board. They can expand it and fill in the circles as they are introduced to the information below. *(constructive, collaborative)*

The Middle Class in England

Just as there are several levels of the middle class in the United States, there are several levels of the middle class in England as well. The upper-middle class consists of wealthy professionals, merchants, stockbrokers, and other well-to-do individuals. The remaining middle classes hold less prestigious positions and receive lower pay.

Those in the upper end of the middle class may send their children to exclusive independent (sometimes called *public*) schools, which are the equivalent of private schools in the U.S. They might also belong to one of the posh London clubs frequented by the aristocracy and landed gentry. But many in this category attend state (what we would call "public") schools. In recent years the government has tried hard to make educational opportunities more equal for members of all classes, and to a certain extent this has been achieved. Cambridge and Oxford universities are also available to members of this class, or any class, who qualify scholastically.

The sport of cricket, an example of understated enthusiasm and correct sportsmanship, belongs for the most part to the middle classes. Golf is particularly popular with the upper-middle class.

Rising above the middle class is more difficult in England than in the U.S. A middle-class English person's income can go up with a better job. And sometimes members of the upper-middle class can be richer than members of the aristocracy, but they remain in the middle class. One must be born into or marry into the aristocracy. To be a member of the landed gentry, one must own large estates. Occasionally someone will marry into a higher class, but it is not a common occurrence.

The Working Class in England

It is not necessary for someone to be employed to be called "the working class." The term generally refers to a lower economic level of society. Members of the working class might hold jobs as factory workers, cooks, maids, and certain office workers. Soccer is a sport quite popular with the working class. They usually attend the state schools, although a few may be selected to go to a prestigious private school on a scholarship. A certain accent makes it easy to identify members of this class. Some famous people with working-class backgrounds include members of the Beatles and actors Michael Caine and Sean Connery.

The *cockney* form one of the most fascinating and colorful groups of the working class. Living primarily on London's east side and within the sound of the bells of a certain church, St. Mary-le-Bow, they speak in an accent very difficult for the average U.S. ear to understand. First-time visitors to London who happen to get a cockney taxi driver for their ride through town may find themselves bewildered by their driver's way of speaking. The cockney pronounces *th* like *f* or *v*, changes *ou* to *ah* and *a* to *i*, and drops the *h* at the beginning of words. So "thing" becomes *fing*, "about" turns into *abaht*, "daily" spins into *die-ly*, and "house" becomes *'ouse*.

Activities

1. Complete the Mind Map on the British class system. *(constructive, collaborative)*

2. Discuss: What are the differences between the classes in England? How is the British middle class different from the U.S. middle class? *(interpretive)*

3. Ask students to rent the movie *Oliver!* and study it for its accents. Can they tell the difference between lower-, middle-, and upper-class accents? Are there different kinds of lower-class accents? Have them try to imitate the accents, with one group of students as upper class, one as middle class, and one as lower class. *(cross-cultural, constructive)*

Lesson 3

The Group

The emphasis on the group has been around much longer than individualism, and in many societies it still plays the dominant role. But groups are formed quite differently around the world. Being aware of how someone views her own group can be a stepping-stone to cross-cultural understanding. The following incidents actually took place and demonstrate how cross-cultural mistakes can be made when one misunderstands another person's group loyalty. Many years ago, before the civil war broke out in Lebanon, one of the authors had gone to that country to write a magazine article about the children who lived there:

> I had wanted to talk to many different types of youngsters, so one day I visited an Armenian school. The children whom I interviewed were about twelve years old, and they were quick to tell me how their ancestors came from Turkey. I immediately thought back to some of my experiences in Turkey, and, in the way of making small talk, I said that I had found the Turks to be very warm and hospitable. There was immediate silence. Something had gone wrong, and from that point on questions were answered politely but coolly.

Journalist David Lamb tells of the following incident in *The Africans: Encounters from the Sudan to the Cape* (1982):

> One day in Uganda I was talking with a U.S. diplomat at the embassy. His secretary entered the office and said a man was waiting to see him. "Is he Ugandan?" the diplomat asked. "No, he's Acholie," she answered.

In both of the above scenes, people from the U.S. made mistakes because they did not understand the importance of group identity.

SIDEBAR

TERMS TO KNOW

What is the difference between

a country

a nation

a tribe?

Nation, Country, Tribe

The first incident involved a group known as a *nation,* which is not always the same as a *country.* A *country* must have a government, usable land, a stationary population, and an organized economy. Sometimes people share a common culture and language along with emotional ties to their heritage. These people, however, may not have a land to call their own, so they cannot qualify as a country. They are, however, a *nation.* The Tamils of Sri Lanka are an example of a nation (Demko, 1992). At the time of the author's interview, the Armenians were recognized as a nation of people divided across two borders, the Soviet Union and Turkey. Back in the early 1900s, the Turks forced many of the Armenians to leave the country. During the mass exodus, many Armenians lost their lives. Some of the refugees who managed to make it out settled in the Arab country of Lebanon. Each generation of Armenians continued to tell the story of the forced migration. The author had forgotten her history lessons as she attempted to make pleasant small talk with these young people. But she hit a nerve, a very sensitive nerve, when she spoke about the warmth and hospitality of the Turks, who were the old enemy of the nation of Armenians. (The Soviet Union crumbled in 1991, and the Armenians formed their own republic. The Armenians in Turkey, however, have no land of their own and simply have remained part of a larger population.)

The second incident illustrates loyalty to a *tribe* rather than allegiance to a country. Members of a tribe usually share a common ancestor. There are close to two thousand different tribes in Africa, the second largest land mass in the world. Europeans—the British, Germans, Portuguese, French, Italians, Spaniards, Dutch, and Italians—headed south to colonize that great continent and at the same time profit from its wealth of natural resources. These foreign colonizers applied their own superficial boundaries around land masses, creating countries for their own benefit. For the most part, these new boundaries have had little meaning for the members of the native tribes. Indeed, their loyalties often are directed more to their tribes than to their

country. In the incident above, a member of the Acholie tribe, whose members live in the eastern African country of Uganda, went to the American Embassy to see an official on a business matter (foreign governments establish local offices, known as *embassies*, in other countries). The U.S. diplomat, an official in the embassy, asked what he thought was a perfectly natural question. He wondered if the caller was a Ugandan or perhaps someone from the U.S. His secretary was a Ugandan, and she answered in a manner typical of her culture. She identified the visitor by his *tribe* rather than by his country.

Groups can be much smaller than nations or tribes. In Latin and Arab cultures, group emphasis is on the extended family. In both cultures, relatives play an important role in decisions regarding all family members, as we learned in the previous chapter. While two of the authors were living in Mexico, they talked with a young English woman who was married to a Mexican man. She told us how surprised she was to discover after arriving in Mexico that her husband called his family to tell them about everything they were doing, even their social engagements. But she was even more shocked when two of his brothers went along on furniture shopping trips. She was accustomed to making all her own decisions and doing what she wanted, when she wanted, without any of her family involved. But in her new Mexican family she discovered that the family's involvement provided a sense of sharing and a desire to bring others in to help make decisions that might be difficult for one individual to make.

Did You Know?

The Japanese like to bathe together in large communal baths that can be found in many neighborhoods. Men and women have separate sections. Each individual must wash with soap and water before going into the giant tub (more like our indoor pools) in which the water is kept about 100 degrees fahrenheit.

Did You Know?
Rice has had an important role in strengthening the group concept in Japan. Rice is the staple of the Japanese diet, and it takes a group effort to grow it. The irrigation system needed to grow rice is a complicated one, and an individual cannot do it on his own. So farmers have always worked together. Very few people farm today in Japan, but these old attitudes of cooperation are still strong. There is always the feeling that they must work together to survive on Japan's islands.

Activities

1. Discuss and clarify the difference between a country and a nation; a tribe and a country. List characteristics of each on the board. *(interpretive)*

2. Divide the class into small groups. Find a map of the countries of Africa and hand a copy to each group. Explain that many of the borders of these countries were determined by European colonists who came down to Africa and imposed their own rule. But many Africans do not feel loyalty to the areas within these borders; rather they feel loyalty to their tribes. If one were to draw a map of the tribal loyalties in Africa, it would look like hundreds of tiny little countries. Such a map can be found in *Why in the World: Adventures in Geography* by George J. Demko, Jerome Agel, and Eugene Boe (New York: Anchor Books, 1992), p. 39.

    Discuss: How would you feel if another country, such as France, came to your region of the U.S., conquered it and told you that you now lived in a country that was a French colony, called Nouveaupays. Would you feel Nouveaupaysian or would you still feel loyal to your fellow Americans? *(constructive, cross-cultural)*

3. With the students' input, make a list on the board of things, people, or groups to which we feel loyal (school, family, ethnic group, temple, city, country, etc.) Then ask each student to choose from that list, add to it if they wish, and make their own list of things, people, or groups to which they feel loyal. Have them rank their loyalties, with the most important at the top.

    Compare and contrast the students' sentiments. Or assign a group of students to be statisticians who will

tally up the responses and present the statistics to the class. *(constructive, interpretive)*

4. Have the students conduct a small group project with the following assignment: Draw a map of your town, city, or region and indicate the areas that are strongly populated by certain ethnic groups. Label these areas by ethnic group. If time permits, they can conduct interviews with residents from these various areas to discuss their ethnic loyalties versus their loyalties to city, region, or country. Discuss: Why do members of ethnic groups often live in the same areas? *(constructive, collaborative)*

5. Assign group reports on "nations" without countries around the world, such as the Tamils. The groups could present their reports by role-playing members of these nations who speak about their plights. *(constructive, collaborative)*

The Group in Japan
The Japanese emphasis on the group extends far beyond the family. It runs through every facet of their lives. Every Japanese person's life is centered in a group, and exclusion from such a structure, whether it be in school, at work, or at play, is tantamount to nonexistence. To meld, to be at one with others, is not only socially important; it is essential for survival. A Japanese proverb says, "The head of the nail that sticks out is pounded down." In other words, if you are different, if you stand out, you will be put in your place or made to conform to others.

Did You Know?
Japan has what many sociologists call a *shame society*. Parents usually make their children feel ashamed rather than guilty about misbehaving, and the shame serves as a form of punishment. Any feelings of remorse a person may have are usually associated less with what the person has done and more with the shame or embarrassment he or she has brought to his or her family or group. Not conforming to the rules will force someone to be outside the group, and in a culture where being accepted by the group is necessary for functioning within society, exclusion has serious consequences.

The concept most fundamental to understanding the emphasis on the group in Japanese culture is called *amae* (ah-mah-ee). It is a fascinating concept that governs individual Japanese beliefs and behavior as well as the structure of Japanese society. Literally, it means "to look to others for affection," and it implies a deep emphasis on social interdependence. Whereas U.S. children are taught to be self-reliant and to express their individuality, Japanese children are taught early on to express their loyalty to each other and their dependence on and responsibility to the group to which they belong. In fact, the word *individualism (kojin-shugi,* koh-jin-shoo-gee) is shameful, implying selfishness rather than self-reliance.

The best model of amae is the relationship between an infant and a parent, where dependence is natural and taken for granted. The Japanese have a word for that relationship: *ninjo* (nin-joh), which means "spontaneously arising feeling." Amae relationships within Japanese social groups are called *giri* (gee-ree), or the kind of interdependence that is like an unwritten social contract, a sense of duty and obligation to those who are members of a social group, such as a classmate, a fellow club member, or a co-worker. Just as people in the U.S. rarely think consciously about individualism, Japanese people don't think about amae; they simply live it as they grow up and establish bonds beyond their families, to their school homerooms, their study groups, their clubs, and later their companies (Doi, 1973; Kato, 1992).

The Japanese depend on the group throughout their lives for approval and gratification. One might say that they are who they are because of whom they are dependent upon. Just as the Japanese mother indulges her child when he is young but still retains her authority over him, the group becomes his authority as it offers him social approval. It rarely is difficult for the Japanese child to move from the indulgent world of early childhood to the more strict and demanding world of school in Japan because he or she has learned that obedience to authority and strict pressures to conform to the group are like a form of affection. With that, however, is the threat of being abandoned or ostracized by the group. Few things are more devastating to a Japanese person. Because of the Japanese culture's emphasis on the authority of the group, Japanese people learn always to place the desires and needs of the group before their own individual desires and needs.

The Japanese have a term for those people who are outside the group: *tanin* (tah-nin), or "other people." Tanin includes all people with whom one does not have a ninjo

SIDEBAR

Kao (kow)—that is the Japanese word for "face," as in the expression "saving face" or "losing face." It is a very important concept in Japanese culture, tied to an individual's sense of self-esteem. To maintain group harmony, a Japanese person does whatever he or she can to save face, in others and in him or herself. He or she will try to avoid any action that would bring humiliation or embarrassment to himself or herself and others (Kato, 1992). Nothing can be worse to a Japanese person than feeling that all eyes are on him or her if he or she fails at something, as when a teacher scolds or criticizes that student in front of his or her classmates.

or giri relationship. One's parents, for example, would never be considered tanin because the child's bond with them is unbreakable—nor would the members of one's company or one's school study group. As long as someone is tanin, the Japanese person has no real relationship with him.

If you wanted to draw a picture of how the Japanese culture conceives of relationships, it might look like this:

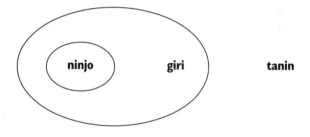

The degree of group loyalty is strongest towards the center. The inner circle contains one's family, the next circle contains one's friends, classmates, and co-workers, and the outer circle contains everyone outside one's group, whom one will most likely simply ignore. The Japanese will ignore the world of strangers until that world presents a threat or a source of interest. Then they tend to act superior to them—an old battle strategy. If that does not work, and the Japanese can no longer ignore the strangers, they will attempt to identify with them and adopt their ways, since amae teaches the Japanese to be comfortable with identifying and assimilating (Doi, 1973). This behavior explains why the Japanese are so eager to incorporate some aspects of U.S. culture and why it is not impossible to adapt to life in the U.S. Many Japanese youth love U.S. rock stars, designer fashions, and sports, both here and across the Pacific Ocean.

A concept closely related to amae is *wa* (wah), or "harmony," a concept the Japanese hold dear. Wa works horizontally among members of a group while amae is more vertical, working between members of groups in a hierarchy (the next lesson covers hierarchy)—between a person and those who have authority over that person, for example. Japanese people will do anything to maintain wa in the group (Kato, 1992). They will avoid confrontation and conflict. A Japanese child would almost never directly confront or provoke a classmate because he or she has always been taught that such behavior is childish and immoral.

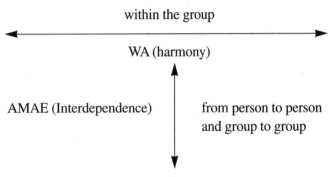

within the group

WA (harmony)

AMAE (Interdependence)

from person to person and group to group

Starting with preschool, children begin to identify with a group outside the home. On the first day, each youngster carries a book bag made by his or her mother; the school has sent home the exact instructions for putting the bag together. Once in first grade, the children spend many days repeatedly placing their pencils at the top of their desks, their notebooks on the right, switching their outside shoes for inside ones, standing up, sitting down, bowing, taking notes, and learning to answer questions. Nothing is left to chance, and academic lessons do not begin until these rules, which teach each student to conform to the group, are firmly learned.

In Japanese elementary schools, the homeroom (*kumi,* koo-mee) is a very important place. Each contains about forty to forty-five students with one teacher for two years. It is there that Japanese children learn to develop deep loyalty to the group. Within the homeroom group, the students have smaller groups, called a *han* (hahn), in which they study and do projects together. Each homeroom has a student leader and each han has a student leader, but the kind of leadership they learn to practice is quite different from the dominant, charismatic leadership so often praised in U.S. schools. The Japanese students

Did You Know?

In Japan, schools sometimes reinforce the concept of the group by measuring the girls' skirt lengths before classes begin. The measurements must conform to the regulations, and even the hair length is checked.

Did You Know?

Cleaning the school in Japan also brings a sense of working together for the good of a cause. Teachers and youngsters alike scrub halls, mop bathrooms, pick up trash, and do other jobs left to custodians in the United States.

learn to lead with humility and caring. The main role of the leader is to maintain harmony within the group by helping to build consensus and cooperation among all the group's members. Good leadership involves the ability to unite the members of the group by calm persuasion, not by demands. The homeroom teacher looks not for talent in the leaders but for the ability to get along with others and to help them get along with each other (Duke, 1986).

School is family, and teachers and administrators do not feel that discipline ends as each child heads home. Teachers visit each student's home to meet the mother and discuss any problems, and they also have been known to patrol the neighborhoods to make certain no child is up to mischief. If a high school student receives a traffic ticket, the school feels responsible for his behavior. This is in sharp contrast to the typical U.S. reaction to such a situation. A group of U.S. neighbors complained to the local high school that students were speeding through their area on the way to class. They were told by the principal that the school had no authority over the students outside the school's grounds.

Japanese junior and senior high school students also loyally identify with their homerooms, where they remain for most of the day. Teachers come to them for each subject, with the exception of science and art for which the students travel to laboratories and studios to take advantage of special equipment. Even lunch is brought to the classroom rather than having the students move to a central cafeteria. Friendships are made within this homeroom, not outside the school. There really is little time for students to get together after school hours because many of them move on to *juku* (joo-koo) (school-after-school) classes, which enrich their academic lives and help to prepare them for entrance exams to high schools and universities. Not everyone is dedicated to a serious academic life, but many are, and these students do not even want to be seen sipping a soft drink in a local hangout during the school week.

For adults, the company for which they work becomes almost an extended family, and their loyalty runs deep. Employees rarely change jobs for more pay or for the chance to enhance their own careers. They wait for promotions based on seniority and age. The company in turn looks after its individual members, even to the point of playing matchmaker if a young person is having difficulty finding a spouse. Employees proudly wear their company's pin for group identification and sing the company's song with great enthusiasm.

Despite their group orientation, the Japanese have some avenues for expressing their individual identities, such as the cultivation of tiny gardens, arranging flowers, writing in diaries or composing *haiku* (hie-koo), among other art forms and hobbies. Japanese literature provides them with the opportunity to participate in the search for identity, for many works widely read are about the personal search for selfhood in a world where conformity is demanded at every turn. The Japanese tend to like what they call the "I novel" which is a deep and honest introspective description of the author's emotions in an oppressive society. Japanese individuals also are encouraged to develop a specific hobby or individual skill, such as golf, judo, music (playing the violin), or any of the activities mentioned above, and many Japanese will flaunt their devotion to their hobbies and skills for others. These give people a source of self-respect and individual self-worth (Reischauer, 1988).

One opportunity the Japanese student has to shine individually is in the university entrance exams. They make it necessary for one to forget about one's group bonds and attempt to stand out above his or her peers for those few coveted spaces at the top universities.

Activities

1. Have the class help to draw on the board a Mind Map of "the group" in Japanese society. What aspects of Japanese behavior and values are related to their emphasis on the group? Go over any new Japanese terms and add those to the Mind Map. *(interpretive, constructive)*

2. Discuss the difference in leadership styles valued in Japan and the U.S. What are some characteristics of good leaders in the U.S.? What are some characteristics of good leaders in Japan? Why do these characteristics differ from one culture to the other?

   Discuss the importance of the han in the Japanese homeroom. For a week, have the students form and work in hans. Have the group choose a different han leader each day. This leader must practice the Japanese form of leadership, trying to create consensus and maintain harmony within the group.

   At the end of the week, discuss the students' experience of Japanese leadership and group cooperation. What did they like and dislike about the experience? *(cross-cultural, constructive)*

3. Discuss: What are some benefits to making group loyalty more important than individualism? Can the students think of any instances in U.S. society in which people are encouraged to work cooperatively in groups instead of independently as individuals? What are the advantages and disadvantages to a group orientation? *(interpretive, constructive)*

4. Draw the figure of the ninjo-giri-tanin relationships on the board and go over each term. When the students feel they understand these concepts and their relation to one another, ask them to draw and label a similar picture of their own equivalent to ninjo, giri, and tanin groups. Who is included in these groups? *(cross-cultural, constructive)*

Lesson 4

Hierarchy

Just like class, the system of *hierarchy* is not the same in the various cultures in which it is found. Both Japan and India have forms of hierarchy, but the systems in the two countries are quite different. In Japan both groups and individuals take their places at different levels on this imaginary staircase, yet there is a strong feeling of egalitarianism, of people being equal. In India the opposite is true. There groups of people, not individuals, are placed above or below each other in a caste system, which is rigid and unbending. There is no sense of equality among castes.

Hierarchy in Japan

Japan does not have a class system. This is very difficult for people in the U.S. to understand, even those who have spent a great deal of time in the country. One important factor contributing to Japan's lack of a class system is the fact that the Japanese do not have the great division of incomes that one finds in the U.S. The head of a corporation in the U.S. often receives a salary many times greater than the employees or factory workers. He or she will be in the upper class while many of his or her workers will be in the middle or lower class. The head of a Japanese corporation, on the other hand, will receive a salary closer to that of his workers. Moreover, there are few in Japan who can be classified as underprivileged or poor (Reischauer, 1988).

Instead of a class system, the Japanese have a hierarchy. Picture a giant stairway, and each person has a specific step on which to stand. There might be a few people on one's own step—such as an old classmate or some individuals with whom one works—but nearly everyone else in the culture will be above or below another individual. The only person who has no one above him is the emperor.

Hierarchy begins within the family. Brothers and sisters do not call each other by their first names, but instead use "elder sister" or "older brother." At school, a boy who fails to add *san*, a sign of respect, to an upper classman's name can find himself in serious trouble. The older boy may decide to teach him a lesson by involving the younger student in a physical fight.

Beginning in junior high school, students are required to wear uniforms. Hierarchy takes over again, as students in the upper grades tell younger ones how these uniforms should be worn. Age definitely has its privilege in Japan, and it also has power. Throughout life, the Japan-

ese always show respect to those only slightly older than themselves.

The sense of hierarchy continues throughout life. When meeting for the first time, Japanese are anxious to know exactly where the other stands on the imaginary staircase. It is important to discover the other's status in order to know how deeply to bow and how to speak with him or her. The quickest and easiest way to discover another's status is through the exchange of business cards. One's position and the company for which one works establish a person's exact spot in the hierarchy. Companies in Japan have their own hierarchy. The company for which one works is even more important than the actual position one holds within that company. This means that a president of one of Japan's giant corporations is more important and higher on the stairway than the president of a small company, even though their salaries, their memberships in clubs, and their homes are very similar. People who come from the very best universities are recruited by the big corporations. About 3 percent of all college graduates come from Tokyo University, but about 25 percent of all corporations presidents in Japan have graduated from that school.

Hierarchy also carries a sense of responsibility. A boss becomes almost a father-figure to his employees, looking protectively into their private lives. Many in the U.S. would consider such interest an invasion of privacy (Reischauer, 1988).

Friendships made during one's early school years often last a lifetime, and they are one of the few relationships in which individuals do not find themselves on the stair-steps of hierarchy. With these school-day friends a certain equality is shared. But with nearly everyone else with whom one comes in contact a ranking system will exist.

The group and hierarchy serve the Japanese person well. They give him a sense of belonging and a willingness to accept his station in life—his job, for example—without having always to compete for a higher position (Reischauer, 1988).

Activities

1. Ask each student to draw a picture of a Japanese hierarchy on a piece of paper (they may choose the figure of a ladder, a stairway, branches of a tree, a path up a mountain, etc.) Then have them place people on the various levels of the hierarchy and label these people. Who stands where? What determines where one stands in Japanese society (one's age, one's company, one's position in the company, one's level of education, one's profession)?

   Now ask the students to draw a picture of a U.S. hierarchy on another piece of paper. Is such a task possible? If so, what would such a hierarchy be based upon in the U.S.? In other words, have the students place people, including themselves, on the various levels of the hierarchy and label these people. Who stands where? Why? Who receives more respect? Why?

   How is a U.S. hierarchy different from the Japanese hierarchy? (A U.S. hierarchy may be based on racist or sexist practices, for example.) We aren't supposed to have a hierarchy in the U.S. but many would say we do. What kind of hierarchy do we have? Is it a fair one? Does it seem as fair as the Japanese hierarchy? Why is there a sense of security in a society with a hierarchy? *(constructive, cross-cultural)*

2. Have the students practice a sense of Japanese hierarchy for a day. For simplicity's sake, the hierarchy will be based on age alone. Each student, then, will carry a "business card" with his or her birth date written on it. As students work together, talk, go to lunch, etc., they must first bow and present to each other their business card. The one who is younger must then bow a little deeper and show great respect for the older one (the students can choose their forms of respect). At the end of the day, or at your next class meeting, discuss how your students felt about their experience of hierarchy. *(cross-cultural, constructive)*

Did You Know?

Indians of the subcontinent usually end their meals with *paan*, a mixture of beetle nuts, spices, and lime wrapped in leaves. It is supposed to aid digestion, but it also stains the teeth.

Hierarchy in India: The Caste System

A Glimpse of the Past:

The sun had just settled over the dusty horizon, but a red orange glow still hovered across the tiny shacks, pieced together from tin cans, cardboard, wooden boxes, and any pliable material that could be fashioned into a shanty's wall. The narrow, alley-like streets, shadowed by the crowded shacks, were crammed with half-naked children and poorly clad adults scurrying home from jobs as sweepers of the cities' streets. They were considered so low in social position that anyone who came in contact with them had to cleanse himself immediately. A Brahmin, descendant for 3,000 years of priests and scholars and the highest of India's castes, would have to wash himself six times if their shadow fell on him.

Inside one of the dark hovels, Rama, a thin, tired woman of thirty-five crouched near the door. As she waited for total darkness to fall, she thought how fortunate she was to have a roof over head. Many people slept on the streets. As soon as the town was cloaked in total darkness, she would be allowed to venture from her tiny, one-room quarters, where she lived with her husband and seven children. Their water supply was nearly gone. It would be impossible for her to visit the local well because she would contaminate it by her very presence. Instead, she must walk three miles to another well where she would be allowed to fill her water jugs for her family.

The year was 1930, and Rama and members of her group, known as the Purada-Vannan, were not allowed to appear on the streets until after dark. If anyone's eyes were to fall on Rama or members of her group, that person would become impure. Rama and her people were the lowest of the low in all India because they washed the clothes of the untouchables.

The nighttime wanderers, the Purada-Vannan, no longer exist. Such harsh traditions have been declared illegal in India. The caste system in that country, in theory, has not existed since the constitution of 1947 outlawed such practices and assured everyone equal opportunities. Many of the strictest traditions, such as those associated with the Purada-Vannan, have disappeared. However, laws do not completely wipe out attitudes of discrimination. Today, particularly in the villages where 70 percent of India's population lives, the caste system still prevails socially if not legally. It is in the big cities—where people often do not know each other's personal background—that individuals can lose their caste identities.

Caste versus Class

What is a caste system and how does it differ from a class system? Some *class systems* allow for mobility. It is possible in some class systems, depending upon many circumstances, for an individual to move up or down into a higher or lower position within society. But in a *caste system*, you are born into a certain position, and mobility in or out of it is nearly impossible. Each caste has a definite position in society with one group above or below the other in the hierarchy. While the caste system is closely tied to the Hindu religion, it is not part of this religion's actual beliefs.

How the Caste System Began

Although no one really knows for sure, there are several theories as to how caste started in India. It is believed to have dated back to approximately 1200 B.C. One theory is similar to the Judeo-Christian story of Noah and the ark. According to the Indian's tale, Mahanuvu, a very famous man of his times, took seven people who were sorry for their wrongdoings on board his own ark when he received word that a great flood was coming. After the waters went down, the seven people left the ark and went around India dividing people into four major castes (Baker, 1990).

Another popular story is that the four major caste divisions came from the Almighty God, Brahman. From the mouth of this great god came the highest caste known as the Brahmin. From the god's arm came the next caste level known as the Kshatrya. From the god's thighs came the Vayshya, and from his feet came the lowly Sudra (Baker, 1990).

Did You Know?
The Hindus of India believe that when one dies, one is reborn into another life. *Karma* is the sense that what a person has done in a past life will influence how he or she will live in the next life. A person is born into a certain caste because of behavior in his or her past life. If he or she is virtuous, there is a possibility to be reborn into a higher caste in the next life. But if a member of a high caste, such as the Brahmin caste, commits sins and crimes, or is greedy and lazy, that person may be reborn as something as low as a pig.

Caste Divisions

There are four basic caste categories, or *varna* (war-nha), in India. Certain purification rituals as well as occupations are associated with each caste. The highest caste, the Brahmin, have a 3,000-year heritage as priests and scholars. Even today many of these Brahmin still serve as ministers and teachers. The Kshatrya (sha-tree-ah), the next highest in rank, are the warrior caste. Today that translates into being members of the police force and army. Many of them also are very wealthy property owners. The Vayshya (why-shee-ah), the next highest caste, serve as merchants, businessmen, money lenders, and landowners. The lowest caste, the Sudra (shoo-drah), serve the upper castes as carpenters and blacksmiths (Baker, 1990). There are many subcastes as well. Within the Sudra caste, for example, there are thousands of these smaller groups.

There are millions of *untouchables*. Some people consider the untouchables so low in this hierarchy that they do not even qualify for a place in the caste system. In the past they held menial positions as sweepers and latrine cleaners. One story goes that the untouchables descended from native tribes who were conquered long ago by invaders with lighter skin from the north. Modern-day Indians of higher castes descended from these conquerors.

In the past, castes depended upon each other because certain jobs could only be performed by people within certain groups. Today, however, many people hold jobs that cross over caste lines, and with this crossing some feel that a certain amount of security is lost. By law, people can no longer be kept from jobs because of their caste. Mahatma Gandhi, a great nonviolent freedom fighter in India, gave the untouchables, the name of *Harijan* (hahr-i-jahn). The word means "children of God," and the name was designed to counteract the stigma attached to this lowly ranked group. Gandhi also fought to give these people the right to enter temples and shrines, a privilege previously denied them.

Today, there are quotas assuring Harijans a certain number of places in government jobs, positions in parliament (the Indian legislative body), and places in universities. They are also guaranteed a minimum wage. Many people in India argue against these quotas, just as people in the U.S. complain about affirmative action programs. Establishing quotas, say many Indians, just keeps the caste system going because it recognizes the fact that it still exists.

Newcomers to India are often bewildered by this very strict segregation that places each caste group on a precise step in the hierarchy. The Bradley family, discussed at the beginning of this chapter, was hurt and confused when they attempted to interact with the high Brahmin caste. In turn, when Indians go abroad, they face problems in interacting in a flexible class society. The relaxed class system of the United States at first can prove confusing for them.

Activities

1. Ask students to rent and view the movie *Gandhi.* After they have seen the movie, discuss any aspects of the caste system that were represented in the movie.

   Then have the students write a short essay describing the traits they admired about Gandhi. Are there any U.S. heroes and heroines who have had traits similar to Gandhi's? *(interpretive, constructive)*

2. Discuss: If the caste system is illegal, how can it still linger on in people's attitudes in India? Do we have anything similar in the U.S.? (Changes in U.S. law—civil rights legislation and integrated schooling, for example—have not eradicated racist attitudes.) *(interpretive, constructive)*

3. Role-play a caste system. Have the students number off 1, 2, 3, 4. For one day have all those who have been designated 1 sit in one section of the room; those who were named 2 sit in another section, etc. Have the class decide what each group or "caste" is allowed to do. Perhaps group 1 will not be allowed to take a drink that day from the fountain closest to the classroom. Instead, members of this caste will have to journey to the far end of the building for water. Those in group 2 may not

be allowed to enter certain areas of the playground. The class should design its own caste system, deciding on rules, jobs, obligations, etc. The type of punishment that comes with breaking a caste rule should also be planned. But do not make the rules and regulations strictly punitive. Try to show how one caste must depend on another for services or products. One caste could be in charge of distributing books and papers.

Shortly before the close of the day, ask the students to drop their caste identities. How did the students feel about their caste experiences? List some of their reactions on the board. Try to solicit positive as well as negative comments. Was there anything beneficial about such a system? If so, what was it? If there are negative comments, be sure to ask them to explain why they did not approve of the system.

You might want to follow this exercise with a writing assignment. Possible topics include: the student's experience of the caste system that day; one of the castes of India, how it lives today when the caste system is illegal; the achievements of Gandhi; the differences between a class and a caste system.
(cross-cultural, constructive)

Resources

Baker, Sophie. *Caste: At Home in Hindu India.* London: Johnathan Cape Ltd., 1990.

Beteille, Andre. *The Backward Classes in Contemporary India.* Delhi: Oxford University Press, 1992.

Cooper, Jilly. *Class: A View from Middle England.* London: Corgi Books, 1980.

Cooper, Robert and Nanthapa Cooper. *Culture Shock! Thailand . . . And How to Survive It.* Singapore: Times Books International, 1984.

Demko, George J., et al. *Why in the World: Adventures in Geography.* New York: Anchor Books, 1992.

Doi, Takeo. *The Anatomy of Independence.* Tokyo: Kodansha International, 1973.

Duke, Benjamin. *The Japanese School: Lessons for Industrial America.* New York: Praeger, 1986.

The Economist Business Traveller's Guides: Britain. New York: Prentice Hall Press, 1987.

Feiler, Bruce. *Learning to Bow: Inside the Heart of Japan.* New York: Ticknor & Fields, 1991.

Furnas, J. C. *The Americans: A Social History of the United States, 1587–1914.* New York: G. P. Putnam's Sons, 1969.

Harris, Neil. "American Manners." *Making America: The Society and Culture of the United States;* edited by Luther S. Luedtke. Chapel Hill: University of North Carolina Press, 1992.

Kato, Hiroki and Joan S. Kato. *Understanding and Working with the Japanese Business World.* Englewood Cliffs: Prentice Hall, 1992.

Lamb, David. *The Africans: Encounters from the Sudan to the Cape.* New York: Random House, 1982.

Marwick, Arthur. *Social History of Britain: British Society Since 1945.* Harmondsworth: Pelican Books, 1982.

Pessen, Edward. "Status and Social Class in America." *Making America: The Society and Culture of the United States;* edited by Luther S. Luedtke. Chapel Hill: University of North Carolina Press, 1992.

Reischauer, Edwin O. *The Japanese Today: Change and Continuity.* Cambridge: Belknap Press [Harvard University Press], 1988.

Stewart, Edward C. and Milton J. Bennett. *American Cultural Patterns: A Cross-Cultural Perspective,* rev. ed. Yarmouth, ME: Intercultural Press, 1991.

Trudgill, Peter. *Coping with America: A Beginner's Guide to the U.S.A.* Oxford: Basil Blackwell, 1982.

Moral Values

Goals

This chapter explores how cultures define and teach their moral values. The information, proverbs, stories, and activities are designed to help your students achieve the following goals:

1. To understand that every culture maintains certain moral codes for beliefs and behavior, but that these codes may vary from culture to culture.

2. To see that a culture's moral standards are based on its secular (non-religious) values, on its religious values, and on the way it regards the natural and supernatural worlds.

3. To experience the wit and wisdom contained in cultural proverbs and to see how proverbs are one way a culture teaches its moral values to its members.

4. To see that stories are another important means by which cultures promote their moral values. Students will read and interpret a sample of stories from other cultures, stories whose purpose is to impart some moral lesson.

5. To learn a bit about several of the world's major religions and to see that religious teachings often underlie a culture's moral values.

6. To understand the importance nature and the supernatural plays in the spiritual and ethical lives of the Japanese and of the Navajos.

Note: While the main discussion of this chapter will focus on some moral issues in several different cultures, the *Did You Know?* boxes will continue to cover many of the dos and don'ts associated with proper etiquette in various cultures.

Cross-Cultural Attitudes and Skills

As students work toward these goals, they will develop the following cross-cultural attitudes and skills:

1. They will continue to grasp the idea that their culture plays a strong role in determining their beliefs, in this case beliefs about what is right or wrong, good or evil, productive or unproductive. The better they understand the role culture plays in how they think and act, the more willing they will be to accept other cultural ways of thinking and acting.

2. They will continue to develop their interpretive skills as they try to unravel the meanings of proverbs and stories from other cultures.

3. They will explore their own cultural roots by investigating and telling their own cultural and family stories. As they share these stories with their classmates, they will participate in an essential cross-cultural activity: making their cultural differences part of a process of sharing and discussion.

4. The collaborative work they will do in their activities will strengthen their abilities to communicate, listen, debate, and come to consensus; activities that are important for becoming active and responsible participants in a pluralistic culture.

GENERAL INTRODUCTION

Every culture has a moral code, whether or not people are aware of it, agree about it, believe in it, or follow it. A moral code is a culture's shared, often unwritten system of standards or values for behavior: it teaches us to reward certain behavior considered right or good and to punish behavior considered wrong or bad. In a country as large and diverse as the United States, it may be difficult to pinpoint a uniform moral code. But there are certain ethical standards most in the United States would agree upon, such as that *stealing is wrong* under most circumstances or that *murder is wrong* in most situations.

Did You Know?

When comparing how certain cultures interpret their moral codes, one finds some interesting differences. What one culture may consider morally wrong another culture may regard as right. In Mexico, for example, people have a very strong desire to tell others what they want to hear. Some in the U.S., who are often accustomed to "telling it like it is," can misinterpret this Mexican behavior as not telling the truth. But within the parameters of the Mexican culture, such behavior is not considered lying but simply a means of pleasing the person with whom one is having a conversation.

Did You Know?

Behaving in the right or correct way is so important in Mexico and the rest of Latin America that a rude person is labeled *mal educado* (**mahl** ay-doo-**kah**-do), or "poorly educated." *Un mal educado* is a person who is rude, boorish, and insensitive. Mexicans, however, do not simply concern themselves with correct etiquette. The meaning goes far beyond this to include kindness and understanding towards all those with whom one comes in contact.

While a culture's secular values play a strong role in establishing moral principles, religions provide one of the strongest foundations on which these principles are built. Many religions have sacred writings: the Torah for Jews, the Bible for Christians, the Quran for Muslims, and the Vedas (Books of Knowledge) for Hindus. At a very early age, children begin to learn lessons and passages from these sacred books. But some religions have no written word. The African Religion—the name given to the spiritual beliefs that spread through the indigenous peoples in the southern two-thirds of the African continent—has no sacred writings, yet the people are deeply religious. Native Americans have no sacred book that tells of their spiritual beliefs and have no word for "religion" in the hundreds of languages and even more dialects spoken among their peoples. To label a thought or deed as "religious" would be to separate the secular and sacred worlds, and to the Native American this is not possible. A sense of spirituality runs through every facet of Native American life. When religions have no sacred writings, beliefs spread orally, often through tales related by wise old storytellers of the community.

Stories and proverbs are two ways cultures teach their young members moral values. If one traveled around the world, one would discover something amazing: the same basic story, moral, or proverb may be told, perhaps in a little different way, in many different cultures throughout the world. How did that come to be? How could two or more vastly different cultures, thousands of miles apart, be telling similar stories and teaching similar moral lessons? One of many theories is that travelers along the ancient trade routes carried the stories with them and told them to members of the cultures they visited. In any case, people around the world have developed their own moral principles while borrowing, modifying, and adapting principles from other cultures to fit their own needs. We shall be examining a selection of proverbs and stories told around the world to see what moral lessons they promote.

This chapter concludes with a lesson that explores the relationship between nature and the spiritual and ethical life for followers of the Shinto faith in Japan and for the Navajo tribe in North America. Both of these groups believe that nature is full of meaning and offers instruction in the moral life; living life well requires a close relationship with the natural and supernatural worlds.

Lesson 1

A wise man who knows proverbs reconciles difficulties.
(African/Yoruba proverb)
Proverbs are the coins of the people. (Russian proverb)

Learning Moral Values Through Proverbs

Proverbs provide a fast and easy means for learning some of a culture's moral values. These pithy sayings make their points forcefully, quickly, and in a style that is easy to remember. Proverbs may take the form of questions, declarative statements, or simply lines in a song. They come from many different sources: the law, religion, superstitions, wise individuals, fables, historical events, heroic occasions, and traditional customs. For the most part, proverbs reflect a culture's secular moral values, even if they once came from a religious teaching.

Many cultures share the same proverb; while the meaning remains the same, sometimes the wording may be different. For example, the Bible says, "An eye for an eye, a tooth for a tooth." The Nandi, a group of people in East Africa, tell their people, "A goat's hide buys a goat's hide and a gourd a gourd." Experts tell us that the meaning of these two sayings is the same. Can the students detect the similarity?

On the other hand, a proverb may sound just like one found in another culture, yet have a different meaning. People in the U.S. say, "The clothes make the man." In the U.S. a good appearance makes a favorable impression. Yet in Germany, the same expression has a very negative meaning. It refers to an individual who is trying to impress others by dressing in a very expensive manner. The saying in Germany criticizes personal vanity.

In the United States, Benjamin Franklin is probably the best-known proverb writer. His ideas and sayings were not original. Franklin took many old European sayings, gave them a local twist, and wrote them into his famous Poor Richard's Almanac. They have served many well as young and old alike repeat his catchy sayings and often apply them to lessons in right and wrong behavior.

Activities

On page 181 are some proverbs from around the world. They are listed by the areas from which they come. Copy the list for your students.

1. Divide the class into small groups and assign a selection from each area to each group. Ask the groups to interpret—or at least guess—the meaning of each proverb. Have the students paraphrase each proverb: What kind of behavior does the saying praise or criticize? Ask each group to share with the class their favorite proverb from the list and to explain its ethical teaching. *(cross-cultural, interpretive)*

2. Have the students pair up and read through all of the proverbs together. As they read through, they should label each proverb with the kind of behavior that is criticized or praised (words such as "greed," "selfishness," "nosiness," "honesty," "kindness," etc. are suitable labels). Then ask each pair to make columns on sheets of paper; each column should be titled with one of the labels given to the proverbs. In other words, there will be a "Greed" column, a "Selfishness" column, an "Honesty" column, etc. Under each column they should rewrite (or cut and paste) the proverbs that fit under that category. They should make sure to note where the proverb comes from. If they find a proverb from one culture that is nearly the same as one from another culture, they should mark it with a star.

   One of the points of this exercise is for the students to discover that cultures sometimes share similar ideas of what constitutes right and wrong behavior. Therefore, this activity should be concluded with a discussion of the similarities between proverbs and their meanings, similarities made evident in their columns. You might also want to discuss the ways proverbs are written (i.e., their brevity, conciseness, wittiness, use of images, etc.). *(cross-cultural, interpretive)*

3. Make two columns on the board, one labeled "Right" and the other labeled "Wrong." Ask the students to suggest examples of behavior that are considered right or wrong in the U.S. and list them under the appropriate heading. Some discussion and debate should be encouraged. Then have each student choose two examples from each column and write their own proverbs for each example. Post their proverbs around the room or include them in the student's portfolio. *(constructive)*

A SELECTION OF PROVERBS FROM AROUND THE WORLD

U.S.

God helps those who help themselves.

The love of money is the root of all evil.

Honesty is the best policy.

A good deed is never lost.

DANISH

An honest man does not become a dog simply to get a bone.

The one who holds the ladder is no less at fault than the thief.

God will help you if you help yourself.

RUSSIAN

A hard-earned penny lasts a lifetime.

Next to the rotten apple the good one also spoils.

Some people are masters of money and some are its slaves.

ARAB

Consider the problems of others and you'll be content with your lot.

Work at a task for 40 days and it will be overcome.

If lying saves, then truth saves more.

CHINESE

The wise man does not store away treasures. By giving more, he has more.

A great talker never lacks enemies.

Do not attempt to stand on two boats.

JAPANESE

Wealthy people have many worries.

He who chases two hares will not catch even one.

If the hands are empty the mouth is empty.

MEXICAN

Kind acts, not words, are the true language of love.

He who promises much is most likely to fulfill very little.

A good deed is the best prayer.

AFRICAN

Greed never finishes. (Swahili)

If God dishes you rice in a basket, do not wish to eat soup. (Sierra Leone)

One mouth cannot drink from two gourds at one time. (Uganda)

Stolen things bring in misfortune. (Kenya)

Lesson 2

Learning Moral Values Through Stories, Part I

Stories are one of the best tools for cross-cultural understanding. Reading a story is like traveling to another culture; it offers us the opportunity to experience what the world is like for other persons, even if fictional. As we read about the lives of others, we are immersed in their perspectives and the rich details of their existence. We encourage you to use stories from other cultural viewpoints in all areas of the curriculum.

For now we have chosen stories specifically geared toward the subject of this chapter—the teaching of moral values and behavior in various cultures. Therefore the kinds of stories we have selected are a bit two-dimensional compared to more realistic fiction. They include a religious writing, a legend, a fable, and two folk tales from cultures other than the United States. These stories were told and written especially for teaching moral lessons, and we can find such stories in most cultures around the world. Some of these kinds of stories are passed on through a culture's oral traditions by storytellers and parents.

Legends are stories about some famous event, place, or person. They may be based on fact but later embellished almost beyond recognition to become stories that teach a moral lesson by entertaining the listeners. To the storyteller and listeners alike, they can be taken as true accountings of the past.

Myths, folk tales, and fables are told to account for the origins of the world, why humans act the way they do, why nature is the way it is, etc. While they usually concern themselves with gods, superhumans, and animals, they often impart very human moral lessons.

Did You Know?

Superstitions sometimes dictate social behavior. In Japan chopsticks should never be left standing upright in a bowl. That is an indication that the food has been left for the dead.

Activity

In the following two lessons, your students will read samples of a religious writing, a legend, a fable, and two folk tales from cultures around the world. Each story has been told to model and teach a moral lesson.

Copy the stories for the students. Divide the class into groups and have the groups read and discuss each story together. Discussion questions are included after each story. Background information has been provided to share with students as an aid to their discussion. *(interpretive, cross-cultural)*

Background Information for "How the Buddha Responds"

The first story comes from *The Sutra,* a sacred writing of Buddhism. The religion began in the sixth century B.C. when Siddhartha Gautama, a wealthy young prince of northern India and a Hindu, decided to leave his wife, son, and life of luxury to search for the truth. Protected by the high walls of his many palaces, the wealthy young prince had never seen illness, death, or poverty. That is, until one day when he was returning from a hunting expedition. Along the way, he was startled to see a man writhing in pain, a dead man being carried to his cremation, and a feeble old man shuffling along the road. Before reaching the confines of the palace, he saw a humble, contemplative monk begging for food. But in spite of his hunger and poverty, the monk appeared happy and content. At that moment the prince decided to leave his young wife and son in order to search for truth and enlightenment. Gautama eventually found the answers he was seeking and became very wise. He was given the name of Buddha. It was the beginning of a religion that was to spread eastward from India across Asia to the islands of Japan. Today more than 500 million people follow the teachings of the Buddha.

From a very early age, children of this faith are taught to resist violence and cherish all life; that while there is no supreme god to punish or reward a person, everyone has the potential for spiritual awakening or enlightenment; that everyone should practice self-restraint; that each individual should respect the belongings of others; that only truth should be spoken; and that no one should take part in producing any object that would be dangerous to another's health or weaken the mind. At some time during their lives, boys are expected to serve as monks. The period may be for only a day, perhaps a week, or it can be for a lifetime if the young man decides to dedicate himself to the search for enlightenment.

Buddhism stresses nonviolence. In the above story, the Buddha shows that by not responding to violence, the wrongdoing is thrown back on the person who is committing it. It is similar to Christianity's "turn the other cheek" ethic.

Background Information for "A Story of Nasreddin Hodja"

Throughout the Middle East, dozens and dozens of stories circulate about a man named *Joha* (joh-ha). His name changes from one country to the next. In Turkey, where this particular story is told, he is called *Nasreddin Hodja* (nas-red-in hoh-ja), and in Iran he is known as *Mullah Nasreddin* (moo-lah nas-red-in). His most common name is *Joha,* particularly within the Arab Middle East. Some scholars believe Joha actually lived in the thirteenth century, in which case the stories can be classified as legends. In this particular tale Joha, or Nasreddin Hodja, as he is called here, appears in the mosque, the Islam house of worship, on Friday, the day of worship. He comes in the role of a *shaikh* (shake), a religious leader but not a clergyman because the Islamic religion has no priesthood, ministry, or rabbinate, as do Christianity and Judaism.

Islam has five basic beliefs or pillars, as they are called, on which the religion is built. Muslims proclaim that there is no other God but Allah. They observe the fast of Ramadan, at which time they take no liquids or foods from sunrise to sunset for one month. The fasting is in commemoration of Mohammed's first revelation from the angel Gabriel, which told him what his purpose in life was to be. Each Muslim is to give a certain percentage of his income each year to the poor. If in good health and financially able to do so, each Muslim is expected once in a lifetime to make the *Hajj* (hahdj), a pilgrimage to Mecca where the religion began. All the faithful are to pray five times a day, and on Friday at noon these prayers should be said in the mosque. Usually only men and boys go to the mosque, but women, who do attend, sit in a special section reserved for them.

In this story Nasreddin Hodja appears at one of these Friday services to speak to the worshippers. In his witty way, he really is asking them why they have come to the mosque. Rather than seek true answers, the people respond with clever, quick rejoinders. Nasreddin is not satisfied. He feels the people are being hypocritical about coming to the mosque, and he wants them to search for their real reasons for being there.

Background Information for "The Lion and the Mouse"

Fables are short tales dedicated to teaching moral principles. This kind of story probably originated with the ancient Greeks and early Asians. It later found its way into European literature. Among the most famous fables are those credited to a sixth-century B.C. Greek slave known as Aesop. However, the Arabs have practically identical stories under the title of *Fables of Luqman.*

"The Lion and the Mouse" is one of Aesop's many fables, with which your students are probably familiar. One of the principles it illustrates is what the Christian religion calls the Golden Rule—Do unto others as you would have them do unto you. One can find this principle in many religions and philosophies around the world. It often is worded a little differently but the central point is that you should treat others as you wish to be treated. In this fable, the lion treats the tiny mouse with kindness and thereby spares his life. The mouse, in turn, does the same for the lion. This fable illustrates other moral themes as well, such as the value of being witty (the lion does a favor for the mouse because he gets a kick out of the mouse's cleverness), the importance of depending on one another, and the belief that good deeds will be returned. Your students will probably think of others.

HOW THE BUDDHA RESPONDS

A mean and wicked man heard that the Buddha was teaching that evil acts should be returned with love and kindness. He sought out the Buddha and abused him. But the Buddha said nothing and only pitied the man who was cruel to him. Finally, when the man had stopped his cruelty, the Buddha asked him, "Son, if a man refused to accept a gift made to him, to whom would it belong?" The abuser quickly answered, "It would belong to the man who offered it."

"My son," said the Buddha, "I refuse to accept your abuse, and ask that you keep it for yourself. Will this not be a source of unhappiness for you?"

The Buddha went on to tell his tormenter that when a mean and wicked individual attacks a good person, it can be compared to looking up into the heavens and spitting. The spit does not soil nor disturb the heavens, but falls back on the one who committed the act.

The man listened to the Buddha and left very ashamed of what he had done. He came back, however, to become a follower of the Buddha.

Statue of Buddha

Discussion Questions:

1. Who are the characters in this story? Describe them.

2. How does the Buddha respond to the man's behavior?

3. What does the Buddha teach the man?

4. How does the man respond to what the Buddha has told him?

5. What is the moral lesson of this story? If there is more than one moral lesson, describe some other lessons that you learn from the story.

6. Is the moral lesson similar to one taught in the United States?

7. Can you guess from which culture or cultures this story comes?

A STORY OF NASREDDIN HODJA

One Friday sometime in the thirteenth century, in the Anatolian town of Akshehir [part of present-day Turkey], the Shaikh [pronounced "shake"] Nasreddin Hodja mounted the minbar [pulpit] of the Grand Mosque and addressed the congregation. "O believers," asked Nasreddin, "do you know what I am about to say?" "No, we don't," chorused the congregation. Nasreddin paused dramatically, then said: "If you don't know what I'm going to say, then what's the use of my talking?" And he descended from the minbar. The congregation looked at one another in confusion.

A week went by, and when Friday came, Nasreddin once more climbed the steps of the minbar and addressed the congregation. "O believers, do you know what I am about to say?" This time the congregation was not going to be caught napping. "Yes," they all answered. "We know what you are about to say." Nasreddin again paused dramatically. Then he said, "Since you all know what I'm about to say, there's no need for me to say it." And he descended from the minbar. The congregation was bewildered. Finally, they decided that next Friday, one half of them would answer "no" to the shaikh's question, and the other half would answer "yes."

A week went by, and when Friday came, the faithful hurried to the mosque. Nasreddin mounted the minbar. "O believers," he said, "do you know what I am about to say?" "No!" shouted half the congregation. "Yes!" shouted the other half. Nasreddin paused dramatically. Then he said, "Very good. Those of you who know tell those who don't." And he descended from the minbar.

Reprinted with permission from *Aramco World* (Houston: Aramco, 1971).

Discussion Questions:

1. Who are the characters in the story? Describe them.

2. What does Nasreddin Hodja say to the congregation on the first, second, and third Fridays? How does the congregation answer him?

3. If you were in the congregation, how would you answer Nasreddin?

4. Why do you think Nasreddin Hodja says the things he does? What do you think he means with his last statement to the congregation?

5. What are some possible moral lessons to be learned from this story?

6. Can you guess what area of the world this story comes from?

THE LION AND THE MOUSE

Once upon a time a fierce and dangerous lion lived in the jungle. All the animals feared him. One day, while the lion lay sleeping, a tiny mouse approached him. The mouse was so small he could not tell that the great mound of flesh before him really was a lion. "Ah, a mountain I must climb," the mouse thought to himself, as he looked at the enormous animal. With that he scampered up the lion's tail and along his back. The lion felt something tickling him and immediately woke from his deep slumber.

The lion was angry when he saw the tiny mouse. "I shall eat you," he proclaimed. But the mouse argued back, "Why eat me? I am so small, you will still be hungry. Besides, who knows. Someday you may need my help."

"You are very funny," roared the lion. "How could I ever need a mouse? But since you are so witty, I shall let you go." With that the mouse scampered away, and the lion promptly forgot him.

A short time later, hunters came into the jungle and captured the lion. They tied him up with sturdy rope and then left him on the jungle floor while they sought help to move the lion to their campsite. The lion tried in vain to tear at the rope and free himself. He was desolate and realized the end was near. Suddenly, he felt a funny sensation running across his back. It reminded him of the tiny mouse that once had annoyed him. To his astonishment the same tiny mouse abruptly appeared in front of his nose.

"I shall eat the rope," declared the little mouse. "I love ropes, and besides, I can help my friend." With that he proceeded to chew away at the strong rope with his sharp teeth, and within moments, the rope had split apart.

"I bless the day I decided not to eat you," cried the lion. "I saved your life, and you saved mine!" The lion lunged merrily through the jungle with the tiny mouse laughing happily, as he rested in the giant animal's tangled mane.

Discussion Questions:

1. Who are the characters in the story? Describe them.

2. What does the lion do for the mouse? Why does he do this favor?

3. What does the mouse do for the lion? Why does he do this favor?

4. What kind of behavior is rewarded in this story? What moral lessons can you learn from this story?

5. Is this the kind of story that might be told in the United States?

Learning Moral Values Through Stories, Part II

Refer to the instructions in Lesson 2 for the two stories contained in this lesson. Then proceed with the activities that follow.

Background Information for "The Stone-Cutter"

In this folk tale from India, children readily discover that wishing for more and getting it do not necessarily bring happiness. The story illustrates that being unhappy with what you have and being greedy for more can only result in further discontentment; one is happiest when one accepts and makes the best of his or her present position in life.

Hinduism is one of the oldest religions in the world and dates back thousands of years before Christianity or Islam. The Hindu religion contains many myths and legends concerning its gods. Basically, Hindus believe in one God, Brahman, meaning "World-Soul." But three other gods are actually a part of, or a manifestation of, Brahman. These gods are Brahma, the creator; Vishnu, the Preserver; and Shiva, the Destroyer. Shiva is the most famous god, often pictured with four arms, one leg extended outward and a second leg standing on a dwarf of evil. Shiva is not considered an evil god, but simply the one who, in a sense, "cleans house," destroying to make way for creation. There are many other gods who are offshoots or different manifestations of the three gods.

Hinduism is the dominant religion in India, and Hindus strive to leave behind the harsh material world and eventually be united with Brahman. To do this, the human soul must be born again and again until he finally is united with Brahman. How an individual behaves in this life will determine whether or not he or she comes back at a higher level in society and thereby be closer to union with Brahman. If he or she has not led a good life, he or she must come back with a lower status. The record of one's good and bad acts is an individual's *karma*; Hindus believe that a good deed reaps good things and that a bad deed results in bad things. There is a religious ritual to be observed for everything in life: getting up, eating, bathing, etc. Hindus also believe in nonviolence, truthfulness, self-control, detachment from the material world, and deep respect for all human creatures. Many Hindus are vegetarians, and hardly any Hindus will eat beef because they

Shiva

William Rockhill Nelson Gallery of Art, Atkins Museum of Fine Arts, Kansas City, Missouri

believe the cow is a sacred animal. Cows roam freely through the countryside and city streets.

Background Information for "Who Is the Greatest of Them All?

In this folk tale from the Bushmen in southern Africa, the ostrich proves that wisdom and cleverness are more powerful than brute strength. She illustrates that she is the "greatest of all," despite her lack of teeth. She is clever enough to beat the lion without having to kill and eat him; she simply knocks him unconscious. The ostrich is the Bushmen's favorite bird. Many of their tales feature her as a wise and courageous example to humans.

This story reflects the Bushmen's belief that it is more important to be wise and clever than to be strong. The Kung Bushmen (one of several Bushmen tribes) call themselves "the harmless people," for they, like most Bushmen, would rather run from conflict, or submit, than fight. Fighting is not in the Bushman spirit—unless it is absolutely necessary, as when they need to defend the land, water, and animals they consider their own.

Unfortunately, it is this reluctance to fight or compete with their powerful European and Bantu neighbors that slowly is leading to the Bushmen's demise. There are more than 100,000 Bushmen living today. They used to live as nomadic hunter-gatherers, free to wander and subsist in the wild, especially and most recently (in their long history) in the Kalahari Desert. Most have moved or been moved, however, into areas of Angola, South Africa, and Botswana where water is more accessible. Only a handful of Bushmen still live with the kind of freedom and self-sufficiency their culture has enjoyed for thousands of years (Lewis, 1996).

THE STONE-CUTTER

A young and often unhappy stone-cutter once lived in the mountains of India. Each day he toiled at his work, carving huge blocks of stone from the mountainside and then crushing them into tiny pieces that were to be sold in the nearby village. One day as he traveled down the mountainside toward the market where he planned to sell his stones, he passed a magnificent palace in which the *rajah* (rah-jah, meaning "ruler") lived with his beautiful wife. He could see the couple sitting in their cool and lovely courtyard playing a quiet game.

"Oh," the stone-cutter said to himself, "there is the most powerful and fortunate man in the world. How I wish I could sit all day in a palace courtyard and play a game!" With that, his wish came true.

The stone-cutter was now a rajah, and he sat each day in the palace courtyard, under the clear blue skies and bright sunshine. But the stone-cutter was not happy. "The sun," he said to himself, "is more powerful than a rajah because it can burn the rajah's skin. How I wish I could be the sun!" With that, his wish was immediately granted.

"Ah," he thought to himself, as he shone from the bright blue skies onto the earth below. "At last I am the most powerful thing in existence!" But at that very moment a delicate white cloud floated past him, blocking his rays and casting a shadow on the earth.

"You are not so powerful," said the floating cloud. "I have more power than you because I can keep your rays from reaching the earth."

The sun thought about this for only a moment and cried to himself, "How I wish I could be a cloud. Then I would be the most powerful object in existence." With that, his wish was granted.

A strong wind began to blow the cloud about. "You are not so powerful," howled the wind. "I am stronger than you because I can shove you where I please!" "The wind is right," thought the cloud, and again he wished that this time he could become the wind. His wish was immediately granted.

Just as the wind began to blow freely around and over the earth, a mountain appeared to block its way. "You are not as powerful as I," shouted the mountain, "because I can block your way." The wind was very discouraged and disappointed. "Oh how I wish I were a mountain," he complained. His wish was immediately granted.

Now he loomed majestically over the quiet valley beneath him and raised his haughty head into the skies above him. "I know I am the strongest and most important thing in existence," the mountain said to himself. "Now I am truly happy!" But just then a man began to chip away at the mountain's side. He cut big blocks from the mighty mountain and then crushed them into tiny pieces.

"What a fool I have been," said the great mountain. "That little man with his chisel is more powerful than the mountain. If only I could be a stone-cutter again, I never would wish for anything more." His wish was immediately granted.

Each day the man who had just returned to earth in his old role as a stone-cutter counted his blessings. How happy he was to be back at his old job. How proud he was to be a stone-cutter! Now he knew that he was the strongest and most powerful thing in the world.

Discussion Questions:

1. Who is the main character of the story? What is he like? What happens to him?

2. Why does the stone-cutter always want to be something else?

3. What does the stone-cutter learn in the end?

4. What did you learn from this story?

5. What is the story's main moral lesson? Are there other lessons in the story? What are they?

6. Is this the kind of story that would be told in the United States? Why or why not?

WHO IS THE GREATEST OF THEM ALL?

In the early days of the race
of Bushmen,
an argument rose up
between the Lion and the
Ostrich.

"I am the greatest of all,"
boasted the Lion,
"for look at my teeth
—large, white, and
strong—
and you, like a child,
have not one!"

At that, the Ostrich replied,
very firmly,
"Ah, but I am very wise,
for I am many winters old."

"I am much much more
many winters than you!"
Lion roared.
"Therefore,
let's hear your call,
the call of the wild."

"Arrrrgh! Arrrrrgh!"
she cried.

"ROOOOAR!
ROOOOOAR!"
Lion bellowed,
and his sound echoed
throughout the desert.

Ostrich sat calmly fanning
herself
with the papyrus branch
from the heat of Lion's
roar.

"Well, I see,
you are not frightened
of me.

But you have no teeth
with which to kill,"
Lion challenged.

"I am tall,
I am great,
great as you.
So let us go now
and hunt as two,"
she replied.

On safari,
Lion attacked an eland.
Ostrich attacked the calf.
Lion tore off chunks of meat
and chomped.
Ostrich couldn't chew but
drank blood instead.

Lion roared once more,
"Hah!
You cannot chew meat with-
out teeth.
Come here! I'll eat you,
too!"

Ostrich ran quickly away
and hid behind the ant-hill.
Lion approached and circled
around the hill.
Ostrich moved accordingly.

"Whack! Whack!"
All of a sudden,
Lion was blind.
For Ostrich, with her two-
toed feet,
scratched clods of dirt from
the hill
and threw them at him.

But still he hollered,
"Wait! Wait!
Can't you see?

I am the greatest,
I am he!"

Ostrich continued to throw
ant-hill clods
until the Lion's lights went
out.
Then she yelled
at the top of her lungs
for all to hear,
"Oh yes,
it is true I have no teeth.

But I had a plan,
and just look at you.

Now who would you say
is the greatest today?"

───────────────

Reprinted with permission.
I. Murphy Lewis, *Why
Ostriches Don't Fly and
Other Tales from the
African Bush*
(Englewood, CO: Libraries
Unlimited, 1996).

───────────────

Discussion Questions:

1. Who are the main characters in the folk tale? Describe
   them. How are they different? How are they alike?

2. What is the subject of their argument? How do they
   attempt to prove their points?

3. Who wins the argument? How? Why?

4. What is the moral lesson of this tale? What character
   trait does it praise? What trait does it criticize?

5. Whose side were you on when you first read the story?
   Who did you think would win? Why?

6. If this tale were re-told in the U.S., which character
   would win the argument? Why? What does that say
   about moral values, as you see them, in the U.S.?

7. Can you guess what area of the world this tale comes
   from?

Did You Know?

Sub-Sahara African parents discipline their children and teach them moral values through proverbs and story-telling. They rarely use direct reprimands or instructions. Proverbs and story-telling are such an important part of the culture that each Sunday morning for an hour-and-a-half on Tanzanian TV, schools compete in a rigorous contest to determine who can recite the most epigrams and morally based tales. An enthusiastic master of ceremonies cheers the teams on and often asks a child, "Where did you learn that story?" "From my grandfather," is a typical answer. "He wants me to be a good boy."

Did You Know?

Indians who live in Malaysia do not tell their children goodbye when they are leaving the house for school in the morning. That brings bad luck. Instead, they say, "Go and come back." Children also do not say goodbye but "I'm going and I'll come back."

Activities

1. After the groups have discussed each story (this will probably take several days), assign one story to each group. Their assignment is to use the story to prepare some kind of report or presentation for the class. These presentations may take many forms:

- Students can turn the story into a play and perform it for the class with costumes and props.

- They may turn the story into a filmstrip by drawing scenes from the story on a long, narrow strip of paper and devising some means to display the filmstrip as it moves across the "screen." (For example, students can take a small box, cut a square in it for a screen, and stick pencils through each end of the box. Each end of the filmstrip is then taped to a pencil and rolled around one of the pencils to move the strip across the screen.)

- They may simply tell the story to the class and then explain it, with each group member having the chance to speak.

- They could prepare a report on the religious or cultural background of the story.

- They could find another story from that culture and perform it.

Encourage their creativity and their use of many media, and there is no end to what they might do. *(collaborative, constructive)*

2. Have the class create its own Culture Storybook. Each student will need to investigate his or her cultural backgrounds (most people have more than one) and find a story from one of those backgrounds. The story may be a folk tale, legend, myth, fairy tale, etc., from their culture. Just as important are true stories about a cultural hero, such as Frederick Douglass or Martin Luther King, Jr. Equally important are stories that parents and grandparents can tell your students about their own experiences. Any kind of story is acceptable as long as it pertains to each student's cultural background and illuminates some aspect of that culture. Sources for these stories include the public library, places of worship, and families. (Note: This kind of activity may be difficult for adopted children. They may wish to use the cultural backgrounds of their adopted families or use the cultural background of their birth parents if they know anything about it.)

Ask each student to write or rewrite the story neatly in his or her own words and then present it to the class. Then each story will be placed in the class Culture Storybook. The Storybook will also need good organization, illustrations, a table of contents, and a cover, so editors and artists from the class will be needed. Have the class present the book to other classes and display it in a school display case. If the class can raise money, they may also want to have the book copied so that each student has his or her own copy. *(constructive, cross-cultural)*

Lesson 4

Lessons from Nature and the Supernatural

Sunsets, waterfalls, rainbows, and earthquakes: nature can be beautiful, soothing, awe-inspiring and terrifying. Every culture around the world has developed ways of appreciating and coping with the forces of nature. Some cultures, especially those in the West, have traditionally tended to regard nature as something to be conquered and tamed for human use. Fields have to be irrigated and fertilized to produce more food, forests have to be cut down to provide more paper goods, and marshes have to be filled so new mini-malls can be built. Many other cultures, on the other hand, believe that humans must learn to live in harmony with nature or at least show great respect for its power. The Shinto faith in Japan, for example, is a religion that promotes the worship of nature; its influence on the Japanese culture can be seen in the Japanese love for harmony and tranquility. The Native American Navajos, like many other Native American tribes, have a strong belief in the supernatural; nature, for them, is full of spiritual meaning. They feel that humans must respect the awesome powers of nature and try to live harmoniously with it because it is filled with ghosts and spirits of gods and the dead.

The ways members of a culture regard nature have an important influence on how they live and act and on what they consider of value in life.

Activity

Ask your students the following questions:

What is the purpose of a field?

What is the purpose of trees?

What is the purpose of a river?

What is the purpose of unexplored territory?

Is it more important to leave nature alone and enjoy it or to do what we want with it to suit our own purposes?

Is nature meant to be conquered and tamed or to be left alone and respected?

Which is stronger: People or Nature?

Explain that Western cultures have for the last few centuries believed that nature was created for humans to conquer and use for their own development. That belief persists today but it is now challenged by a growing belief that we are destroying the natural world, that it was not created for the sole use of humans, and that now we need to protect it.

Did You Know?

Shogatsu (shoh-gaht-soo), New Year's, is the most important day of the year in Japan. On New Year's Eve, everything closes down so that families can spend their time together. Occasionally, families will take hotel rooms so that out-of-town relatives and the city people can all be together for the holiday. But the hotel is far from festive on New Year's Eve and is in fact extremely quiet with the lights dimmed very low. The next morning, many are up very early for *Hatsuhinode* (haht-soo-hi-noh-day), New Year's Day Sunrise. The Japanese believe that by praying to this most important of all gods, the sun, they will have happiness and good luck during the coming year.

Explore this dilemma further by having groups of students look through several newspapers for any articles that have to do with the conflict between humans and nature, such as an environmentalist group's protest against new construction, Greenpeace's latest activities, new developments in global warming, the effort to save an endangered species, etc. After the groups have chosen and discussed their issues and then shared them with the class, vote to select one issue and stage a debate with half the class as environmentalists and half as industry representatives. See if the debate changes any minds. *(constructive, collaborative)*

Shinto

In Japan, one of the country's major religions has fostered not simply a respect for nature, but a worship of it. The Shinto faith and Buddhism are the two dominant religions of Japan. The Japanese are quite comfortable belonging to both faiths at the same time. Shinto is native to Japan and dates back to the time when the islands were first inhabited by people. The name Shinto means "the Way of the Gods," and the religion began as a simple form of nature worship. Through the centuries, the followers of the Shinto faith have believed that the gods' spirits rested in every aspect of nature—rocks, trees, flowers, mountains. It was therefore important to communicate with nature, to live in harmony with it, not to conquer it.

Did You Know?

One of the most important Shinto celebrations for children is *Shichi-Go-San* (shee-chee-goh-sahn), a festival for three-, five-, and seven-year-olds. On November 15, three- and seven-year-old girls and five-year-old boys dress in traditional Japanese kimonos and travel to the shrines to pray for long life and good health. Parents always buy *Chitose-ame* (see-toh-see-ah-may), the long white sticks know as the "thousand-year candy," which is sold on the shrine's grounds to ensure the children a long life.

Shinto also supplied its followers with accounts of how the Japanese islands and the country's imperial family came to be. According to Shinto tradition, the islands were created by the union of a god and goddess, and these islands were the first and most beautiful ever to be created on earth. Later, the couple produced the sun-goddess, Amaterasu. The story claims that Jimmu Teno, Japan's first emperor, was a direct descendant of Amaterasu. This royal line has never been broken, and today's emperor supposedly traces his ancestry back to that first imperial ruler and the sun goddess. Whether or not the Japanese take these stories literally doesn't seem to matter. The tales have tended to provide a sense of national and social unity (Seward, 1972).

Throughout Japanese history, the sun has been a focal point in people's lives. Known as the "Land of the Rising Sun," Japan honors this heavenly body by placing it in the center of its flag. The sun is glorified in line after line of Japanese poetry, and many people rise early to watch its arrival in the eastern skies. Each year, thousands of brave Japanese climb Mt. Fuji, the country's highest mountain peak, to watch the sunrise. But the Japanese love for nature does not stop with the sun. Japanese art often depicts scenes of natural beauty, and their music frequently centers on the theme of nature. A generation ago, girls attended *ikebana* (i-kee-bah-nah) classes (flower arranging) as a prerequisite for marriage. While such training may not be considered as important today, the classes still are extremely popular among Japanese women. Their great love for nature has led the Japanese to develop a special vocabulary for activities associated with nature, such as flower-viewing and moon-viewing (Christopher, 1983).

It is important to let the Shinto gods know when the natural surroundings are about to be disturbed. A priest is called to a construction site before building begins so that he can inform the gods what is about to take place. He also informs the sea gods before a ship is launched. These ceremonies are really more traditional than religious, but they remain an important part of the lives of Japanese people (Taylor, 1983).

Shinto has no special day of worship. Some people pray to the gods daily in their homes while others travel to the shrines on a weekly basis, but more commonly on special holidays. One of the most important rituals that takes place during visits to the shrine is the purification rite. At the entrance to each Shinto shrine is a simple tall gate known as the *torii* (tor-die). The gate consists of two high columns, crowned by two crosspieces. There usually are three consecutive gates, each one of which progressively purifies the worshipper as he or she passes through.

The emphasis on purification ceremonies is considered one of the main reasons the Japanese place such importance on cleanliness in their lives. Most Japanese wash themselves very carefully with soap and water *before* stepping into a bathtub, so as not to dirty the water. They substitute slippers for shoes both at home and at school to avoid getting the floors dirty. Visitors and natives alike need have no fear about eating in any Japanese restaurant, even those tucked away in back alleys, because they will be clean.

Shinto followers believe that nature teaches people to live a balanced, agreeable life and to maintain *wa* (wah), harmony, with those around them. This requires, among many other things, the desire to help others save face. A woman from the United States living in Japan told us a story that illustrates the importance of maintaining harmony:

I placed an order with a salesman in a local department store for a set of dishes. The salesman spoke excellent English, and he appeared to understand exactly what I wanted. But when the dishes were delivered to my apartment, I discovered that they were the wrong ones. I called the store immediately and spoke with the man who had sold the dishes to me. "You sent me the wrong dishes," I said rather irritably to him. "Impossible, madam," he replied and then proceeded to hang up before I could say anything more. I thought about it for twenty-four hours, and then I called him back. "I love the dishes you sent me," I said. "But my husband really dislikes them. What should I do?" His reply came swiftly: "We shall be out immediately to pick them up."

From *Windows to the World: Themes for Cross-Cultural Understanding.* Copyright © 1996 by Phyllis Kepler, Brooke Sarno Royse, and John Kepler

Did You Know?

The sand paintings used by the Navajo in their complex healing ceremonies are made from powdered sandstone, charcoal, gypsum, and clay sprinkled onto a sand base which in turn rests on a blanket. The intricate designs, which sometimes take as many as a dozen people a full day to create, follow specific patterns, and there are hundreds of these patterns. Acts of nature, such as lightning, are sometimes depicted in these pictures. While chants and prayers are said, the sick person is placed on the painting so that the healing forces from the picture can flow upward into his or her body. After the ceremony, the sand painting is destroyed, but members of the family are allowed to keep a tiny portion of the sand. The remaining sand is dumped north of the house, the side where evil always exists (Maxwell, 1978).

The woman learned an important lesson in how to interact successfully with the Japanese. Her first call had served only to accuse and embarrass the salesman. That made him look bad and created conflict. The next call allowed him to save face because she was not blaming him for a mistake. She maintained a harmony by avoiding direct conflict and allowing him to correct the situation without looking bad. The Shinto belief in living in harmony with nature teaches the Japanese also to care about living in harmony with their fellow human beings.

Activities

1. Discuss: What does it mean to live in harmony with nature? How does the Shinto religion in Japan express this belief? What does nature teach followers of Shinto about how to live? Go over the story about the woman from the U.S. and the dishes. What did she learn about maintaining harmony in Japan? (*interpretive, cross-cultural*)

2. Ask the students to think of a recent instance when they or someone they knew was in conflict with someone else. Pair them up and have them describe the situation to their partner. Then ask them to role-play the situation, first as it happened and then as if they were Japanese and trying to maintain harmony in the situation.

What could they have said or done to help the other person save face and to avoid any anger or conflict? Ask some of the pairs to perform the scenarios for the class, and have the class discuss the differences in each situation. (*constructive, cross-cultural*)

3. Get a book on Japanese flower arranging (*ikebana*) from the local library. Study with the students some pictures of Japanese flower arrangements and ask them to describe some of their characteristics. Share with the students some of the principles of ikebana. Then have the students make various flowers out of paper or other media and arrange them according to some of the principles of ikebana. Display them in the class or have the students give them as gifts to their families. (*constructive*)

4. Get a book of Japanese *haiku* (hi-koo) from the local library, read a few samples to the students, and discuss their themes and structure. Note the ways the poems center on aspects of nature. Have the students follow the haiku model and write their own haiku. Compile the poems in a book, and ask some of the students to illustrate it. (*constructive*)

The Navajo and the Supernatural

The Navajo, like other Native American tribes, have traditionally believed in the power of the supernatural and the spiritual to guide their lives. They have lived with the closest of ties to the natural environment, so much so that chores as ordinary as hunting require special procedures with religious meaning. That would be like people from the West having elaborate religious rituals for a chore such as grocery shopping. The Navajo have believed that since animals have souls, just like people, they must be killed, butchered, and eaten with respect, according to certain rules and techniques. If these are not followed properly, the animal's soul will report the indignities to other animals who, in turn, will not allow their bodies to be killed (Driver, 1972).

According to traditional Navajo belief, there are two major groups of personalities who dwell in and on this earth, the Earth Surface People and the Holy People, and both groups are filled with mystical creatures who far outnumber the Navajos themselves.

Did You Know?

The indigenous African region includes a strong belief in animism, an assumption that all natural phenomena have souls. A waterfall, for example, may be the home of spirits. There is no written scripture in this religion, but believers find many different ways to express their faith. In addition to the legends, myths, and folktales handed down by word of mouth from generation to generation, there are numerous ceremonies and festivals, such as those honoring the harvest, which help the people demonstrate their faith. Believers in the African religion worship not only in temples but also under trees, among the rocks, and in caves, which are designated as sacred. In many African societies, a man on the run can hide within these sacred natural settings with no fear of being harmed. Elaborate geometric figures with religious significance grace many of their buildings, and natural phenomena like birds, trees, and insects have special religious importance. The chameleon, for example, is considered a symbol of security (Mbiti, 1975).

The Earth Surface People, created by the Holy People, include not only humans who are still living on the earth but also the ghosts of those who have died. Ghosts are unpleasant, evil creatures who stay around to haunt all those who ever did them harm. They also target the places where they have died for special revenge. It all results in many Navajo being extraordinarily fearful of death and anything associated with death. Their fear runs so deep that they often move very ill or elderly relatives from their homes and place them in small shelters nearby to reduce the risk of their dying in the *hogan* (**ho**-gahn), or home. But if someone dies at home, a hole is cut into the north wall, the evil side of the structure, through which the body is removed. The hogan then is usually burned to the ground (Maxwell, 1978).

Humans and ghosts are not the only Earth Surface People. There are also witches. Witches are wicked tribal members who come back at night in animal disguises to bring trouble. Their spells can be cast over innocent people, causing illness and even death.

The Holy People live inside the earth but travel around outside the globe on rainbows, lightning, wind, and thunder. The Holy People have great power—they created the Earth Surface People, for example. Some of them are generous and life-giving, and others can bring destruction and death. They have one creature in their midst who is always kind and helpful. She is the most important of all the Holy People: Changing Woman. She is the one who has taught the Navajo how to live in harmony with nature. In an elaborate ceremony called The Blessing Way Chant, the Navajo act out the first time humans were allowed to watch Changing Woman bring natural forces such as storms, lightning, wind, and animals into harmony with one another (Driver, 1972). Changing Woman also built the Navajo's first house from turquoise and shells, and she gave the people the gift of corn (Maxwell, 1978). Changing Woman is married to the Sun. But the Sun can be destructive at times, causing plants to shrivel and die. Many other members of the Holy People travel among the Navajo, such as Spider Woman, who taught them to weave, and Spider Man, who predicts approaching disasters. The infinite number of other gods, along with all the witches and ghosts, have kept the Navajo on a never-ending process of pleasing the spirits and protecting themselves from them.

It is difficult for non–Native Americans to understand the significance of ritual in the Native American's life. Some of us may consider a ritual to be an extra, time-consuming activity, but for a Native American, rituals are central to his or her life, just as important as—if not more important than—eating or sleeping. These rituals take lots of time, especially for the men. One-third of their lives may be taken up with rites and rituals designed to protect themselves and their families or to cure existing problems. An ill patient, for example, may be treated through a complicated ceremony that lasts anywhere from one to nine days. During this ceremony, they attempt to get rid of the evil spirit causing the sickness and bring the patient in closer harmony with the natural and supernatural world (Driver, 1972).

The Navajo have many different ways within their ceremonies to achieve their goals, including singing, constructing elaborate sand paintings, conducting purification rites, praying, and chanting. To an outsider, these ceremonies, often referred to as "The Chants" or "Ways," appear colorful and entertaining. But to a Navajo, these activities are serious and essential for their lives. The Navajo have even been known to cure their tribal members when modern medical techniques have failed. No one knows for certain why this has been possible. Observers re not sure if the healing has been a result of the Navajo's own tribal medicines or of the moral support brought to the patient by the ceremonies (Driver, 1972).

Those who have studied the Navajo point out that while people outside the Native American community might label their beliefs and activities as superstitions, the tribal people believe that there is always evidence to prove their beliefs. For example, a Navajo would explain a piece of dirt falling off the roof as the work of an evil spirit on top of the building. Someone outside the culture, on the other hand, would say that the dirt fell off simply because of the wind. A Navajo might return that even the wind has spiritual qualities. To the Navajo and to the observer, each explanation is based in reality (Leighton, 1947). The point to keep in mind is that how we interpret the forces of nature, or of anything, is often a result of being raised in a certain culture.

Navajo children's lives are also closely associated with nature and the supernatural. Parents, for example, tend to avoid severe punishment when the children misbehave because it is believed the souls of deceased ancestors rest within the children's bodies. Hitting a child would be the same as striking an elder. Boys are praised when they bring back their first game, but they never eat it. The animal goes to other tribal members, while the young hunters stand by to watch the celebration. Girls do not eat the first berries they bring back but instead are praised by the adults. These are steps the family takes in encouraging the children to become good providers later in life for their own families (Driver, 1972).

At the age of seven, boys and girls take part in a special ceremony to induct them into adulthood. Two adult males disguise themselves as Holy People and dance and scream to frighten the young people. The gods smear sacred cornmeal on the boys and lightly switch them with yucca leaves, and then they spread the sacred meal on the girls. When the gods suddenly remove their masks, the children relax and realize that these are not supernatural creatures but people they really know. Each child is allowed to try on a mask to look at the world through the eyes of the Holy People.

These close ties to nature and the supernatural are firmly in place by the time most Navajo children become adults, and in adulthood they carry on the sacred traditions of their culture.

Activities

There are abundant resources available to teachers for study of Native American cultures. These are just a few suggestions for activities related to this lesson.

1. Discuss: How do the Navajo regard nature? Why is nature so sacred to them? What does nature teach them about how to live? Draw a Venn diagram on the board and ask the students to list differences and similarities between the ways Navajos and Shinto followers relate to nature. *(interpretive, cross-cultural)*

2. Have the students do reports on a Native American tribe of their choice and several aspects of that tribe's relationship to nature. The local library is rich in resources for their research. Encourage them to use various media to present their findings—visual, oral, written, dramatized, computerized, etc. *(constructive)*

3. Ask the students to find stories from various Native American cultures at the local library. Have them practice their oral skills by reading the stories out loud to the class or by acting the stories out with other students. *(constructive)*

4. Choose a Navajo ceremony, find some background on it, and study its meaning with the class. *(interpretive, cross-cultural)*

5. Ask a Native American to come to your class to explain some of his or her beliefs about nature and the supernatural. *(cross-cultural)*

6. Read to the class the "Speech of Chief Seattle," found in many recent anthologies of American literature. Discuss and interpret it. This speech, given with dignified defiance in the face of defeat by the European settlers, illuminates another Native American tribe's belief in the supernatural power of nature and the belief that nature will exact revenge for the Europeans' cruelty towards the native peoples. *(interpretive)*

Resources

Arnott, Kathleen. *African Myths and Legends.*
New York: Henry Z. Walck, 1963.

Christopher, Robert C. *The Japanese Mind: The Goliath Explained.* New York: Faucett Columbine [Ballantine], 1983.

Cole, Joanna. *Best-Loved Folktales of the World.*
Garden City, NJ: Doubleday, 1982.

Craig, JoAnn. *Culture Shock: Singapore and Malaysia.*
Singapore: Times Books International, 1979.

Draine, Cathie, and Barbara Hall. *Culture Shock: Indonesia.* Rev. ed. Portland, OR: Graphic Arts Center, 1990.

Driver, Harold E. *Indians of North America.*
Chicago: The University of Chicago Press, 1972.

Heusinkveld, Paula Rae. *The Mexicans: An Inside View of a Changing Society.* Worthington, OH: Renaissance Publications, 1993.

Leighton, Dorothea, and Clyde Kluckhohn. *Children of the People: The Navajo Individual and His Development.*
Cambridge: Harvard University Press, 1947.

Lewis, I. Murphy. *Why Ostriches Don't Fly and Other Tales from the African Bush.* Englewood, CO: Libraries Unlimited, forthcoming 1996.

Maxwell, James A., ed. *America's Fascinating Indian Heritage.* Pleasantville, NY: Reader's Digest Association, 1978.

Mbiti, John S. *Introduction to African Religion.*
New York: Praeger, 1975.

Seward, Jack. *More About the Japanese.* Tokyo: Lotus Press, 1971.

Taylor, Jared. *Shadows of the Rising Sun: A Critical View of the Japanese Miracle.* New York: William Morrow, 1983.

Chapter Seven

Work and Leisure

Goals

This chapter explores aspects of work and leisure in several different cultures. The information, examples from various cultures, and student activities are designed to help your students achieve the following goals:

1. To understand that people in various cultures have different attitudes toward working and that these attitudes are reflected in very different styles of working.

2. To explore their own cultural attitudes toward work and how work fits into their long-term goals.

3. To grasp the concept of a global marketplace and to see how cross-cultural understanding is required for that marketplace to operate successfully.

4. To learn about foreign currencies and to practice calculating the exchange rate among several different world currencies.

5. To understand bartering and to experience a bartering economy.

6. To think about cultural attitudes toward leisure time in the United States, and how they and other people in the United States use leisure time.

7. To learn about some different uses of leisure time in other cultures, including sports and children's games.

Cross-Cultural Attitudes and Skills

As students work toward these goals, they will develop the following cross-cultural attitudes and skills:

1. They will improve their interpretive skills as they continue to think more about the cultural values that influence their goals and perspectives; as a result they will be better able to question and analyze these values.

2. They will practice and hone their communicative and collaborative skills as they participate in group activities and class projects during these lessons.

3. They will learn to view U.S. attitudes toward work and leisure with a cross-cultural eye as they learn about the different attitudes and styles of work and play in other cultures.

4. They will gain a stronger sense of the ways cultures depend upon each other in the global marketplace and of how they, the students, have a role to play in the world economy; thus they are developing a sense of global citizenship.

GENERAL INTRODUCTION

People around the world must work in order to survive. But exactly how people define and perceive work changes from one society to the next. What is considered honorable work for some may be scorned by others. The way of going about accomplishing a task—from designing the office space to working with fellow employees on an assembly line—may also vary across cultural lines. The differences in cultural attitudes toward work are not always easy to recognize. Nevertheless, they can create confusion and conflict among people who attempt to work across cultural borders.

We all want to be successful in our work. Yet not every culture defines success in the same way. Does being successful mean accumulating money or the things money can buy? Or is success more a matter of prestige, power, or security? Some cultures may define success as having a lot of money, but their money does not look like our money. Monetary notes and coins vary with each country, and

metimes they cannot even be recognized as a form of
oney at all by someone from another part of the world.

How people define and use their leisure time also
ries among cultures. Do people skip vacations in order
impress the boss, or do they always take the allotted
oliday time because it is a top priority? What do people
 with this free time? Do they use it to better themselves,
ll in the sun, play a game, or perhaps enjoy a cultural
ent? What kinds of games and cultural events do they
ve in their culture?

Work and leisure are inter-related themes that are
portant to all cultures in some way or another. At times,
ople in different cultures share the same perspectives
 these cultural themes, and at times they differ strongly.
migrants who settle into a new land bring their cultural
itudes toward work and leisure with them and attempt to
still their own perspectives in their children. Conflicts
n naturally follow as the children are caught between the
lues of their parents and the forces of their new culture.
hether we meet people from different cultures abroad
 within our own borders, we must remember that their
finitions of success, their working patterns, and their use
 leisure time may be quite different from many of the
mmon styles and attitudes found in the United States.
mplicating the issue even further is the fact that mone-
y systems differ across cultural lines.

Learning about the cultural differences in attitudes
ward work and leisure will aid your students in discard-
g any stereotypes they or their parents may have about
orkstyles in other cultures. As students begin to under-
nd why these cultural differences exist, they will be
ss likely to label people as lazy, unambitious, or unpro-
ctive. Further, they may gain a deeper, more complex
derstanding of how these themes—work and leisure—
terrelate, in their own lives and the lives of others.

What Went Wrong?

These introductory activities are designed to introduce
the students to the ways work, money, leisure, and success
can act as stumbling blocks in cross-cultural understanding. Most students will not know the correct answer to
each, but that is not the point. The point is to initiate
curiosity and discussion and to stir their interest in
pursuing this topic.

Teacher's Instructions: Divide your class into groups of
four or five students. Hand each group a copy of each of
the following worksheets. Have each group work together
to decide which answer best explains the behavior
described in the "What Went Wrong?" Then, as a class,
each group will explain its reason for choosing the answer.
After each group has spoken, reveal to them the correct
answer and discuss it. An explanation to each one has been
given below. Do the same with each "What Went Wrong?"

Some discussion questions include:

1. Why did your group choose this answer over the other
   answers. Were there clues given, did you simply eliminate the other answers, did you choose by instinct, or
   did you apply some assumptions you already had about
   the cultures mentioned? If you applied some assumptions, what did you already assume about the people
   from that culture?

2. How would you have felt in this situation?

3. What would you have done next?

4. What does this exercise show you about the various
   ways people from different cultures respond to the
   same situation?

n *Windows to the World: Themes for Cross-Cultural Understanding.* Copyright © 1996 by Phyllis Kepler, Brooke Sarno Royse, and John Kepler

Answers and Explanations

WHAT WENT WRONG? #1 = Answer #3

John should not have concluded, based on his observations, that things were bad at the Bangkok factory. The things that confused him are perfectly normal in a Thai plant. Hiring family relatives or close friends for positions is not unusual. Thais are comfortable working with and relying on people they know. Even if the employees are not tied by links of kinship or friendship, they were addressed as such by Bunchob as a sign of respect and to establish a closer relationship. Thais do not adapt comfortably to strict plant regulations concerning hours of work, etc.; therefore Bunchob's job was to make an effort to get to know each worker personally and to develop a family atmosphere in the plant. The workers would then be willing to follow reasonable regulations and to produce more circuits.

WHAT WENT WRONG #2 = Answer #1

Cynthia Jay's confusion shows just how complicated handling money in another culture can be. She faced the problem of "foreign exchange" at the Montreal shop. The U.S. dollar does not have the same value as the Canadian dollar or, for that matter, the Australian dollar or the German *mark or* the Mexican *peso.* The Mexican *peso* does not have the same value as the Argentine *peso* or the Venezuelan *peso.*

How the values are established for each currency is a very complex matter, but comparisons are often made by showing how much of one currency it takes to buy a loaf of bread and then how much it takes in another country's money. The souvenir Cynthia was buying cost a little bit less in Canadian dollars than in U.S. dollars, so she received the small difference in change (Canadian coins, of course). The values of different currencies are revealed when exchanging one for another. The business papers, like the *Wall Street Journal,* and the big banks have a "rate of exchange" that fluctuates daily. This "rate" tells, for example, what amount of U.S. dollars a person will get for German *marks* on that day.

WHAT WENT WRONG #3 = Answer #2

Phil's friend had invited him to attend what is often called Japan's national sport—sumo wrestling. Although sumo wrestling looks very strange to foreigners, it is filled with ancient ritual. Public matches date back to 1600. The bouts last only for a few seconds. The object is to force your opponent outside the circle or to touch any part of his body other than his feet to the floor of the ring. The great body bulk, gained by a special protein diet, helps provide the momentum to force an opponent over the line. Despite the quickness of the bout, great skill is required to move such a heavy body. The elaborate ceremony that each wrestler goes through at the beginning of the match is a traditional effort to drive away demons and evil spirits. The clapping of hands shows there are no concealed weapons. Throwing the salt serves to purify the wrestler and the ring. Six championship tournaments are held each year and shown on television throughout Japan. Phil would have enjoyed the evening much more if he had learned these points.

Student

Worksheet

NAME _____

DATE _____

WHAT WENT WRONG #1

John Stone was assigned by his company to Bangkok, Thailand, in order to manage a factory that manufactured computer circuits. After a few days in his new position, he noticed that the work habits of the employees were strange. They would report late for work, would take unscheduled breaks during the day, and even leave the plant for a short time. He also was amazed to hear that his Thai assistant, Bunchob, called the employees by such titles as "Uncle" or "Big Brother." John thought that someone had hired members of the same family, and this was why the atmosphere at the factory seemed to him more informal than businesslike. John was afraid that this implied that things were so bad he might have to close the plant.

What was wrong at the plant? (Circle the answer that best explains the problem.)

1. The workers were all members of the same Thai family, and they felt they could do whatever they wanted at the factory, especially because John Stone was an outsider.

2. The assistant manager, Bunchob, was simply not doing his job to keep the workers in line.

3. Nothing was necessarily wrong at the plant. John Stone did not understand the different way of doing business in a Thai factory.

4. The Thai employees were suspicious of foreigners coming in to order them around, so they tried to make life difficult for John Stone so that he would fail at his job.

Worksheet

NAME _____

DATE _____

WHAT WENT WRONG? #2

Cynthia Jay was excited about her family's upcoming trip to Canada. This would be the sixteen-year-old's first trip outside the United States. When they arrived at downtown Montreal, she ran into a shop to buy a souvenir. She picked out a packet of illustrated post cards and asked the clerk for the price. The clerk told her they cost one dollar and fifty cents. Cynthia had saved some money for the trip so she handed the clerk two one-dollar bills. The clerk told Cynthia she couldn't accept her money. Cynthia protested, "You said the price was $1.50. My money is not counterfeit. Aren't all dollars the same?" The clerk laughed and said, "Definitely not." But then she took pity on Cynthia and agreed to take the U.S. money. Cynthia then handed her exactly one dollar and fifty cents. When the clerk handed her back a few cents in change, Cynthia was really confused.

Why was Cynthia so confused about the money? (Circle the answer that best explains the trouble Cynthia was having.)

1. Canadian dollars are different from U.S. dollars. Cynthia had encountered the difficulties of changing and using money in another country.

2. The clerk in the shop was trying to take advantage of Cynthia.

3. Cynthia's money looked old and dirty. When using our money in another country, people from the U.S. should pay only with new dollar bills. Otherwise the clerks might not believe the money is real.

4. In Canada, people under 18 must be with an adult when using money to buy something. The clerk did not want to break the law, but she felt sorry for Cynthia since she was from another country and probably did not know about the Canadian law.

NAME _____

DATE _____

WHAT WENT WRONG? #3

Philip Lewis was living with his family in Tokyo, Japan. One of Phil's Japanese friends invited him to attend a wrestling match. Phil was thrilled because he had wrestled on his U.S. high school team. The wrestling hall was crowded with thousands of spectators, and Phil thought the matches should be great to watch. But he also was a little confused. The ring was not like the square ones with sides of ropes used for professional bouts in the U.S. In fact, it was just a ring about fifteen feet in diameter drawn on the floor. Then the first wrestlers appeared and Phil nearly burst out laughing. They were huge men, weighing about three hundred pounds with big bellies around which were strapped heavy black belts. They faced each other across the ring and stamped their feet, scattered salt around the ring area, and clapped their hands. Finally, the two men rushed toward each other and bumped together with the force of two tanks meeting on the battlefield. After a few seconds of pushing and grunting, one wrestler was forced over the line on the floor and the other was declared the winner. Now Phil really laughed and told his friend that he had seen all he wanted, and he left.

Was Phil justified in acting the way he did? (Circle the answer that best describes what Phil should have done.)

1. Phil was justified. Since the Japanese version of wrestling went so fast, Phil got easily bored and did not need to stay to see more.

2. Phil was not justified. He should have realized that tradition and ritual are very important in Japan, and so he should have tried to understand this sport.

3. Phil was kind of justified. He should have stayed until the matches were over so he would not offend his friend, but he did not need to take seriously this crazy form of wrestling.

4. Phil was justified. He loved and revered the game of wrestling, at least in its U.S. form, and could not stand to see it in such a different form. He did not have to stay and witness it any longer.

Lesson I

Success and Work

Everyone hopes to be successful. The definition of success and how to achieve it, however, changes from one culture to the next. Each culture usually has some general standard that determines whether or not a person has reached success. In the United States, the possession of money or the things it can buy is considered a measure of success. When someone in the U.S. says, "He is really loaded," they are not being insulting. Rather, they are referring to wealth in a complimentary, even a slightly envious, way. Indeed, people from other cultures generally regard people in the U.S. as more materialistic than other people around the world. Yet there are many other industrialized countries where there is a direct relationship between success and the amount of money and material goods one has. In all of these countries, including the U.S., a spacious residence, a current-model luxury car, beautiful clothes, plenty of leisure time to travel or play, and large contributions to charities are just a handful of the many signs of wealth, and therefore success.

Money and evidence of wealth are not the only signs of success, however. Success in many cultures can be realized through the completion of any worthwhile goal a person sets for himself or herself. For example, the goal may be to stop smoking or to get a high grade on a school test. But these are often just short-term accomplishments on the road to success. Success usually means an achievement or status of longer duration, having a more permanent effect on one's life, and which others will recognize and acknowledge. *Prestige, fame, education, power, titles, honors, awards, a large family, security, respect of one's peers,* or *personal happiness*—all are signs of success. In many cultures, one or more of these may be more highly prized than money.

Even though people can realize success in all areas of life, it is through their work that people from many cultures primarily define their personal success. A student can be successful in school, a factory worker in his or her job on an assembly line, a professional soccer player in his sport, or an attorney practicing his or her profession. They may realize their success by earning money, prestige, fame, power, titles, honors, awards, security, or the respect of their peers. In a money-oriented country like the U.S., one can be considered successful in his or her profession

no matter what that profession is. *Fortune* magazine's list of the wealthiest Americans in the past has included a manufacturer of teddy bears, two men in the pizza business, a producer of rental trailers, and the publisher of the telephone yellow pages. Their wealth is what, for many, defines their success.

In this lesson, we will consider how people work and regard their work in four different cultures: the United States, France, Saudi Arabia, and Nigeria. There are interesting differences and similarities in the ways people from these four cultures conduct their working lives and feel about making a living.

Activities

1. How is success defined in your culture? Write on the board "Success is. . . . , " and ask students to finish the statement by writing a paragraph or two on their personal definition of success. Then have the students form small groups and share their statements with the other members of the group. Ask the group to summarize each person's statement and then to present to the class a list of the group's opinions on success (Success is. . . 1. personal happiness, 2. making a lot of money, 3. having a loving family, etc.). Then compile all of the groups' lists on the board. What definition seems to come up most often? *(constructive, collaborative)*

2. Ask the students to look again at their personal definitions of success. How will they achieve that form of success? Have them write personal mission statements, sometimes called "vision statements." In such a vision statement, the writer will define his or her personal goal

and then explain how he or she plans to achieve that goal. When the students are finished with their vision statements, have them seal the statements in envelopes and give them to you or their families for keeping until the following year, or even until they reach eighteen. It will be fun for them to read the statements again, either yearly or in several years, to see how their visions and goals have changed or remained the same. *(constructive)*

Working in the United States

In the U.S., work is often more than just a necessity; it is considered honorable to labor. Over the centuries, a cultural "work ethic" has developed that dictates that failure to work is a sign of laziness and personal weakness. Indeed, many people admire and approve of the "workaholic." In keeping with this work ethic, the U.S. has fewer national holidays than other industrialized countries. People are often expected to work overtime and even to take pride in doing so, with or without pay. Do-it-yourself and equipment rental stores are in every neighborhood to assist the weekend handyperson. Physical labor is considered a sign of strength and ability. "Moonlighting" and dual-career households are the rule rather than the exception. Either out of necessity or desire, more and more women work both outside and inside the home. Teenagers have become an important segment of the workforce, particularly for fast-food and other minimum wage industries. Students expect to take jobs during summer vacations. Even young children open a lemonade stand or take a paper route to earn money as their parents do. If going to the office is not necessary, modern computer and communication technology enables people to work from the home.

U.S. workers are faced with the problem of balancing the demands of the culture's work ethic with the need for leisure time. Should an employee work longer than a normal shift for overtime pay, or should he or she take a day off for a family picnic? Some employers encourage their employees, if they are truly "dedicated," to reduce or skip vacations. Even professionals and the self-employed find that long hours are part of the job. Young lawyers who join large firms and doctors serving a residency in hospitals are expected, at times, to work almost around the clock. Owners of a bed-and-breakfast inn at a resort area are the last to go to bed and the first to get up and rarely take days off, much less a vacation.

Recently, more enlightened employers have initiated a number of new innovations to avoid over-work—new, that is, for the U.S. Countries like Sweden and Denmark

SIDEBAR

All work, even cotton spinning, is noble; work is alone noble. . . . A life of ease is not for any man, nor for any god.

—**Thomas Carlyle (1795–1881), English writer**

When men are employed, they are best contented; for on the days they worked they were good-natured and cheerful, and, with the consciousness of having done a good day's work, they spent the evening jollily; but on our idle days they were mutinous and quarrelsome.

—**Benjamin Franklin (1706–1790),** *Autobiography*

There is no substitute for hard work.

—**Thomas Alva Edison (1847–1931), U.S. inventor**

long ago took measures to help employees maintain a healthy balance between work and family. For example, there and in the U.S., day-care centers have been installed in some factories and offices so that employees can be near their children during the workday. The same job may be held by two people working in alternate, shorter shifts. Maternity leave for fathers, not just mothers, helps family bonding.

Many physical clues reveal the importance of an employee in a typical, traditional U.S. office. First, the location—which floor and where on the floor—are significant. Generally, the rule has been "out and up." In many traditional places of work, if the employee is sitting near the center of the work area, he or she probably is relatively junior. This is especially true if the partitions of the work station are modular and are not regular walls. An interior room with walls, even windowless, is slightly higher in status. As an employee gains status and responsibility, he or she moves toward the outside walls. The most prestigious offices are those along the outside with windows, particularly the corner office. In most offices with several floors in a building, the term "the top man" can be taken literally. Senior officers usually have their offices on the highest level, and the officers still are predominantly male.

Did You Know?

The method of looking for a job can vary from culture to culture. In the United States, when a person is looking for a position at the career level, he or she usually writes a resume. This is a very brief personal history, usually only one or two pages, which lists the person's experience, education, honors, membership in organizations, and interests. Accomplishments are highlighted in order to make the individual look as good as possible. A British job applicant will also write a resume, but it is quite different from the U.S. version. British employers look with skepticism upon resumes that emphasize honors and accomplishments. A low-keyed, understated listing of your background is far more acceptable.

The size and the furnishings of a work station or office further reflect the status of the employee. Most companies establish some form of rank, grade, or title for each position. Each employee gets the type of desk, chair, and other fixtures allotted to his or her grade. Senior employees are sometimes rewarded with the privilege of decorating their own offices.

Much of this is changing, however. Many innovative companies, particularly those in advertising and high technology, do not have offices along outside walls. Everyone, including senior managers, works in one large room with modular partitions. The philosophy behind this layout is that people work more happily and productively as teams and in community-oriented workplaces than in walled-off spaces. Furthermore, the term "the top man" is becoming less and less accurate as more women work their way into the top positions at U.S. corporations.

Openness, informality, and accessibility are characteristics many U.S. companies try to develop. Senior executives are sometimes called by their first names, and many try to remain accessible to any employee. The expression, "My door is always open," captures this spirit. People in the U.S. tend to make many of their friends at work and to get together with workplace friends on the weekends. It is said that more business is done by people in the U.S. on the golf course than in the boardroom.

Activities

1. Assign the following project: Interview a working adult about his or her work. The interview should include the following questions. *(constructive, interpretive)*

Questions about attitudes toward work:
What do you do for a living?
Why do you work?
How do you feel about working?
What do you get out of working?
What do you dislike about working?
Would you rather not work? Why or why not?
What would you do if you did not work?

Questions about the workplace:
What is your position within the company?
What does your workplace look like, how is it laid out?
Where do you sit or stand to do your work?
Do you have a boss? Where does she or he sit or stand to work?
Do you have people who work under you? Where do they sit or stand to work?
Are you on a first-name basis with everyone?
Are things casual or formal at your workplace?
Do you have friends from work?

When the students have completed their interviews, there are many ways to go with this activity. They could include one or all of the following:

- Compile the interview responses in a Cultural Work Book for the students to review, make comparisons and contrasts.

- Have each student do a narrative write-up of the interview, as if he or she were writing for a newspaper. What conclusions can the student draw about this particular perspective on and experience of work in his or her country? Compile these write-ups in a mock newspaper called *Our Country's Workers,* or a title of their choice.

- Assign a group of statistically minded students to the task of compiling and tallying the responses of all the interviews. Assign a group of narratively skilled students to the task of summarizing the variety of answers that have to do with feelings and perspectives. It is up to them how to conduct such a task. How will they quantify the results? How will they treat answers that are subjective? When they have compiled and summarized the results, discuss the conclusions with the class in terms of cultural attitude toward work and the typical or various ways workplaces are structured.

2. Have the students look through magazines and newspapers for advertisements that in some way reflect images of working people or attitudes toward work. (They may also videotape TV commercials, if possible). Each student can then choose an ad, analyze it, and share the ad and its implications with the class. What predominant images and attitudes are depicted in advertisements? Are these accurate pictures of how most people in their country feel about work? What would someone from another culture think about these workstyles and attitudes if he or she saw these advertisements? *(interpretive, cross-cultural)*

3. Ask the students to draw a picture of the ideal office or worksite. What makes the workplace ideal (productivity, teamwork, happiness on the job, for example)? Are there bosses and subordinates, or is everyone of equal status and even pay? Where do people sit? Label them. What kind of walls are there, if any? Are there windows? Where do people go to eat lunch? Where are the clocks? Is it warm or cold in there? Is it light or dark? How do people talk with one another? Are they allowed to talk? The students will think of many more considerations. Post their drawings and attach explanations around the room. *(constructive)*

Working in France

Business does not hold as important a place in French society as it does in the U.S. If a French boss were to ask an employee to forgo his August vacation to stay and work on an important project that might bring a promotion, chances are that the employee would turn the boss down with little hesitation and leave. Actually, this incident probably never would happen. The French try to keep their business and social lives definitely separate. August is the traditional month for a holiday in France. Everybody who can leave Paris does, and the city almost goes into hibernation. Only the most necessary caretakers and those catering to the tourists stay. No one would try to disrupt the vacation plans of the average worker.

The French do not have the same concept of work found in the United States. The French believe that one's life should be lived with grace and style. Yet they have joined the ranks of "do-it-yourselfers." Gigantic hyper-

Did You Know?

Japan, a country notorious for workers who keep late hours at the office, is going through a trend to encourage its citizens to take more time off from their jobs. In February 1992, Toyota began publishing a seasonal company magazine giving middle-aged employees ideas on how to spend their leisure time *(Japan Times)*.

markets offer everything for the home, including tools, supplies, and hardware. Projects often include fixing up the cottage in the country, which is the weekend getaway home enjoyed by Parisians fortunate enough to have one.

The French tend to be highly "polychronic," which simply means that they are capable of doing many things at once. They are flexible about agendas, schedules, appointments, changing plans, and being interrupted. For many cultures, including the U.S., a business meeting must have an agenda listing the topics to be discussed at the meeting, and many people would be uncomfortable if the discussion strayed from the list. But the French consider such straying normal. Encouraging the participants to express their thoughts and feelings about a matter is more important than covering everything on a checklist.

French authority is highly centralized. Paris has been the hub of everything French for centuries: government, education, the arts, and business. The same is true in the

PROVERBS ON WORK

Work half done is no work at all. —Slovakian

All work and no play makes Jack a dull boy. —English

Hard work never killed anyone. —Yiddish

Do not put off today's work until tomorrow.
—African (Ovambo)

Hard work makes a skillful worker. —Danish

Lack of work brings a thousand diseases.
—Indian (Hindi)

The hardest work is to do nothing. —U. S.

Did You Know?

People in the U.S. can be competitive even among friends. Many people try always to "keep up with the Joneses"; that is, to compete with one's friends and neighbors to have as much as they have in terms of nice cars, the newest stereos, the most exotic vacations. But with the French, customarily, friendship excludes competitiveness. The concept of "keeping up with the Joneses" appears completely baffling to the French.

Activities

1. Using a Venn diagram as a graphic aid, discuss the differences and similarities between U.S. and French attitudes toward work and styles of working. *(cross-cultural)*

2. Discuss and list on the board how the French rank some of the top professions. Then take a class survey and ask the students to name some top, highly regarded, and respected professions in the U.S. Vote and rank them on the board. Why do we respect these professions more than others? How does the class's ranking compare to the French ranking? *(constructive, cross-cultural)*

Working in Saudi Arabia

It is not possible to understand the attitudes toward work in Saudi Arabia without looking at its history. Saudi Arabia is a young country, which came together politically in 1932 when a man by the name of Abdul Azis ibn Abdul Rahman al Saud brought the many tribes under his control and declared himself king of Saudi Arabia. It became the only country in the world to be named after an individual, Saud. Before it became a kingdom, Bedouins roamed the desert in search of grazing lands for their herds. By tradition, work was not honorable, except perhaps the kind of work associated with tending the flocks. There was a particular aversion to doing anything that involved physical labor, and farming was considered a dishonorable occupation. Gradually, since the birth of Saudi Arabia, most Bedouins have exchanged their nomadic existence for a settled life and have moved into the cities.

Although a U.S. oil company gave the Saudi king $50,000 in 1933 for the right to drill for oil there, it was not until after World War II that the oil industry began to boom. With the enormous wealth created by oil, hundreds and hundreds of new jobs were created. Saudi Arabia was emerging rapidly from a quiet, undeveloped desert land into the late twentieth century. With this development came enormous economic activity in all sectors of the country. New roads, schools, offices, hospitals, hotels, restaurants, and shops had to be built, and people were needed to construct them and to operate them. Plumbers, electricians, mechanics, office workers, as well as financial and business managers were required. One of the major problems in that fast-growing and wealthy country was finding people to fill the jobs. The old Bedouin traditions still remained important, and the people did not want

typical French office layout. The senior person will not be found on the edge of those with whom he or she works, but in the center hub surrounded by his or her group. A newcomer joining the group will usually be placed furthest from the central hub of authority. In addition, French business is considerably more formal by U.S. standards. One would rarely call one's boss by his or her first name. Workers seldom socialize together after hours.

Business in France is not considered the top profession. The French rank government service as number one, followed by medicine, law, and engineering (Hall, 1990). University professors and those with careers in the arts, such as painters and writers, are held in high regard. The French educational system plays a large part in determining one's career. This is true in the U.S., but only to a certain extent. Graduates of the top Ivy League universities, such as Harvard or Yale, and other acclaimed private and state universities, such as Stanford or Michigan, often have better chances than graduates of some other schools of getting prestigious jobs when they graduate, yet they are never assured of a position just because they went to these schools. Graduates of the most prestigious French institutions, *les grandes ecoles* (lay grahnd **ay**-kohl), on the other hand, can be confident of a place in the elite group of graduates who monopolize positions of power and influence in French business and government. Because of the lofty status of these schools, students work extremely hard to gain admission, just as Japanese students strive to get into one of the top universities in Japan.

to take positions that might soil their hands. They did not, in fact, want any part of manual labor. Many people took jobs at much lower pay in order to sit at a desk rather than accept a post that required physical exertion. The government tried valiantly to create training programs for its citizenry, but they had few takers. For example, in the 1980s an Airway Training Facility with twenty-seven teachers had absolutely no students (Mackey, 1987).

It was not only contempt of physical labor that followed the Bedouins into the city, but many other attitudes and traditions that made working an unpleasant activity. The importance of family made dedication to a job very difficult. Allegiance to an employer became an affront to God and obeying rules of a business was to suffer personal dishonor (Mackey, 1987). The government has had difficulty convincing people that work is not only honorable but has religious and social value. There still is a shortage of trained personnel in the country, but there are many schools available to help the problem.

These negative attitudes toward physical labor have softened, and one sign is that machines, once simply replaced when a part malfunctioned, are now being repaired (*The Economist,* 1987). Yet the aversion to manual labor in Saudi Arabia has not completely disappeared, nor has it in many other Arab countries. A middle-class

Did You Know?

Without honor, money and material things are of little significance in the Arab world. Some still-nomadic Bedouins, for example, live relatively poor and simple lives. They take great care of their camels without any sense that this activity is less honorable than any others. Farming, however, is considered a much less respectable occupation. Money also does not compensate an Arab who has no sons or whose daughter's public conduct discredits the entire family.

office worker usually will not wash his car or mow his lawn on the weekend. Youngsters customarily will not weed the garden or carry out the garbage. It is important to keep in mind that it is not laziness that prevents people from taking these positions of manual labor, but a centuries-old sense of tradition and honor.

In spite of these obstacles, numerous businesses have developed in Saudi Arabia, and many people have made great sums of money. Yet even in these successful businesses, many of the old traditions still prevail. Offices, for instance, may appear similar to those in the United States while beneath the surface they operate very differently. Housed in high-rise buildings, equipped with the latest in office machines, and staffed by many English-speaking managers, many of whom may have studied at a U.S. university, these businesses are the embodiment of modern efficiency. But one must look beneath the facade to discover how work is conducted. Hiring relatives is not frowned upon but considered an Islamic tradition in which family loyalties are strengthened. Decisions are not necessarily made by high-ranking officers but often by a father figure in "an extended business family." The father figure expects loyalty, honesty, and hard work from his subordinates, just as a dad in a real family does, and he generously rewards those who follow the rules (*The Economist,* 1987).

Business meetings are reminiscent of the councils that took place in the guest tents of the Bedouin leaders. The host greets and talks with everyone, and no one should expect to get down to business immediately. Interruptions come often, as Arabs follow a polychronic time pattern, and meetings will be long. If someone arrives late

SIDE BAR

Who are the Bedouins? The Bedouins are the nomads who roam the deserts of the Middle East, often working as shepherds and goatherds while living in tents made of black goat's hair and other products provided by their animal herds. Today, less than 10 percent of the Bedouin population still follows the wandering lifestyle. The groups who roam together are related and usually trace their ancestry back through the males in the family. They have developed a strong sense of bonding and an attitude that pits their group against the rest of the world. The Arabs often quote a proverb that no doubt had its roots in early Bedouin traditions: "I and my brothers against my cousin; I and my cousins against the world." The Bedouins are known for their hospitality, generosity, and sense of honor, all characteristics that have followed them as they have moved from the desert to a settled life in the cities.

for the gathering, everyone assumes he or she probably had something more important to do (*The Economist*, 1987).

Businesses in the United States often expand with bank loans on which the borrower must pay interest. In the U.S., much is made of the changing interest rates that are announced by the government. But interest cannot be charged in Saudi Arabia because it goes against Islamic tradition. In the United States people buy grains from harvests that have not even ripened yet. This is called buying commodities in a futures market. In the futures market, grains are bought at one price with the hope that when they are finally harvested they actually will sell for a lot more and thus a profit will be made. But the Saudis will not allow such transactions because they consider it gambling, and this, too, is against Islamic traditions. Another policy, quite different from that found in the United States, is that life insurance cannot be sold. Businesses, however, can buy insurance to cover fire, accidents, and shipping (*The Economist*, 1987).

Although less than 10 percent of the women work outside the home in Saudi Arabia, it is quite different from a couple of generations ago when women were expected to stay strictly behind the walls of the family compound or in a special section of the home known as the harem and could not attend school. Today, girls not only go to elementary and secondary schools, but some go on to the university. When entering the workforce, women must take positions that do not require working with men, so this means either working in separate rooms or in occupations in which men will not be found. Since boys and girls never attend school together and must have instructors of their own sex, teaching is a popular profession for women. A number of women have formed banks that are strictly for female patrons, and other women have started their own businesses, in which men often serve as managers. It has been rumored that one-third of the wealth in Saudi Arabia today is held by women. Medicine is the one area in which many restrictions have been dropped. Women doctors may work with men.

Activities

1. Discuss attitudes toward physical labor and working styles (including women in the workplace) in Saudi Arabia. Do the students understand some of the cultural roots of these attitudes? What are they? In other words, why do many Saudi Arabians dislike physical labor? Why is a business conducted like an extended family? Why are meetings often long? Why won't the Saudis allow commodities trading or life insurance? Why must

men and women work separately in most jobs? Being able to answer these questions shows that the students are taking great strides towards cross-cultural sensitivity and a deeper understanding of an Arab culture. (*interpretive*)

2. Using a Venn diagram, discuss and list the differences and similarities between U.S. and Saudi Arabian work-styles and attitudes towards work. Make the same comparisons and contrasts between the French and the Saudis. (*cross-cultural*)

Working in Nigeria

West Africa's Nigeria, like its other sub-Saharan neighbors, is an extraordinarily complex collection of culturally diverse tribes and nationalities. More than four hundred different ethnic groups, and almost as many mutually unintelligible languages, exist within its borders. Also like its neighbors, with the lone exception of Liberia, it once was occupied by a European power, England. Nigeria achieved independence in October 1960 and became a modern state. The people in the north are primarily Muslims, while the majority of southerners are Christian. These three facets of Nigerian culture—hundreds of indigenous languages and customs, colonial influences from the West, and religious creeds—have worked to shape the country's workplace.

The "right connection," usually a tribal affiliation, often plays an important role in the selection of an employee, as well as later promotions. Employers tend to classify tribes with various characteristics. For example, the Ibu of southeast Nigeria are known for their industriousness, but employers sometimes eye this reputation with a little skepticism. The Ibu may want to take charge, they reason. Tribal stereotyping, therefore, can work to the advantage or disadvantage of a prospective candidate. Family alliances are also extremely important in seeking a job, and once that job is obtained, no one forgets his or her family back in the rural areas. Money goes to all of the relatives, sometimes as many as fifty, on a regular basis. These generous gestures cause financial hardships and at times financial ruin (Enahoro, 1987).

Just as certain characteristics are attributed to various tribes, families are known by their trades or skills. These familial groups take great pride in these proficiencies, handed down from generation to generation. Employers often seek out certain families when recruiting for various positions within their organizations or companies.

Companies in Nigeria do not rely solely on tribal or family affiliations in selecting their staffs. Other qualifications, of course, are considered: education and the ability to speak English among them. Because of the British occupation of the country, everyone knows at least one or two words of English. The British had agreed not to allow missionaries to travel into the Muslim northern areas of the country, where education centered on the Quran. In the south, however, children were taught under the English educational system. As a result, people in the south today usually are more proficient in English than those in the north, although currently all schools are required to teach the English language. But in the north there is a shortage of qualified English teachers, and children begin to learn the language at a later age or sometimes not at all.

According to one U.S. citizen who worked several years on a personnel panel in Nigeria, employers are also often concerned with very personal issues. Job interviews, she explained, can become very confrontational, with employers even asking a candidate why he combs his hair in a certain fashion. Once hired, the new employee will probably be asked to swear a traditional oath of allegiance to the organization.

Power in the Nigerian businessplace can be very centralized. The boss makes the decisions, and there is little, if any, delegation of responsibility (Moran, 1991). In the south, employees are more apt to raise issues with their bosses than in the very hierarchical north. The key to successful business relationships, however, is trust and confidence in those with whom one is working. Friendships take precedence over accomplishment.

Promptness is not a high priority in the workplace. An office may be scheduled to open at 8 A.M., but workers drift in at various intervals, which no one seems to mind. Work does not begin immediately because there are dozens of questions to be asked. "Did you sleep well?" "How is your body?" (when someone has been ill). "How is your new bride?" (up to four wives are permitted among the Muslims). "How is the family?" And on a terribly hot day, "How is your sweat?" People are friendly, warm, and interested in one another to a degree that is difficult for a Westerner to understand.

Women have entered the Nigerian workplace. They are more readily accepted in the Western-influenced south, but in all areas of the country there are entrepreneurial opportunities for the female sex. Sometimes they open little shops or perhaps a stand in the local marketplace. Women never appear at work in trousers, but instead wear two wrap-around skirts, one discreetly tied on top of the other, with a Western-style blouse.

Lagos, the capital, with a population estimated at three million, throbs with the pulse of both Westerners and Africans seeking new opportunities fueled by abundant reserves of oil and other raw materials. An overtaxed infrastructure, however, drives residents to distraction. Too many vehicles and roads in disrepair create horrendous traffic jams and missed appointments that test the Nigerians' flexible attitude toward time. Some commuters report four-hour trips each way between home and office. An unworkable telephone system forces people to leave offices and travel to communicate directly with others, resulting in long periods of absence from their own workplaces.

While Western influences are gradually seeping into the homes and workplaces of Nigeria, its people are still guided by a cultural heritage which has endured for centuries. In keeping with the respect shown to the elderly, for example, Nigerian companies may adopt pension plans for their employees. Still, they are considered inadequate substitutes for the care and attention provided senior citizens by families.

Activities

1. Discuss the information given about the Nigerian workplace. Ask students to list the characteristics that stand out for them regarding attitudes, working styles, relationships on the job, and so on. List them on the board. Which characteristics are similar to the U.S. and which are different? Compare and contrast them to characteristics of working in France and Saudi Arabia as well. Using Venn diagrams may help. *(interpretive, cross-cultural)*

2. Assign a small research project for which groups of students will choose a country in Africa and conduct research on working styles and attitudes in that country. What are they? Why do they exist? Resources include books at a local public or university library, consulates of the countries they are studying, foreign graduate students at a local university, perhaps even employees of large multinational companies who do business in Africa. Have students present their findings to the class. Compare and contrast their findings among the African cultures studied. *(collaborative, constructive)*

Lesson 2

Work in the Global Marketplace

Practically every type of work has international, hence cross-cultural, dimensions. Many of the largest corporations in the U.S. are owned by foreign nationals, and, in turn, U.S. companies have extensive operations in other countries. Modern supermarkets now feature fruits and vegetables from around the world. Conventions, trade shows, sports events, and vacations bring millions of foreign visitors to the U.S.; they are lodged in hotels, fed in restaurants, and do business with shop owners and clerks of all kinds.

International commerce is abolishing national boundaries. This buying and selling across countries' borders is known as the global marketplace. It is imperative that the students of today and the businesspeople of the future understand that they will function not in a domestic (within their country's borders) but in a global economy. This will require open-minded attitudes, flexibility, and intense sensitivity to cultural differences in the ways people do business around the world. When business is lost because of a misunderstanding or disagreement about prices or delivery terms, these factors can be adjusted for the next transaction. When cultural "goofs" take place, such as those mentioned in the activity below, there is a danger of losing the business forever.

Being fluent in the language of the country with which one plans to do business is, of course, a big plus. But it certainly is not enough. Translating can bring all kinds of problems unless the individual doing it is also aware of the culture of that particular country. As products are introduced across cultural lines, the promoter must understand how the language is used, the attitudes toward time, the use of space, moral values, relationships, whether the individual or the group is valued more, as well as attitudes toward work, leisure, and money. These, of course, are the themes discussed in this book. In a culture where women do not take an active role in the workplace, for example, promoting products that will save the homemaker time will not be effective. Space-savers, such as plastic containers that will stack on top of each other, will be particularly meaningful in a culture where homes are small and closets nonexistent; a U.S. plastic container company found sales did well in Japan. Commercials in Taiwan often center on the family because of the importance of familial relationships.

In the following activities, we will look at some of the kinds of problems that can arise in the global marketplace as well as the cross-cultural sensitivity that is necessary to operate in it successfully.

Activities

1. Listed below are some examples of problems companies encountered when trying to promote their products in other cultures. Divide the class into groups, and give each group one of the problems to discuss. Hand one person in the group the "Answer" folded up. Instruct him or her to keep the answer secret until the group has finished its discussion. After they have come up with their own answer to the problem's questions, have the answer-holder read the actual outcome to the problem. Ask the group to discuss the outcome and compare it with their answer. It will help if they keep in mind some of the themes discussed in this book. When each group is finished with their problem, have each group present the problem and then the outcome to the class.

Each scenario actually happened and has been reported in *Big Business Blunders: Mistakes in Multinational Marketing* by David A Ricks and *International Marketing* by Philip R. Cateora. *(collaborative, cross-cultural)*

- A U.S. toothpaste company promoted its product in Southeast Asia by advertising it in the same manner as it did back home. It told the people that by using this product, they could have white teeth. It used the punch line, "Wonder where the yellow went?" Two very serious mistakes were made. Can you figure out what they might be?

  Answer: The question, "Wonder where the yellow went?" was considered by many of the people in Southeast Asia as a racial slur. The second problem was that many people did not consider white teeth an advantage. They chewed beetle nuts, which stained their teeth an acceptable dark color.

- A U.S. company attempted to promote its business in the Middle East by showing a picture of a business executive with his feet on the desk. The local people were insulted. Why?

  Answer: In the Middle East, showing the sole of your foot is considered a very serious insult.

• A European firm decided to sell its product in Thailand, and it hired a local Thai person to translate its English advertising slogan, "Out of sight, out of mind," into the local language. What do you think might have gone wrong when the translation was made? How might the meaning of the slogan have been interpreted?

Answer: The translator knew the words, but not the subtle variations in the meaning of the slogan's words. He translated the slogan as "Invisible things are insane."

• A U.S. company decided to take advantage of the consumer demand for golf equipment in Japan and began to ship golf balls to that market. The balls were packaged in convenient groups of four balls. The Japanese did not buy them. Why?

Answer: Four is considered a very unlucky number in Japan because the word for that number in Japanese is very similar to the word for "death." Anything numbered four, like the package of golf balls or a fourth floor in a building, is avoided if possible, just as the thirteenth floor often is not numbered in buildings in the United States.

• A British company tried to sell its comfortable leather shoes in Saudi Arabia. They were extremely well made and had sold very well in England. But the company was not so successful in Saudi Arabia. What went wrong?

Answer: The weather is very warm in Saudi Arabia, even in the winter. Enclosed leather shoes are not comfortable in that climate. Italian sandals are more practical because they are cooler.

• A Chinese firm wanted to export a sewing machine to the United States. They named the machine "Typical." The people in the United States who were going to market it said that "Typical" was not a good name, but the Chinese could not understand why. Why was this a problem for the Chinese?

Answer: The Chinese told the people in the U.S. that they saw other U.S. products named "General," or "Standard," so they did not see what was wrong with their name. (What products or companies in the U.S. have the words "General" or "Standard" in their titles?)

2. Have the class think of other U.S. products that could be sold in other countries. What problems might arise in the marketing or selling of these products? *(cross-cultural)*

3. Divide the class into groups. Ask the students to pretend they are manufacturing and selling an electric rice cooker in two areas where rice is a basic part of the diet—East Asia and the Middle East. Market research shows that the Chinese like their rice cooked so it will be fluffy and warm. The Japanese prefer their rice to be warm and sticky. People in the Middle East actually like to have a slight burnt taste to their rice. Also, the Japanese keep their rice cookers on the counter, whereas the Chinese put theirs away out of sight.

   As chief designers for their company, how would the students make a cooker that would meet the needs of all these different cultures? Ask the students to draw the rice cooker. Have them share their solution with the class. *(constructive, cross-cultural)*

Answer: They would have to install an electric thermostat on the cooker to allow for heat adjustment to meet the tastes of the different cultures. The appearance would have to be attractive so that Japanese women could display the cookers in their kitchens.

4. Divide the class into groups. Ask them to choose a U.S. product and a country in which to sell it. Have them devise an advertising campaign for selling that product. Can they come up with a campaign that will have broad appeal and not offend anyone? They may want to do a little research into the cultural attitudes and economic needs of the country. It would be useful for them to choose a country that has been covered in this book so that they can draw a bit on what they know about the country's interpretation of some of the cross-cultural themes.

   Have the students present their campaigns to the class and display them. You might want the class to critique their campaigns. *(constructive, cross-cultural)*

Lesson 3

Money and Currency

Every country in the world, and even smaller social units such as tribes, have their own form of money, or currency, which is used to buy and sell goods and services. Today, most countries' currencies consist of paper bills and metallic coins of various sizes and amounts that are issued by the government. But many other objects have been used as currency over the centuries. One of the most commonly used objects, found particularly in Western Africa, was a small ocean shell about the size of a thimble called the "cowrie." Pictures of these shells appear in caves occupied by prehistoric humans. The shells were held and paid as individual pieces or a number of them were strung on strings to represent a greater value. Instances have been recorded when an African seller refused gold in favor of cowrie shells. They have been the currency of choice for certain special payments such as a "brideprice"—the money paid for a wife—or payment of fines.

Currencies have usually fallen into two categories: those which have practical use such as rock salt, iron, cloth, feather bands, and wampum; and those used for ornamentation such as gold, silver, and rare stones. No true money existed among the North American native tribes prior to the coming of the Europeans. The Native Americans used shells, beads, and furs (Driver, 1972).

In some cultures, it is acceptable for one to show off his or her wealth. Women in some African tribes carry their wealth with them in the form of gold bracelets lining their arms. In other cultures, it is considered in poor taste openly and unnecessarily to display one's money or jewels. In most cultures, the choice is one of personal preference rather than social custom.

The desire to get and save money is not found only in today's financially sophisticated societies. Some simpler and relatively isolated tribes such as the Kapauku in Western New Guinea have developed their own lifestyles built around acquiring wealth. Although their money is the cowrie shell, the Kapauku use it in the same way that more industrialized countries use their money for profitable purchase and sale of all goods and services. The Kapauku are motivated by a desire to become rich, for those in their culture who are wealthy acquire power and higher social standing (Nanda, 1987).

Before currency came into widespread use, and even after its introduction, trade was accomplished by means of *barter*. There are areas in Africa even today where people never have had any use for currency (Zaslavsky, 1973). In a barter economy, you exchange an object or service for goods or services from another party, and no money is involved. For example, a bushel of potatoes might be considered payment for some plumbing repairs or a bicycle tire. Bartering is not simply a primitive method of buying and selling. In today's international trade, many barter transactions on a large scale are conducted. A typical transaction might find Russia exchanging millions of barrels of oil for an equally large shipment of wheat from Poland.

The barter process reveals much about another culture, about what kinds of objects and services it values, about what its economic needs and desires are, and about

SIDEBAR

PROVERBS ON MONEY

Money grows on the tree of patience.
—Japanese

Much money, many friends.
—German

He who loves money must work.
—African (Wolof)

Money is power.
—United States

If we have not money, let us have honor.
—Turkish

Make money honestly if you can, but make money.
—United States

Money talks.
—English

He who has money can do what he pleases.
—Greek

SIDEBAR

SOME CURRENCIES AROUND THE WORLD

COUNTRY	CURRENCY
Bolivia	peso
Ecuador	sucre
France	franc
Gambia	dalasi
Iraq	dinar
Israel	shekel
Italy	lira
Japan	yen
Kenya	shilling
Laos	kip
Netherlands	guilder
Norway	krone
Sri Lanka	rupee
Vietnam	dong

what it feels is worth giving up in exchange for other things. The process of bartering across cultural lines illustrates how people value goods and services differently. The bartering process requires skill at cross-cultural negotiation and communication in order to conclude a transaction successfully.

Activities

1. Have the class practice converting U.S. currency into another currency and vice-versa. Cut out the latest listing of foreign exchange rates from the newspaper and copy it for the class. First, have the students familiarize themselves with the names of currencies in some of the countries listed. Illustrate several exchange computations for the class.

   Then pair up the students, and assign each pair a particular currency. One member of the pair will then convert a certain amount of his or her U.S. dollars to the foreign currency held by the other person. They will need to work together to compute the exchange. Then the pairs can convert a certain amount of the foreign currency back into U.S. dollars. Have the pairs repeat this process several times with different amounts.

   Another way to do this is to set up a kind of currency exchange market. There will be six or seven booths, four or five representing a "bank" in a particular country (chosen from the list of exchange rates) and two representing a U.S. bank. Assign some students to operate the booths and others to be world travellers. As the travellers start out, they will carry with them play U.S. money. As they visit each country, they will need to exchange their U.S. dollars for the local currency so that they can buy things in that country. Since information about currency exchange rates among countries other than the U.S. is difficult to obtain (although possible through banks and consulates), the students will need to exchange their foreign currency back to U.S. dollars every time they want to visit another country's booth—hence the reason for two U.S. bank booths to handle the overload. Of course, the students will need to make some play money to represent the foreign and U.S. currency. *(constructive, collaborative)*

   Discuss: What is an exchange rate? Does getting a higher number of a country's currency mean that the currency is worth more than U.S. dollars?

2. Turn the classroom into a bartering marketplace. Assign each student a country. The students must then choose a product or service which his or her country can provide. For example, a student from Saudi Arabia might barter a barrel of oil; one from Argentina could offer beef; a French student might barter some French wine; a Canadian could barter furs, etc. Have the students make representations of their products or services on pieces of paper as well as name tags representing their country.

   When the market begins, the students will mill around the room, introducing themselves to each other, and proceeding to discuss and make fair or profitable exchanges of goods and services. How many cows will one trade for how much wine? Some may decide that an exchange is not worth it. It is up to them to decide. Further, they will need to think about whether they even want or need products or services from a particular country. A person from a warm climate probably will not want Canadian furs, for example.

   After the market, ask the students to share some of their more interesting exchanges or instances where an exchange was not worthwhile. Do they wish we had a barter economy in the U.S.? How would that work? If we had a barter economy, would people be less likely to show off what their money could buy? Would our economy seem more fair? *(constructive, cross-cultural)*

Lesson 4

Leisure Time

About 2500 years ago, the Greek philosopher Aristotle recognized the need for people to enjoy leisure time (Kando, 1980). He realized that the sophisticated and advanced Greek civilization had reached a point at which its citizens no longer needed to spend all of their time working and sleeping. The time left in a 24-hour day could be used for relaxation and pleasure. Yet it was in another advanced civilization, that of Rome, where, because of its large population, mass recreation was really popularized. Gladiator fights, chariot races, and other spectacles held before thousands in the Circus Maximus played to the sense of brutality of the audience. In fact, the word "leisure" comes from the Latin word *licere,* meaning "to be permitted." Today, leisure is thought to be synonymous with "free time."

The different activities in which people engage in their leisure or free time is limited only by their imaginations and their wallets. If one has sufficient money and leisure time, he or she may engage in some rather creative free-time activities. *Fortune* magazine conducted a survey of what some top executives do for relaxation. Among the more imaginative ones were

• Heli-skiing in Canada	• Volunteer fireman
• Trekking in Nepal	• Canoeing in the Artic
• Computer chess	• Showing champion dogs
• Growing orchids at home	• Ballooning

Yet what may be leisure for some people or some cultures may be work for others. Digging a garden and planting flowers in the dirt is fun for some, but for others spectator sports like soccer or football are the way to get away from the work routine.

For still others, volunteer work is the answer. Many people in the U.S. use their hours of free time to help others. Teenagers often distribute mail and deliver flowers to patients in local hospitals. Adults dedicate long hours as volunteers without pay. They may clean up and repair blighted areas, assist in tutoring programs, work at the Special Olympics, or help the aged. These activities often earn the volunteers praise and respect from members of their communities. Yet in some cultures these voluntary programs are looked upon with suspicion. When a group of U.S. women living in Paris attempted to introduce a volunteer program to the American Hospital in that city, they were met with resistance. "Why would they want to do this for free? They will take away the jobs of paid employees," the hospital staff argued. The program finally was accepted, however, and has proved to be successful. But what is well-intended in one culture can be negatively interpreted in another.

At the other extreme are those who spend their leisure time simply curled up in a comfortable chair with a good book or glued as couch potatoes in front of the TV.

People in many cultures enjoy their leisure time both as observers and as participants. We will look at both types—passive leisure in which one is a spectator and active leisure in which one takes part in the activities.

Activity

1. Discuss: What is leisure time? Why do we have it? What purpose does it serve? Is it as important as work? How do we earn leisure time? How do we get to deserve it?

   List on the board the students' response to the following question: What is the best thing to do during one's leisure time? When you have a list of ten answers, go back through each one and ask, "What purpose does this activity serve?" Label the purpose next to the activity. When you are finished, count how many of the activities had some kind of purpose beyond "having fun."

   As a result of this kind of probing, students will start to think about how people in the U.S. regard the use of leisure time. In the U.S., many people think of leisure time as an opportunity to better themselves or produce something; therefore the line between leisure and work is rather thin. Others in the U.S. (and in many other cultures) think of leisure time as a period in which one does not need to have a purpose to his or her activity; leisure is therefore totally separate from work. *(interpretive)*

Passive Leisure: Spectator Sports

There are several sports and games that are an essential part of one culture or of a group of related cultures, but which seem strange to others. One of the most insensitive acts is to insult or joke about these sports to one of their fans. Some of these sports include:

- Rugby football in England and former commonwealth countries
- Cricket in the same countries
- Sumo wrestling in Japan
- Jai-lai in Mexico and Latin America
- U.S. football

Without a doubt, the world's most popular sport is football, not the U.S. version but what is called "soccer" in the U.S. One hundred and seventy-eight nations fielded teams to vie for the quadrennial World Cup held in the U.S. in 1994. Over one billion people, almost one-fifth of the world's population, watched the opening ceremony and game. More than thirty billion watched all fifty-two games held in nine U.S. cities. The final championship game was played in the Rose Bowl in California. No other sport in the world could enjoy such a large audience.

Although there is evidence that a somewhat similar game was played in China around 200 B.C., the modern version was invented and standardized in England. While professional soccer in the U.S. has been slow to catch on, except for the modified indoor version, it is a major sport at the high-school level. For example, in Illinois some 239,000 boys and girls play the game on over 300 teams for boys and 150 for girls (*Chicago Tribune Magazine*, May 22, 1994).

The intensity of soccer fans abroad is legendary. Waves of them will march arm-in-arm, their team's colors on scarves, jackets, hats, and other apparel, to and from the stadium. Inside, many of the stadiums have a moat separating fans from the playing field. Bags are searched for unauthorized objects that could be thrown or otherwise disrupt the game. If the national team of a country is playing, activity comes to a standstill in that country during the game. The noise from fans is deafening, even in a huge outdoor arena. Referees often have to be escorted off the field by police guards at the end of a game.

A spectator sport not nearly as universally enjoyed as soccer is bullfighting. It has seemed a bloody, gruesome, insensitive display to its non-fans. The bull is killed, and the men and other animals participating are likely to be injured or worse. Every bullfighter is gored by the horns of the bull many times during his career. To its *afficionados* (ah-**fi**-see-oh-**nah**-dohs), those who understand and appreciate the event, bullfighting is an elegant ballet displaying the courage and skill of both the animal and the men. Ernest Hemingway saw the bullfight as the supreme example of showing grace under pressure.

Two of the authors, while living in Madrid, Spain, were given a quick course in understanding the event from a long-time bullfight admirer. It is a spectacle, he repeatedly emphasized, which incorporates delicate grace, emotion, ritual, color, bravery, and skill. It is not a competition; no one wins. From the opening trumpet fanfare until the last *Olé* (a shout of approval) has been sounded by the audience, a saga of life and death is played out on the sands of the plaza. Danger is always lurking. The fighting bull is just as wild as a lion or tiger, and more dangerous because it requires no provocation to attack.
If he displays extraordinary bravery and nobility, his death is pardoned. The most famous bulls are those of Miura, from Seville, Spain, which have killed many famous bullfighters.

The number of passes made by the *matador* (maht-ah-**door**), the principle performer, are surprisingly small, ten with the larger cape and ten with the *muleta* (moo-**lay**-ta), a smaller, heart-shaped cloth draped over a wooden stick and used in the latter part of the bullfight. Both the cape and the muleta are bright red—not because the bull reacts to this color (it is color-blind), but because red disguises the color of blood that may splash upon them.

The motions for each pass are rigidly defined, but every matador has his own style. The performance of the matador, his helpers, and the bull are meticulously reviewed by the press just as if it were an opening of a new ballet. If the bull is fierce and the matador skillful, the crowd signals that the matador should be awarded an ear cut from the bull's head. Two ears are awarded for a particularly outstanding fight, and a tail is added for a sensational performance.

Activities

1. Discuss: What is your favorite way to spend leisure time? What are some common pastimes in the United States? *(constructive)*

2. Discuss: What sports or activities do you like to watch? What is the favorite passive use of leisure time in the U.S.? Why? What is so important about that event? What meaning does it have for people in the U.S.?

   What do you think of soccer and the bullfight? Why aren't these two activities as popular with people in the U.S. as they are with people in other cultures? *(interpretive)*

3. Assign a class report on the bullfight. Groups of students will research one aspect of the bullfight and present that aspect in a large class report. Aspects include the running of the bulls before the fights, the kinds of bulls used, the role of the matador, the roles of the other participants, the goals, the rewards, and the symbolic significance of the event. When the class has finished its research, stage a mock bullfight with students role-playing spectators, bulls, matadors, commentators, etc.

   After the bullfight, discuss its symbolic significance for both players and spectators. Do we have any events in the U.S. that also have symbolic significance? *(constructive, cross-cultural)*

Active Leisure: Children's Games

Children around the world share a common bond. While their education may be different, the games they play, the emphasis on winning or losing, the amount of time devoted to these activities, and the importance placed on them are often very much alike. Some secret form of communication seems to develop as youngsters from different cultures begin to play together. Games may be one of the strongest bonds existing among people, young and old alike, around the world. The Olympic Games bond athletes with common goals, a sense of sharing, and an opportunity to learn about people from other parts of the world. But games on a much more informal scale and among much younger people also serve to bring individuals together. The following is an example of how, through play, a youngster from one culture bonded with a group of children from a very different society. Two of the authors had received permission from the Hungarian government to place their four-year-old daughter in a factory-workers' day-care center in that country's capital city of Budapest.

At that time, suspicions and animosities hovered between our part of the world and Eastern Europe, of which Hungary was a part. We had gone to Eastern Europe on a research project, and one of the areas we were looking into was child care. Thinking it would be fun for our daughter to meet local children, we had asked if we could enroll her in the nursery. We will never forget the reception our daughter received from the Hungarian children. As she walked into their midst, they excitedly ran toward her, smiling, all jabbering at once, and several threw their arms around her. Quickly, they pulled her into their play group. Although our daughter and the Hungarian children could not verbally communicate with each other, they had no problems conveying their ideas and thoughts, and they quickly joined together for a race across the school's courtyard. Children at play understand each other. We were to experience such incidents in many other areas of the world, but none was as poignant as this Eastern European episode because we were in an area of the world that was supposedly at odds with our country.

Children were playing games two thousand years ago, as wall paintings in the ancient Egyptian tombs tell us. They were tossing balls, spinning tops, and hugging dolls in the ancient civilizations of Greece and Rome. The Bible's New Testament alludes to children's play and a form of mock wedding that young people apparently performed. All are activities not unknown to young people today in many different cultures.

Activity

In the sixteenth century, the Flemish painter Peter Bruegel memorialized children's games in a delightful oil painting he recorded on a wood panel. Page 219 shows a reproduction of this famous piece of art, which today hangs in the Kunsthistorisches Museum in Vienna, Austria. According to art historians, there are no fewer than eighty-four games depicted, many of which are still played by children all over the world.

Show the painting to the class. How many games can they find and identify in the painting? Which of these games do children still play in the U.S.? *(interpretive)*

Answer: Among the games and activities portrayed in Bruegel's painting are leapfrog, gymnastics, tumbling, top-spinning, hide-and-seek, hoop rolling, stilt walking,

Painting by Peter Bruegel / From the Kunsthistorisches Museum

riding a hobbyhorse, swimming, tree climbing, mock tournaments, tug-of-war, follow-the-leader, king of the castle, mumblety peg, blowing soap bubbles, balancing a broom on the hand, making mud pies, swinging, piggy-back fighting.

If any of today's children are unfamiliar with the traditional games, this can perhaps be blamed on the advent of organized juvenile sports' teams and video games. While most kids will have difficulty recognizing many of the painting's worldwide games, they can confer with adult members of their families who can probably describe how they took part in these activities as children. A family member who was born in another culture may also be able

to identify many of the activities in Bruegel's painting.

Ball Games

Balls are found in nearly every culture around the globe. The very early balls, which probably dated back to five thousand years ago, were likely to be smoothed and polished round stones. But through millennia, as balls evolved from stone to marble, wood, pottery, or perhaps animal hides filled with sawdust, they have often served as a magic symbol. Even today in an African tribe in the former French Cameroons, girls take part in a ritual ballgame to hasten the rainfall (Arnold, 1972).

Did You Know?

A very popular game in Nigeria, called *ayo* by the Yorubans, is played on a board with twelve cups, or "houses," and forty-eight seeds. The object is to capture or "eat" your opponents through artful but controlled moves of your own seeds.

Activity

Many ball games are shared by children around the world, sometimes with just a few alterations. Dodge ball, for example, is played both in the U.S. and Japan with only slight differences. At other times, ball games appear to have a common heritage but vary quite a bit in the way in which they are carried out. Such is the case with cricket and baseball. Some will argue that baseball has nothing in common with the English game of cricket, but those who have studied the two games believe they share the same heritage. Read the following description of cricket to your class. Then ask them if they see similarities between this game and the game of baseball. What are the similarities? What are the differences? A Venn diagram may be of assistance. Do the students think baseball might have evolved from cricket? *(interpretive, cross-cultural)*

Cricket is played on a circular field and involves two teams of eleven members each. The purpose of the game is to score runs. Two wickets, or groupings of three sticks each, are placed in the ground approximately 22 yards apart. A "bowler," similar to a baseball pitcher, throws the ball from one wicket toward the other wicket in an attempt to strike the second wicket. The batsman tries to prevent this by hitting the thrown ball with a bat held somewhat like a croquet mallet. Once the ball is hit, runs are scored by the batsman and another teammate running between the two wickets until the ball is picked up and thrown back to the wicket area.

Board Games

Board games also have an ancient history. Rather than on an actual board, the first games of this type were probably played on the ground with shells or stones. The themes of board games are inspired by thrilling events, such as battles, races, hunts, and territorial conquests, that people

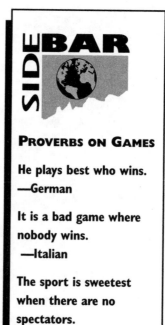

SIDEBAR

PROVERBS ON GAMES

He plays best who wins.
—German

It is a bad game where nobody wins.
—Italian

The sport is sweetest when there are no spectators.
—English

want to remember and experience again and again through the replaying of these board competitions.

Checkers, which also traces its origin to antiquity, is typical of a board game in which symbolic men are taken as they would be in battle. The game is played around the world, although sometimes under a different name and with slight variations. In England it is known as *draughts* but the rules are the same as in the U.S. In Spain and Turkey, however, the rules are a bit different: in Spain, the piece can move both backward and forward; and in Turkey, side movements are permitted. In the U.S., only forward maneuvers are allowed.

Sometimes a culture borrows a board game from another society and makes it strictly its own. The most popular board game in Japan, *Go,* originated in China over four thousand years ago. Unlike checkers, where players take pieces representing men, this game involves taking territory. Two players place either their 180 white round stones or their 180 round black stones on the intersections of nineteen vertical and nineteen horizontal lines, all of which add up to 360 crossing points. If a player can use his stones to completely surround his opponent's stone, he has taken the territory. The player who takes the largest amount of territory is the winner.

Board games on occasion cross cultural lines with few changes. Such is the case with Monopoly®, which remains almost intact despite a name change in some countries. In the British version, squares on the board have been renamed: Boardwalk becomes Mayfair, the name of one of the most exclusive and expensive neighborhoods in London; and the railroads all change to the names of London train stations, such as Kings Cross.

During the Cold War, when the communist countries would not allow people to own their own real estate, Monopoly® became a popular game in Bulgaria, a communist country. The Bulgarians enjoyed the game in spite of the fact that they often did not understand all its principles. For instance, they could not fathom why individual players would be required to pay the hospital a fee or pay interest on "shares." Even more mysterious was the competition to buy "houses" and "hotels" when all such buildings were owned by the government in their country. Nevertheless, the game was a hit, in spite of the fact that the participants did not always understand all the plays. Names on the Monopoly board change in Bulgaria, too.

Jail turns into ЗАТВОР (Zatvór)

Chance is ШАHC' (Schànc)

and Free Parking becomes

БЕЗПАТЕН МАРКИНГ
(Besplàten Parking)

John Locke, a well-known British philosopher from the seventeenth century, was a major instigator of educational games. Today, educational games are very popular in the U.S. and elsewhere in the world. Bulgarian children learn much of their geography, for instance, from a game called *Atlas*. A very large circle is drawn in the ground with a smaller circle in the center of the larger one. The big circle is divided into pie-shaped pieces, each one named after a continent. The smaller center circle is Bulgaria. The teacher selects one child to stand in the center circle. Then he or she shouts out the name of a country or some significant geographical point and the children run to the correct slice of pie, or continent, in which that country is located. The first one to reach the correct space is the winner who can now stand in Bulgaria, the center.

Sports today probably forge stronger unifying bonds between cultures than any other aspect, with the possible exception of popular music. TV networks around the world pay millions of dollars for the right to televise the Olympic Winter and Summer games, and the number of participating teams keeps getting larger. A decade ago, who would have predicted that professional U.S.-style football games would be played in England and Japan? Athletes become worldwide heroes. Hakeem Abdul Olaju-

won, the son of middle-class parents in Lagos, Nigeria, was simply a foreign student at the University of Houston until he was discovered by a National Basketball Association scout and converted to stardom in the international basketball world.

Activities

1. Discuss the ways Monopoly was confusing to the Bulgarians. What games do we play that would be strange to someone in a foreign country? Would it be difficult to play Trivial Pursuit® with someone from Russia or China? Why? how about Pictionary?® cards? If you were to try to market a game in other cultures, what considerations would you have to keep in mind? (language—Can it be translated? Will it make sense to those in the other culture? Will it offend anyone?, etc.) *(interpretive, cross-cultural)*

2. Are many video games cross-cultural? Why? Divide the class into groups, and have each invent an idea for a video game that could be played in any culture. *(constructive, cross-cultural)*

3. Play the Bulgarian game Atlas with the U.S. as the center. Is this a fun way to learn geography? *(constructive)*

4. Hold an international game day. Have groups of students research games from other cultures and make the necessary preparations to play them. If your class includes students from other cultures, ask them to share games from their cultures. On game day, invite other classes to come play these foreign games. *(constructive, cross-cultural)*

Resources

Arnold, Arnold. *The World Book of Children's Games.* New York: World Publishing, 1972.

Cateora, Philip R. *International Marketing.* Homewood, IL: Irwin, 1990.

Cooper, Robert, and Nanthapa Cooper. *Culture Shock: Thailand.* Singapore: Times Books International, 1984.

Doing Business in Nigeria. New York: Price Waterhouse, 1994.

Driver, Harold E. *Indians of North America.* Chicago: The University of Chicago Press, 1972.

The Economist. Business Traveller's Guides: Arabian Peninsula. New York: Prentice Hall, 1987.

Enahoro, E. O., editor. *Culture and Management in Nigeria.* Lagos: Lantern Books, 1987.

Greenfield II, Arthur. *Anatomy of a Bullfight.* New York: Longmans Green, 1961.

Hall, Edward T., and Mildred Reed Hall. *Understanding Cultural Differences.* Yarmouth, ME: Intercultural Press, 1990.

Kando, Thomas M. *Leisure and Popular Culture in Transition.* St. Louis: Charles V. Mosby, 1980.

Mackey, Sandra. *The Saudis: Inside the Desert Kingdom.* Boston: Houghton Mifflin, 1987.

Myers, Robert. *Nigeria.* Oxford: Clio Press, 1989.

Nanda, Serena. *Cultural Anthropology.* Belmont, CA: Wadsworth, 1987.

Randle, J. K. *Who Is Fooling Who?* Lagos, West African Book Publishers, 1985.

Ricks, David A. *Big Business Blunders: Mistakes in Multinational Marketing.* Homewood, IL: Dow Jones-Irwin, 1983.

Wellemeyer, Marilyn. *On Your Own Time: The Fortune Guide to Executive Leisure.* Boston: Little, Brown, 1987.

Zaslavsky, Claudia. *Africa Counts: Number and Pattern in African Culture.* Boston: Prindle, Weber & Schmidt, 1973.

A FINAL WORD:

Today, as we search for ways to achieve cross-cultural understanding, we must look not only at the foods, clothing, housing, and arts of other nations. We must also earnestly seek a means to understand people who are different from us and to learn not simply how they act but why they function in certain ways. We need to realize that interacting successfully across cultural lines requires more than "a tolerant attitude"; it requires a sense that we have so much to gain in our cross-cultural relationships. A final story from one of the authors illustrates this point:

In the 1960s, my husband, John, and I, along with my brother and his friend, drove a van from Paris, France, to New Delhi, India. My brother and his friend had just completed their medical residencies back in the U.S. When we reached Afghanistan, that Middle Eastern country that is shaped like a leaf and about the size of Texas, we discovered there were few roads. Rather than travel along paved highways, we were forced to follow tire tracks that cut through the sand of the vast, lonely desert. Most of the people there were too poor to own cars, and when they wanted to visit their friends or relatives in neighboring villages, they either boarded small buses or rented space on top of trucks that were delivering supplies to these desert towns.

Late one night as we were driving across the desert, we came across a truck that had toppled over, spewing its rooftop passengers across the sands. We grabbed the bandages and medicines we were carrying and ran toward the badly injured victims. "We're doctors," we shouted. "We're Americans. We want to help." But we looked funny. I was not covered by the chador (the long, flowing tentlike robe that covered a woman from head to toe with a small stretch of lattice work across the eyes to allow her to see out), and the men in our group did not wear the typical, baggy, pajamalike pants. We spoke some kind of gibberish they simply did not understand. We were strange and different, and they were extremely frightened by us. Through sign language and an attempt to clean and bandage some serious wounds, we attempted to make ourselves understood. The Afghans, however, vehemently refused any help, and they forced us back into our van. We left, knowing that many of those injured probably would

Did You Know?

A familiar U.S. folk tune illustrates how individuals long ago eagerly tried not only to learn about people in other countries but also to imitate them. For generations young and old alike in the U.S. have sung the tune "Yankee Doodle Dandy." One line in the song runs, "he stuck a feather in his cap and called it macaroni." Macaroni does not refer to food in this instance but to a group in England named the "Macaroni Society," in existence at about the time of the American Revolution. The British aristocracy customarily sent their young sons to the continent for a year or so to soak up the culture and lifestyle abroad. On their return, they formed the Macaroni Society to continue their newfound, elegant style of dress. Some joined the military and sported the flashy and stylish uniforms that gave soldiers the nickname "Red Coats." Those Red Coats who served as troops in early America during the colonial period sneered at what they considered the shabby dress of the colonists. When one of the locals stuck a feather in his cap and rode to town "on a pony," the Red Coats laughed among themselves at the feeble attempt to emulate the "macaroni" flair for fashion: "Does he think that feather makes him a 'macaroni?'"

die. Had they only been willing to accept our differences, some might still be alive today. This incident taught me not to fear people who seem very different. I have learned there is much to gain from mutual understanding.

This story demonstrates how a fear of difference could result in tragedy. Every cross-cultural encounter that results in mutual misunderstanding could be considered a tragedy in some sense. It is our hope that the knowledge, attitudes, and skills offered in this course of study will enable your students to understand, overcome, and even embrace the cross-cultural differences they will encounter in their world.

A FINAL ACTIVITY:
INVENT A CULTURE

If you have used all of the themes in this book with your class, then the following activity may provide a satisfying sense of closure to this course of study in cross-cultural understanding.

Divide the class into two groups. The assignment: Invent a Culture. Each group will need to discuss and define the important aspects of the culture they want to invent. A helpful first step would be to list the main cultural themes they have covered—Language (verbal and non-verbal), Space, Time, Relationships, Individual and Group, Moral Values, and Work and Leisure. What are some ways their culture expresses these themes? The following questions may spur their thinking:

How do they talk?
What kinds of body language do they use?
How far apart do they stand?
How do they arrange their homes and towns?
What time orientations do they have?
Do they tend to be on time?
Do they value the present and past over the future?
How would they express that?
How do they form friendships?
How do their families live?
How do they raise their children?
What roles to women play?
Do they tend to value individualism over a group orientation?
What are some of their moral values?
How do they regard work?
What are some important professions?
How do they spend their leisure time?

Other considerations:

What do they call themselves?
Where are they located in the world?
What do they wear?
What do they tend to look like?
What do they eat?
What are some important holidays?

Have each group work on a large presentation of their culture, using drawings, write-ups, and any other visual means. They will need to work as teams, assigning various aspects of the culture to each student for the presentation. The presentation may take the form of a book with sections describing each aspect of the culture. But this presentation must be shown only to you for the time being.

Once everyone in the group understands all aspects of their culture, have the students hold a Cross-Cultural Interaction Day. This activity may take two hours. On this day, each group will act out a few chosen aspects of their own invented culture (those aspects that are most easily acted out) as they mingle and interact with members from the other group who are doing the same thing. The best way to do this is to have most of the group be acting out its cultural themes while a few members go as visitors to interact with the other group, who also has sent out a few visitors. These visitors should return and rotate to let other members of the group visit the other culture. The challenge is for the cultures and the visitors to understand each other, not to confuse each other.

When everyone has had a chance to visit the other culture, have the groups meet to discuss what they experienced. Can they describe the other culture? The students should take each theme and try to explain how the other culture expressed the theme. When they think they have the other culture figured out, allow time to have them ask the other culture if their perceptions are correct. The other culture, then, can help to clarify any misunderstandings.

Discuss what the students learned about:

1. How aspects of a culture fit together;

2. Their own invented culture from the perceptions and perspectives of the other culture who was trying to understand them;

3. The best ways to understand another culture;

4. The best ways to communicate with those from a very different culture;

5. The problems involved in cross-cultural understanding and how to overcome them.

Then have the students display their visual presentations for the class, other classes, and parents. You might even want to contact a local cultural center to see if it would allow your students to display their presentations at the center. *(interpretive, constructive, collaborative, cross-cultural)*

Note: We were inspired by a similar project initiated by sixth-grade teacher Bob Brown of the Stevenson School in Schaumburg, Illinois. Some of the countries his students created were named Bullmania, Land of Warmth, Musique, and Meowland (some cities of which were called Cateye Harbor, Whiskers, and Chow Cat).

Index

E

East Asian cultures
  family in, 136–138
  names in, 24–25
  politeness in, 27
  smells in, 21
  time in, 90–93
  togetherness in, 138
  women's roles in, 138
Eastern European countries, names in, 25
Education, in Japan, 158, 170–171
Egalitarianism, 159
Egypt
  family in, 134–135
  time in, 81, 84
Embassies, 167
Emerson, Ralph Waldo, 153–154, 155
Employee, status of, 205–206
England
  class system in, 163–165
  middle class in, 165
  privacy in, 159
  soccer in, 148, 150
  time in, 95–96
  upper class in, 164
  working class in, 165
English language
  British expressions in, 35–36
  number of speakers in, 37
  roots of, 37
Europe
  family life in, 134
  working women in, 135
Expatriate, 80
Extended family, 132–134
Eye contact, 42, 63

F

Fables, 182, 183
Fables of Luqman, 183
Families
  in African cultures, 132
  in Arab cultures, 130, 132
  communication in, 25–26
  in East Asian cultures, 136–138
  in Egypt, 134–135
  in Europe, 134
  extended, 132–134
  in Japanese culture, 130, 139–141, 172
  language in, 24–25
  proverbs on, 133
  role of, in courtship and marriage, 126–127
  in United States, 130

Family space, 65–69
Finger counting, 45
Floors, counting of, 74
Flower clock, 98
Folk tales, 182
Football, 217
Forgiving, 183
Formality in language, 23–24
France
  family space in, 65
  friendship in, 122–123
  working in, 207–208
Franklin, Benjamin, 180
Friday the 13th, 30
Friendliness log, 123
Friendship, 119. *See also* Relationships
  definitions of, 119
  in France, 122–123
  in Korea, 123–124
  in Mexico, 119–120
  proverbs on, 121
  in United States, 121–122
Fuseki, 60

G

Galileo, 85
Games
  ball, 219–220
  board, 220–221
  children's, 218–219
  proverbs on, 220
Gandhi, Mahatma, 174–175
Gautama, Siddhartha, 182–184
German culture, 37
  homes in, 66
  individualism in, 158
  relationships in, 114, 116
  space in, 54, 58, 63
  time in, 80, 83, 88, 102
Giri, 169
Global marketplace, work in, 212–213
Goals
  in studying individuals and groups, 146
  in studying moral values, 178
  in studying relationships, 112
  in studying space, 52
  in studying time, 78
  in studying work and leisure, 198
Go (East Asian game), 60, 220
Golden Rule, 183
Gospel music, 20
Great Britain. See England
Greek culture, body language in, 45